The Family in Business

*Understanding and Dealing
with the Challenges
Entrepreneurial Families Face*

Paul C. Rosenblatt
Leni de Mik
Roxanne Marie Anderson
Patricia A. Johnson

The Family in Business

Jossey-Bass Publishers

San Francisco • Washington • London • 1985

THE FAMILY IN BUSINESS
*Understanding and Dealing with the Challenges
Entrepreneurial Families Face*
  by Paul C. Rosenblatt, Leni de Mik, Roxanne Marie Anderson, and
  Patricia A. Johnson

Copyright © 1985 by: Jossey-Bass Inc., Publishers
         433 California Street
         San Francisco, California 94104
         &
         Jossey-Bass Limited
         28 Banner Street
         London EC1Y 8QE

Library of Congress Cataloging in Publication Data
Main entry under title:

The Family in business.

  (A Joint publication in the Jossey-Bass management
series and the Jossey-Bass social and behavioral science
series)
  Bibliography: p. 303
  Includes index.
  1. Family corporations—United States—Management.
2. Family corporations—United States—Psychological
aspects. I. Rosenblatt, Paul C. II. Series: Jossey-
Bass management series. III. Series: Jossey-Bass
social and behavioral science series.
HD62.25.F36 1985   658'.045   84-43033
ISBN 0-87589-640-5 (alk. paper)

Manufactured in the United States of America

JACKET DESIGN BY WILLI BAUM

FIRST EDITION

Code 8518

A joint publication in
The Jossey-Bass
Management Series
and
The Jossey-Bass
Social and Behavioral Science Series

Preface

It takes only casual contact with a family business or with a member of a business-operating family to realize that family businesses contain substantial potential for problems. The need for self-help literature, for theory, and for research is great, yet relatively little has been written about business families. The neglect of business families and of family businesses is striking. It is as though a crucial part of the lives of millions of people were invisible. As we note in Chapter One, roughly 90 percent of the businesses in America (including many of the biggest ones) are said to be family businesses. Thus, the United States economy is what it is because of the operation of well over 10 million family businesses. This is not a book about the last of the Mom and Pop stores but about millions of businesses, about the lives of tens of millions of people who are in business families or family businesses, and about a good deal of the foundation of this country's economy.

This book is important and needed. So many people and so much of the United States economy are affected by the relationship difficulties that are common in family businesses and business families. Therapists, consultants, and managers who deal with business families or family businesses need to understand those relationship difficulties and to find ways of minimizing or avoiding them. People in business families need to cope with or head off those difficulties. This book fulfills these needs by providing a conceptual overview of the dynamics of business families and family businesses and by exploring the ways people have dealt with those difficulties or might deal with them.

This book reports the results of an in-depth survey of tensions and approaches to dealing with them in a sample of U.S. business families. The book is, first of all, a document for professionals who work with business families. For the professional (therapist, counselor, business consultant, attorney, accountant, fiduciary, and so on) who must deal with the problems of people in business families and of family businesses, this book offers a sense of what the common problems are and of what may underlie them. It offers conceptual tools for wrestling with the problems, perspective to help oneself and one's clients understand the problems, and practical suggestions for dealing with the problems. For some clients, reading this book may help substantially in coming to grips with problems that have seemed insoluble, paralyzingly complex, or perhaps too diffuse and vague to think about clearly.

For people in business families and for people contemplating entering or starting a family business, this book provides an overview of the problems we found to be frequently present in family businesses. Our discussion of problems may provide insight into difficulties that people in business families have known or have been lucky to escape so far. For people contemplating going into a family business or bringing some other family member into a business, we offer information about the common variations from the ideal of easy, productive collaboration that one might expect to encounter. Knowing such things may be helpful in decision making and in preparing oneself and one's family to deal with potential problems.

Chapter One provides a discussion of the images and realities of business families and family businesses. Although business families are often imagined to meet such American ideals as family closeness and economic success, family tensions associated with the business were reported in roughly 90 percent of the families we studied. Chapter One also discusses the definition of *family business,* touching on the complexity present when at any one time only one family member is directly involved in the business or when family members do not themselves define the business as a family one. A key part of the chapter is the introduction to the concept of the interplay, overlap, intermingling, and connection of family system and business system. In business families and family businesses the two systems affect each other and can create trouble for each other. Often there is inappropriate carryover of patterns of interacting, rules, and so on from one system to another. Often the two systems compete for the time, energy, and financial resources of individual family members and of the family collectively. The goals of the two systems inevitably clash some of the time. The competition for resources and clash of goals can create problems, and the ways family members deal with that competition and clash can also create problems. Of course, payoffs can result from the relationship of the two systems—for example, in work assistance to the business from family members and in personal dedication of family members working in the family business—but the potential for serious relationship problems in family businesses and business families is substantial.

Each subsequent chapter expands and elaborates on how to use a systems perspective to understand and cope with the potential problems of family businesses and business families. The problems discussed are described both in the words of the people we interviewed and in more general theoretical terms that will aid professionals and others with an interest in business families and family businesses in conceptualizing and understanding problems and possible solutions.

Chapters Two through Ten explore the sources and consequences of particular problems in business-operating families and in family businesses, and each chapter discusses means of coping with the problems explored in it. Chapter Eleven explores the meanings of what respondents said about the advantages of being involved in a family business. Chapters Twelve through Fourteen provide overviews for professionals of issues involved in coping with the special problems and possibilities of business families and family businesses. Chapter Twelve is written from the perspective of management, Chapter Thirteen from the perspective of therapy, and Chapter Fourteen from the perspective of consulting. Each of those three chapters highlights both conceptual and practical issues. Chapter Fifteen emphasizes what a family member who is not the boss can do in the family business to survive in the business and to be comfortable. Chapter Sixteen provides an overview of the basic conceptual approach in the book and offers a partial summary of the results of the study through a discussion of the developmental cycle of the family business and the differences between smaller and larger family businesses. The chapter concludes with a discussion of what may be involved in realizing the full potential of a family business.

One thing we observed in studying business-operating families that is important for people in such families to understand is that within all families feelings, viewpoints, and understandings differ. For example, one family member may report getting along fine while another has a very difficult time. One family member may find nothing wrong with a situation while another may be seething with anger or continually in pain over that situation. Part of the tension in the family may come from anger or communication problems arising from the differences in feelings, viewpoints, and understandings. Given the differences, it should come as no surprise that what helps one person to get along better in a family business may make things worse for others. Nor should it come as a surprise that family relationships benefit from a tolerance of differences and a willingness to accept that another person's feelings, viewpoints, and understandings are real for that person.

"Perspective" is not a tangible good to be purchased in a store, nor is it a formal system to be acquired from business consultants. Yet "perspective" can be precious to members of business-operating families. That is one of the major gains of reading this book. One can acquire perspective on issues in one's own family or family business or in another family business or business family with which one must deal. To know that parents and offspring often are at odds about how and when business transfer will occur, that brothers often are competitive, that it is difficult in a family business to maintain division of labor, or that offspring in family businesses often feel under great pressure to prove themselves may help some people to see themselves or others as normal rather than crazy. "Perspective" can help one to depersonalize a conflict, to become more objective, to achieve a useful emotional distance, to feel that there is nothing about one's parent, sibling, offspring, or other relative that is creating a problem so much as it is the situation of being in a family business. Knowing that problems one is experiencing are common may make it less lonely to have the problem or may lessen one's feeling that it would take an act of remarkable creativity to solve the problem. That is, knowing that one's problems, however difficult, are experienced by many people may make it easier to live with those problems and may give one more hope that they can be solved, quite possibly without the help of a therapist or consultant but perhaps with such help.

For the scholar with an interest in families in general, a study of business-operating families is valuable for probing family theory. Parent/offspring relations may be unusually complex in the family business and extend well into the offspring's adulthood. This provides opportunity for understanding the development of autonomy and individuation in offspring/parent relationships. The opportunities for family togetherness and enmeshment may be unusually great in the family business. How do family members deal with that? How do people get adequate autonomy when working with relatives? How are nuclear family boundaries affected when related nuclear families are connected through a family business? When some family members are involved in a business together and some are not? When business matters produce a falling out among close kin? Role differentiation theories can also be probed with data from business-operating families. How predictable is role differentiation in one arena of relationship from role differentiation in another? Are the dynamics of development and maintenance of role differentiation similar or connected in the two areas? Business families are unusual in important ways, in ways that enable a probing of a wide range of family phenomena and theories.

This book is for everyone interested in families. If we assume that business-operating families are in most ways like other families, what we learn from them may tell us something about all families. Among the issues important to families in general that receive coverage in this book are the relationships of parents and adult offspring, gender roles, the ways that work and home life are entangled, family togetherness and apartness, indulgence and exploitation in the family, dependence and independence in the family, money, power, and the processes of change and stability in the family.

We have relied heavily in this book on the words of people we interviewed. It seems important to communicate the diversity, intensity, and complexity of their feelings, the reality of their problems, and their wisdom and perspective. Some of what they say clarifies and reinforces our theoretical statements, and some challenges or goes beyond what we have said theoretically. To write a book that speaks to the practitioner and scholar, to people like those we interviewed, and to others interested in family businesses or business families, we thought it vital that we allow readers to know what our respondents said to us. The quoted material has been lightly edited, primarily to substitute pronouns for names and to delete or alter information that might allow a reader to identify a particular business or respondent. Some quotations have been shortened by removing asides, tangential remarks, sentence fragments, repetitions, and clarifications that did not seem necessary to quote.

In finding people to study and in interviewing them, we respected the canons of social and behavioral science research. The details of our research approach are presented in the Appendix. We would be glad to correspond with readers who want to know more methodological details than we have provided there.

The people we interviewed were warm, alive, caring, feeling individuals. They included people who had thought about and struggled for years with the issues addressed in this book and people who claimed rarely or never to have had problems or who answered our questions as though they had never before considered the issues. We spoke with people who were delighted to talk with us, generous with their time, and intensely concerned that this book be accurate and useful. We also spoke with people who seemed annoyed by the interviewer's presence, impatient with the questions asked, and eager to see the interviewer leave. Some people we talked with seemed emotionally distant from the areas of tension and stress we asked about; indeed, some seemed emotionally distant from their own families. Others we talked with cried, shook with anger, and were intensely upset as they talked about issues that had been or currently were of special importance and sensitivity in their own lives.

Everyone we interviewed was a Minnesotan, yet the things our informants said mesh well with a literature based on family businesses and business families throughout the United States, in England, in France, and elsewhere in the world. The issues we discuss involve realities and potential realities for all business families and family businesses in the United States and in societies like the United States'.

Acknowledgments

Many, many people helped with this book. We hope that thanking some of them here does not in any way detract from our appreciation of the many others.

We are very, very grateful to the people who allowed us to interview them. If this book has any wisdom and perspective on their world, it comes from what they said to us.

The research reported here was funded by the University of Minnesota Agricultural Experiment Station, Richard Sauer, director. Sara E. Wright and Michael R. Cunningham provided helpful comments on earlier versions of some of this book.

Gloria Lawrence, who typed numerous drafts of this book, is probably the only person who has ever memorized it.

February 1985   Paul C. Rosenblatt
                                        St. Paul, Minnesota

                                        Leni de Mik
                                        Minneapolis, Minnesota

                                        Roxanne Marie Anderson
                                        Alexandria, Minnesota

                                        Patricia A. Johnson
                                        Washington, D.C.

Contents

Contents

*mental Cycles of Family Businesses • Business
Size • Realizing the Potential of Family and
Business*

*Sampling • The Businesses and the People Inter-
viewed • Contacting People • The Interview
Schedule • Did Members of a Family Tell Things
in the Same Way?*

The Authors

Paul C. Rosenblatt is a professor in the Department of Family Social Science and an adjunct professor in the Department of Psychology at the University of Minnesota, St. Paul-Minneapolis. He received the B.A. degree in psychology from the University of Chicago (1958) and the Ph.D. degree in psychology from Northwestern University (1962), where he studied under Donald T. Campbell. He has previously taught at the University of Missouri, Columbia, in psychology, sociology, and anthropology and at the University of California, Riverside, in psychology and anthropology. He is coauthor, with R. P. Walsh and D. A. Jackson, of *Grief and Mourning in Cross-Cultural Perspective* (1976) and author of *Bitter, Bitter Tears: Nineteenth Century Diarists and Twentieth Century Grief Theories* (1983).

Leni de Mik is a psychologist in private practice in Minneapolis. She received the Ph.D. degree from the University of Minnesota (1984) in Family Social Science and has taught in that department. She has had fourteen years of experience in the planning and administration of educational programs. In her practice, she works with families, couples, and individuals and frequently sees families and members of families who own their own businesses.

Roxanne Marie Anderson is a licensed consulting psychologist in Alexandria, Minnesota, specializing in marital and family therapy. She received the Ph.D. degree in Family Social Science at the University of Minnesota (1982). She is a clinical member of the American Association for Marriage and Family Therapy and a member of the American Psychological Association.

Patricia A. Johnson is a coordinator of in-service education at Children's Hospital National Medical Center in Washington, D.C. She received the B.S. degree from the University of Idaho (1971), the M.S. degree in child development from Iowa State University (1973), and the Ph.D. degree in Family Social Science from the University of Minnesota (1983). She has worked on health-related issues important to children and families for more than ten years.

The Family in Business

*Understanding and Dealing
with the Challenges
Entrepreneurial Families Face*

Chapter One

Overlap of the Family System and the Business System

"My dad was authoritarian, but he was absolutely fair. So whenever my brother and I got in his disgrace, we both knew that we had it coming" (036B).*

"Grandpa goes out for longer lunches now, because he's older and he needs the time more. And I've become more responsible as far as being able to handle it on my own, and I don't mind handling it on my own as much" (062B).

"I don't personally concern myself with hurt feelings in the family as much as the business's needs" (011).

"My mother was never involved in the business. I know potentially she could get involved, but it's been my father's policy to keep her out of the business. He doesn't want to mix the problems in the home. He wants to make the decisions here and not go home and have to argue about them" (120).

*The number in parentheses that follows each quotation is the code number we assigned to the family of the person quoted. When there are two respondents from the same family, each has a different letter following the family number.

"It's probably easier to run a business if you
don't have family who's in, because you have an
extra dimension you have to deal with, and that's
relationships outside of the business" (122B).

The family business is an American ideal. The family
business is often imagined to provide a life of freedom and self-
determination, a life in which hard work and personal initiative
are rewarded with profit, success, financial security, and respect
from the community. When people think of a family business,
they may imagine a business owned and operated by a husband
and wife who are united in their common struggle, with mutual
understanding and shared joy in the growth and success of their
enterprise. The image may also include young children, contributing to the business in small and childish ways at first, then in
progressively more significant ways. Eventually, in that image,
the children may master the knowledge and skills necessary to
take a central role in the business, the parents feeling pride in
the competence and leadership of their grown offspring. The details of the image will, of course, be different for different types
of business: generation after generation running the same Mom
and Pop grocery store; a small repair shop, run by father and
son, growing into a major factory; or a rapidly growing financial
empire involving many relatives, an empire like that of the
Fords or the Rockefellers.

This book is about business-operating families. It is based
on what members of fifty-nine such families had to say. The
story they told in some cases supports the ideal image of the
family business and in many cases reveals a more complex reality, a reality in which tensions are at times great and in which
cooperation is difficult and painful to achieve, perhaps even impossible. As this book makes clear, we believe that involvement
in a family business adds to the load of differences a family
must deal with and puts some restraints on the optimum range
for dealing with differences. In any family, but particularly in a
business family, good people who are sincerely dedicated to
their close kin, who are trying hard to do the right thing, and
who are working competently and with great dedication at their

daily tasks will, we believe, have a substantial risk of at least periodic tension and stress in family relationships. In extreme cases, involvement in a family business may be associated with disastrous relationship problems in the family. We found business families that seemed to have been shattered by business involvement, families in which financial matters or business interactions seemed to have undermined family relationships, and families in which the ideal of intergenerational transmission of the business had become a nightmare of warfare between parent and offspring. Yet the family members studied were not without ways of coping. For example, many of them found ways of dealing with tensions over decisions and of insulating the parent/offspring relationship from the problems that can arise when parent supervises offspring.

What Is a Family Business?

There are no national statistics on the number of family businesses. Even if there were, the numbers would vary with the definitions used for *business* and for *family business.* A common estimate is that more than 90 percent of the 15 million businesses in the United States are family businesses in the sense of being owned (or at least controlled) and operated within a single family (Barnes and Hershon, 1976; Beckhard and Dyer, 1983a; Pine and Mundale, 1983). It is further estimated that family-owned businesses account for a majority of all jobs in the United States and roughly 40 percent of the gross national product (Beckhard and Dyer, 1983a). Nor is it merely the smaller businesses that are family-owned or family-controlled. Roughly 175 of the Fortune 500, the 500 largest businesses in the United States, are either owned or controlled by a single family (Lansberg S., 1983).

Judging by what we found in our interviews, in virtually all businesses owned or controlled by a single family, more than one family member is involved in the business at least some of the time, if not all the time. Even when only a single family member is involved, the heavy time commitment to the business by that single family member depends on the support and tolerance of other family members. It would be difficult for an entrepreneur to say the following if there were no family support of the entrepreneur's business involvement.

> "If I think it's best for the business, I'll come down here on a weekend or I'll have the rest of my family come down here, whatever is necessary, because above all I want the thing to succeed. We have not taken a lot of money out of it" (015).

We define a business as an entity organized to sell goods or services and known to the public—for example, by advertising or by being listed in the Yellow Pages (the business phone book). In this study we did not consider physicians, attorneys, social workers, counselors, and other professionals to be operators of family businesses, because the requirement of formal education in the professions limits the extent to which a family member who lacks similar education can participate in the enterprise. However, our sample included consulting firms run by professionals in a way that would allow family members to participate. Our definition of a business excludes farms, although the dynamics of farm families are almost certainly quite similar to the dynamics of business families. In fact, our previous work on farm families inspired our study of business families (Rosenblatt and Anderson, 1981; Rosenblatt and Keller, 1983; Rosenblatt, Nevaldine, and Titus, 1978).

Different definitions of the term *family business* have different implications for how to understand what is going on in a business and a family. We think a case can be made for defining any business in which majority ownership or control lies within a single family as a "family business," whether or not other family members are directly involved and whether or not family members consider it a family business. A point made throughout this book is that even businesses with only a single family member directly involved require various kinds of support and indirect involvement by other family members. However, for the present study we have worked with a less controversial definition. We define a family business as any business in which majority ownership or control lies within a single family and in which two or more family members are or at some time were directly involved in the business.

The Family System and the Business System

Tension is common. Seventy-nine of the ninety-two persons we interviewed reported tension or stress in family relationships as a result of the business's being a family one. In six of the thirteen business-operating families from which some person reported no tension or stress, another person from the same family offered contradictory information, saying that there was some tension or stress. Thus, there were reports of business-connected tension and stress from 88 percent of the business-operating families in our sample. Judging by what people said about their experiences, few families in business are, over the course of their involvement in the business, free of business-connected tensions. Said one successful entrepreneur, reflecting on her years in business with her children:

> "Family businesses are tough businesses to run. If I was to get into a business again, I would never go in with any of my family" (063A).

One way to understand how being involved in a family business can be a source of tension and stress is to think of the family as a system. From a systems theory perspective (for example, Broderick and Smith, 1979; Greenberg, 1977; Kantor and Lehr, 1975; Wertheim, 1973), all families have patterned ways of interacting, patterned roles, patterns of coming in contact and out of contact. All families have rules they can verbalize and rules they cannot verbalize. All families have ends they seem to work toward. All families overtly or covertly regulate contact among family members and between the family and the outside.

Families not involved in a business enterprise will have interaction patterns, role relationships, rules about conduct and conversation, and patterns of togetherness and apartness governed by their domestic relationships. Whatever it takes to live in their physical and social world and to get the necessities of living accomplished—eating, sleeping, being clothed, meeting psychic needs, connecting with kin, friends, coworkers, and others outside the family, receiving care in illness, and so on—families will typically arrange interactions to somehow fit that world. However, problems may arise (or those already present may become more complex) when the family must relate in an enterprise as well as domestically (Beckhard and Dyer, 1981, 1983a, 1983b; Lansberg S., 1983; Pitts, 1964).

From a family systems theory perspective, members of many families seem to interact with one another in the same ways from setting to setting. They tend to follow the same patterns, to see and define themselves and one another as unchanging across the settings in which they are together. Thus, a person whose family role in one setting is to be well organized and to be the initiator of activity will tend to continue that role pattern in other family settings. Or a person who has developed a pattern of being passive but critical with relatives in one setting will tend to carry that way of dealing with relatives into other settings. Consequently, when family members interact with one another in both the enterprise and the home, they tend to be the same in those two places.

A pattern of interacting that is appropriate in one setting may be inappropriate in another, with the result that the family members may have difficulties when they carry the pattern from one setting to another. For example, consider a couple who deal at home with tensions over major decisions by putting off the decisions. Even dealing with decisions at home that way might be a problem. For example, putting off decisions about repairs to a leaky basement could lead to substantial damage in the basement. If the couple work together in an enterprise where decisions must of necessity be made, putting off business decisions may be even more serious and may threaten the existence of the enterprise. Consider another instance in which a pattern may be less appropriate in the business than at home, one that may have its roots in the earliest days of the parent/offspring relationship but be sustained by parent/offspring interaction in the business. It may be acceptable to everyone in the family for a parent to be nurturant, advice-giving, and sometimes critical or patronizing to a son or daughter at home, but in the business the parenting may be embarrassing to the offspring and may disrupt the offspring's work. Patterns may also originate in the business and carry over to the home, where events may or may not sustain them. The most common example may be the boss of an enterprise bringing the boss role into the home. In some cases patterns seem to originate at home and carry over to the business, and in some they seem to do the reverse. But often, when patterns are similar in business and home, it is difficult to tell where they originated, and perhaps what is most important is that they persist at both places, even if they are inappropriate in at least one of those places.

To understand the risk of carryover from one system to another, one way to think about the problems of combining family system and business system is in terms of goals. The goals of a family and a business are similar, to the extent that all systems have the same requirements—for example, working out effective communication channels, rules about leadership, and rules for developing and enforcing rules. However, the goals of a family almost certainly differ in some respects from the goals of an enterprise. The enterprise must yield profits to survive. Its intermediate goals may include a good credit rating, high priority among suppliers, productive employees, and a stable or growing share of a market. Different families will have different goals, but commonly family goals may include things like a sense of self-worth for individual family members, developing personal and professional competence for individual family members, and achieving feelings of comfort and of belonging together. With so many goals for the enterprise and for the family being different, it is unlikely that what it takes to keep an enterprise viable is identical to what it takes to keep a family going.

People who work at an office or factory far from kin may live their work lives with relatively little direct interference from the family and their family lives with little direct interference from people and events at work. But people for whom a family member is present at the workplace will have to struggle to identify which goals they are working for at any one time.

Some of the time, what is helpful in pursuing one set of goals will be helpful in pursuing another; at other times goals will conflict.

The fact that goals are sometimes in harmony is one reason there are family businesses. A person who loves together-ness and shared experience with spouse and children may wel-come the opportunity to have spouse and children as coworkers and to share work goals with them. A person who wants to be as generous as possible to the family may well hope to transmit ownership of the family enterprise to her offspring. A person who wants a rich understanding of what his spouse does each day may also find a family business a desirable arrangement.

From the point of view of what it takes to produce a via-ble enterprise, family involvement may also be desirable. Fam-ily members may, for example, work longer hours for less pay, may be more dedicated than nonfamily, may be more willing and able to be on twenty-four-hour call to help when needed, and may be more willing and able to be flexible about work conditions. Family members may, in short, give a business more for the wages paid than most nonfamily members would. As Chapter Five indicates, economic ends may be served for both the family and the enterprise by making the enterprise a family one or by making the family an enterprise-operating one.

Despite the possibilities of goal overlap, the goals of busi-ness and family must inevitably differ some of the time. The ways of interacting, the patterns of getting along, the needs for contact, the standards of evaluation, and so on must differ be-tween the two places in ways that can create problems. The re-mainder of this book explores the key areas of difficulty arising when business system and family system overlap. Each chapter rests on a systems theory conceptual base, starting with what has been presented in this chapter, the notion that the family system and the business system have different requirements, yet people are disposed to follow the same patterns of relating to family members in the business and in the home. The carryover of patterns may be inappropriate for one of the two environ-ments of the business family—or for both of them. The chapters that follow bring in additional conceptual elements from systems theory and extend the areas of application of the theory presented in prior chapters.

A common problem in family businesses, confusion over who does what, is discussed in Chapter Two. The sources of the problem include lack of a clear division of labor and the fact that if one knows how to do another person's job, one may well do it. Problems over who does what commonly arise from the dynamics of offspring/parent relationships (for example, parental inclination to control offspring, offspring recognition of parental expertise, offspring respect for parent or resentment of parent). Problems also arise from the dynamics of spouse relationships, where there is a tension between hierarchy (ranking one spouse higher in the business than the other) and equality (one spouse feeling the right to be an equal to the other). Barriers to working out clarity over who does what are discussed, but despite these barriers, the chapter indicates the substantial costs to the family and the business if the confusion is not cleared up. The problem of who does what may be "solved" through someone's leaving the business, and the problem is often solved by unilateral action by a family member with executive authority in the business. A common constructive approach to dealing with the problem is to work out at least a partial or temporary division of labor. Even though there are difficulties in maintaining a division of labor, there are often even more serious difficulties if confusion over who does what is not resolved.

Roughly 50 percent of the business families studied reported tensions over carryover of roles from home to business or business to home. Chapter Three offers a view of the dangers of inappropriate role carryovers, the most common of which seemed to be in parent/offspring relationships. Perhaps what happens most often in parent/offspring relationships in family businesses is a process that disables the offspring (by fostering dependence, incompetence, or lack of confidence) or creates conflict as an offspring strives for independence, respect, and adult identity. In some businesses an offspring leaves. Families that cope often provide a functional and physical separation of parent and offspring or provide for apartness during time outside the business. In Chapter Three the problems and the solutions are discussed in various ways, but the process of individuation is emphasized, the dynamics of developing autonomy and a separate adult identity. Inappropriate role carryover is also commonly present in spouse relationships in business families. A spouse who is the boss at work may try to be the boss at home. At work, the marital role carryover is often expressed in tension over equality and hierarchy. The issue of whether husbands dominate or wives are equal may well cause stress and strain both at home and in the business. The most common way the issue appears in the business seems to involve a wife's desire for equality in business decisions and business status. A wife's striving for equality may threaten her entrepreneur husband, partly because many business decisions are rather arbitrary and not easily defended. Frequently wives are excluded from the business, or business matters are not discussed in the marriage.

Chapter Four discusses tensions over decisions, another common problem in the families studied. Decision problems arise from the dynamics of confusion over who does what and of role carryover, issues discussed in Chapters Two and Three. Decision problems also arise from dynamics that may be present in any business as people with different perceptions, goals, and so on strive for influence, position, and credit for achievements. In intergenerational relationships, tensions over individuation are not uncommonly played out in struggles over business decisions. In marital relationships the struggle over hierarchy versus equality often fuels conflict over decisions. While discussing decisions, people who were interviewed often said, "There can be only one boss." The origin and function of that theme are discussed in Chapter Four. Since there were businesses in the sample that seemed viable while run by more than one boss, the one-boss theme may well be a power position taken in decision struggles, rather than a necessity for viable management.

Fairness of compensation and work load is the focus of Chapter Five. It is clear that what seems fair to one person may seem very unfair to another, and what seems fair today may subsequently seem unfair. Most of the entrepreneurs in the sample were males who were or had been married. In more than

70 percent of the sample a wife was or had been involved in the business, not infrequently in an unpaid or underpaid role. Even when a wife was not directly involved in the business, she typically had to provide substantial support to the business through her work at home, carrying extra chores as she covered for her absent husband and forgoing expenditures on things desired for the household. Some women felt neglected, disappointed, and unappreciated. Even women who worked in the business might feel that way and might in addition carry an undiminished load of home chores. The use of kin in unpaid or underpaid roles is discussed in the chapter from an ethical point of view and from the viewpoint of enterprise development. Offspring also worked at times in unpaid or underpaid business roles. Some offspring seemed indulged, and some who felt exploited had a faith in their eventual reward. In many businesses, both parents and offspring were concerned about the opinions of employees who were not relatives. Would they resent the offspring's favored position? Perhaps to cope with the concerns about nonrelatives in the business, some parents went out of their way to make things difficult for offspring, and many offspring apparently worked very hard in order to prove that they were not being indulged. The hard work by offspring may have many other sources, including high demands placed on the offspring by parents and a sense that offspring of bosses must show by example of their work that they too can lead.

Chapter Six provides an analysis of togetherness and apartness in business families. Family businesses quite often are associated with very high levels of family apartness. Early in business involvement a founder or person who takes over a business may work very long hours, out of contact with family members almost all that time. Even in well-established businesses, many entrepreneurs work longer hours than people who are not entrepreneurs typically work. Some entrepreneurs seemed relatively insensitive to the family problems and resentments that high levels of apartness caused. Some tried to compensate family members for their unavailability with material goods, but the compensation was often not effective in that family members continued to resent the unavailability. In many businesses where family members worked together, they rarely saw one another. Family members who worked together often distanced one another to avoid conflict and satiation or to cool off after arguments. One particular "togetherness" problem in some businesses was that an entrepreneurial husband might feel very uncomfortable if his wife knew much about what was going on in the business. Although togetherness is an issue in some families, there were people who said that they valued the family contact, shared knowledge, and increased closeness of a family business.

As the discussion of supervision in Chapter Seven points out, many people are uncomfortable with the supervisory role. The problems may be compounded when it is a relative who must be supervised. Moreover, a person who is supervised may have difficulty with being supervised by a relative. In supervising relatives, people may hold back or be more harsh than they would be with a nonrelative. Chapter Seven discusses the dynamics underlying these alterations of the normal supervisory process. In many family businesses, in order to avoid the relationship tension that can arise when parent supervises offspring, parent/bosses used nonrelatives to supervise sons and daughters.

Chapter Eight provides an analysis of boundary problems that arise when there is insufficient separation of entrepreneur and business or of family and business. When boundaries are unclear between self and business, family tensions are likely. For example, an entrepreneur may not realize when family needs are different from business needs, may be unwilling to tolerate criticism of the business, and may not want to relinquish business control even when a succession plan ostensibly calls for that. The entrepreneur may be closed to topics not directly relevant to the business and may be preoccupied with the business twenty-four hours a day. When home and business have no clear boundary, people are less clear when what is good for one is not good for the other, and carryover of mood from business to home may be more substantial. Using a home as the business location increases the likelihood of these boundary problems. Employment of a relative is especially complicated when boundaries are unclear. It becomes difficult, for example, to exert authority over the relative or to fire the relative, and the relative may be more likely to ignore lines of authority and organizational limits. The chapter explores ways people go about establishing self/business and family/business boundaries.

In Chapter Nine, money and power are discussed as symbols of excellence, status, and much else. From the perspective of money as symbol, the early scarcity of funds that is so common in family businesses can be seen as a threat to self-esteem, and efforts to promote business growth can be seen as motivated by much more than financial need. The symbolic value of money and power makes concerns over the fairness of compensation understandable as in part concerns about meaning and interpretation. In family relationships those symbols may have even more significance than in other relationships, concerns about fairness reflecting concerns about one's standing in the family. In the interview material, fairness concerns were particularly common in sibling and sibling-in-law relationships. Power battles in business families may start from ordinary differences, but people often dig in because they do not want to lose. In family businesses, battles arise in part from intergenerational dynamics, in part from family members testing where they stand with others, and in part from the need for self-affirmation and assertion of self. A power battle may be a desirable path to necessary change, organizational creativity, expression of feelings, and closeness of relationship, but it can also polarize and lead to coalition formation and actions that are designed to win battles rather than meet organizational goals. There is a predictability to the form and structure of intergenerational power battles. Parents and other senior relatives tend to use seniority, expertise, and the actual control they have of the family business. They may win favor with offspring by not using their power at least some of the time. Younger family members will tend to use their currentness and the threat to leave the business and thereby to make intergenerational transfer of the business unrealizable. Younger people may also offer arguments on ethical grounds, although when feeling powerless they may also be inclined to use unethical ways of circumventing a family member with greater authority than they in the

business. Some parents who were interviewed were concerned
that money might corrupt offspring, and many were concerned about how much pressure to exert on offspring to come
into the business.

A key point in Chapter Ten is that planning for business
succession or inheritance is rare in the families studied. Although an offspring may have worked in the business at an early
age, may have received considerable on-the-job experience, and
may be recognized as the successor, the process of succession
may not have been planned. It can be a difficult situation for
offspring, although many may feel hooked by the money involved, by family loyalty, and by the opportunity to achieve
power and status at an early age. There were also cases in which
no offspring was considered available or willing to succeed to
ownership and control of the business; however, daughters were
almost always overlooked as possible successors. Why entrepreneurs would overlook daughters is discussed at length. Tensions
over succession were present in a majority of the businesses in
which succession had occurred or was occurring. The problems
had many elements. Typically they reflected the senior person's
ambivalence about giving up the business, about trusting the
successor, or about letting changes occur. Offspring who were
potential successors were not necessarily eager to give up their
dependent role and were not necessarily allowed to become
competent. Tensions over succession would often affect other
relationships in the family, particularly the marital relationship
of the potential successor. Some entrepreneurs set a very high
cash transfer price for transfer of the business, which might be a
way to hold off succession but which also reflected their reli-
ance on the income from the transfer of the business to support
retirement. Even after a succession process was far along or
complete, many retiring entrepreneurs continued to influence
the business. There were also successions that had occurred de
facto, even though the succession had not yet occurred on paper, because the potential successor had moved the business
into areas outside the entrepreneur's competence. The keys to a
smooth succession are outlined in the chapter. They begin with
a parent who can give up control and who has other interests

than the business. The successor who is not yet competent needs experience gaining that competence. All parties involved would benefit from accepting change, being flexible and non-defensive, being good at communicating, and being adequately patient. Inheritance is a related problem area. Many entrepreneurs seem reluctant to discuss, perhaps even to consider, inheritance. Yet the interviews show that inheritance matters need to be discussed, that some businesses get into trouble because an inheritance plan does not fit the business and the people who would have to make decisions about the business. Families may avoid serious relationship troubles as a result of inheritance disputes through open discussion of feelings concerning inheritance plans.

How respondents saw the advantages of being in a family business is the topic of Chapter Eleven. Some respondents saw no advantages, and others seemed to have trouble naming advantages because their family business had achieved a taken-for-granted quality. They had not been thinking recently, and perhaps never had, of evaluating their way of life against alternatives. The most common advantage mentioned was freedom—for example, freedom from the control of others, freedom to do what one wants, freedom from criticism, and freedom to use time flexibly. Freedom was mentioned more often by entrepreneurs than other respondents, which may indicate who has the freedom in a family business. The frequency with which freedom was mentioned is somewhat paradoxical, since many of the people who mentioned freedom worked sixty hours a week or more in the family business. Although they felt free, they may have spent less time away from work than most workers do. Another frequently mentioned advantage of being in a family business was a financial one. This was so even though profits were meager in many businesses studied. The monetary advantages included capital accumulation (as opposed to income), the financial advantages of having family members working in the business, and the possibility of writing off some personal or family expenses as business expenses. The financial advantages are difficult to interpret, however, because money is so often a symbol of other things. People who mentioned financial gains might have been able to articulate other advantages if they had gone beyond the symbolic meaning of money. Among other advantages mentioned were prestige and pride, creativity, and the capacity to do good things for one's offspring. One advantage that says something about tensions in business families is that a number of people mentioned improving or building family relationships as an advantage of being in a family business. People talked about sharing pressures, learning tolerance, and working through family problems. Thus, the tensions of being in a business family are seen by some people not as a swamp to be slogged through but as a path to improved family relations.

The entire book contains suggestions for managing the family business, and Chapter Twelve provides an overview of management issues, draws together some of the more important suggestions, and offers some new suggestions. The key to managing the family business is to recognize the separateness of the two systems and the difference in goals of business and family. If that difference is fully appreciated, management does not become simple in a family business, but it becomes in some sense more sane. Management in a family business must deal with goal conflict, particularly conflict of goals between family and business. In matters of the business it is important to keep track of the business goals and what would best serve the business. In matters of direct concern to the family—for example, allocation of family savings or the time of individual family members— family members should participate in decisions. At times the two systems may make competing demands—for example, hire an offspring versus hire a professional manager—and the competition must be resolved with an awareness of the consequences for both systems. A key management tactic in family businesses is to work out a division of labor. Although factors unique to family businesses may make it more difficult to work out a division of labor or to hold to one, a division of labor can reduce problems in almost all family business tension areas. In businesses that are too small or too new to work out any long-term division of labor, a division for the week, the day, or even the hour may be of value. Developing position descriptions is also a useful management tactic. In family businesses such descriptions might usefully include career position descriptions for family members who are likely to move up in the business hierarchy and for family members who will occasionally be called on to help out. Tactics for management are also discussed in the areas of pay, supervising relatives, and conflict management. Although conflict is not necessarily undesirable, a number of detailed recommendations are made for heading off, reducing, or guarding against debilitating and damaging conflict. As with other aspects of family and business dealt with in this book, it seems important that conflict be managed with a sense of mutual respect and of individual autonomy of the people dealt with. It is also important that conflict not spread to other relationships. Suggestions are made at both the level of the individual dealing with other individuals and the level of organizing the business. Management discussion is also extended to selection and training of a successor. Planning is emphasized, as in the education and preparation of the chief officer to carry through the succession process well.

Chapter Thirteen is written for therapists and provides illustrative case material. Although the problems that people from business-operating families bring to therapy are often like those any family might bring, therapy with such families is more challenging because of the linking of family and business. Change in the family may be resisted because of the business, family problems may be aggravated or expressed through tensions in the business, and the business may be a source of family problems or make existing problems more serious. A therapist who is knowledgeable about business families and family businesses may be better able to gain rapport with them, to understand them, and to facilitate desired change in them. The key issues in therapy with business families seem to be ones of boundaries and of individuation. The chapter reviews problems arising from boundary and individuation difficulties, explores resistance to strengthened boundaries and to individuation, and outlines therapeutic approaches to boundary building and the promotion of individuation. The chapter addresses two other topics that seem important in dealing with business families, sexism and money. Sexism needs to be addressed because connection of the family with the business may provide impetus for women to be discounted, treated disrespectfully, scapegoated, exploited, or otherwise put in a position that is difficult for the women and tension-creating in the family. Money is important because it is a focus of tensions, secrets, manipulations, and meanings in many business-operating families.

Chapter Fourteen provides a framework for organizational consulting with family businesses. Consultation with family businesses may be more challenging than consultation with other types of organizations because of problems in defining the client and focusing the consultation. There may be ethical and other complexities in working only with the family member who has asked for the consultation. The most significant challenge in consulting with a family business is, however, to deal with a business system that is linked to a family system. Problems when consulting with interlinked business and family systems include dealing with resistance to change in the business caused by its linkage to the family, identifying family members not directly involved in the business who are having an impact on the business, and helping the business meet business goals while respecting the reality and validity of family goals. The consultation process with a family business ideally aims to give the organization long-lasting problem-solving tools. The consultation is facilitated when the consultant enters the situation with openness to the uniqueness of each family business. The consultation process includes defining goals that are manageable and respecting the separate realities of the people in the system. Often a consultant must redefine things or get beneath the surface. A valuable aspect of consultation in a family business is often the facilitation of communication. A consultant's problem solving for a family business may involve promotion of planning, mediation of discrepant plans and goals, and evaluation of family constraints on organizational functioning. Consultants legitimate change, both changes that they help initiate and those that were on the way before they arrived. Legitimation may involve expert endorsement or guidance, and it may involve engineering some kind of ritual to acknowledge and deal with the losses that are inevitably a part of the change process.

Chapter Fifteen touches on key issues for people to consider in working for a relative. Perspective, the capacity to step back from a situation to reframe and analyze it, is an important tool for anyone but especially for somebody working for a relative. Other important tools are communicating, striving to maintain a balance of togetherness and apartness, defining work roles clearly, and functioning in the work situation with flexibility and learning as personal policies. Entering a family business with an understanding on all sides that it is a trying-out situation, that either party may decide things are not working out well enough and may terminate the employment, may help to maintain family relationships. In working for a spouse, a key issue is to deal with the tension between equality and hierarchy. Openness about the issue and self-conscious organizing to deal with it may pay dividends. In working for a parent, it is often important to address issues of dependency, to be aware of parental needs, to have done work outside the family business in order to gain perspective and experience with being supervised, and to be able to communicate with one's parent/employer about problems in the business relationship.

Chapter Sixteen provides an overview of the basic conceptual approach used in this book. When the family system and the business system are interconnected, both systems may have problems because of inappropriate carryover from one system to the other. The two systems may support each other, but they also may compete for resources, and the interconnection may create problems when one system benefits at the expense of the other. The chapter offers a partial summary of the results of the research reported in this book and perspective on the diversity of business families and family businesses through a discussion of the developmental cycle of the family business and the differences between smaller family businesses and larger ones.

Although this book provides no recipe for peace in the family business and in the business family, it offers some hope to people who are thinking of starting a family business and to families experiencing tension in an established business. Some families seem to get along well. Some families have headed off problems or solved them, and some families have learned to live with problems and find them less distressing now than in the past.

Chapter Two

Tensions over Who Does What in the Business

"It's pretty hard to define roles within a family business. Some members see what other members are doing, and they tend to want to do that rather than what they are supposed to do" (119, who works with his wife and three of his children).

In any organization the potential exists for confusion, tension, and stress over who does what. People are capable of overstepping or disagreeing about role boundaries, about who should do what. Lines of leadership may be unclear, or people in leadership roles may give mixed messages ("Do it but only when I don't want to do it" or "I want you to be responsible for that task, but I want to control when, where, and how it is done"). When new situations arise, it may be unclear who should act, and people may disagree about who should do what. Family businesses seem to have a great potential for confusion, tension, and stress over who does what. Thirty-two respondents, representing twenty-seven businesses, reported tension in this area. Since tensions and stresses over who does what are entangled in many other areas of tension and stress, the present chapter is to some extent an overview of much to come.

Sources of Tension

One source of problems over who does what that seems common in family business is that a person who runs a family business often wants family members to know how to do various jobs, including at least some aspects of the business operator's job. A substitute will be needed if the business operator becomes ill or is otherwise unavailable or if an employee is temporarily absent. Extra help will be needed in a heavy work season. The person running the business may also want assurance that when he or she dies, a spouse or an offspring can operate the business.

> "My wife is very knowledgeable, and she has been my mainstay for a good thirty-six, thirty-seven years now. Like I said originally, she's my back-up person. If I need somebody in a hurry, she's available. It isn't like asking an employee ahead of time. She's there" (116A).

> "My husband would want me to do more than I sometimes felt I wanted to do. He would want me to be more up to date on different sales approaches, money forecasting, budgeting, and I just didn't feel that I wanted to give that much time to it. He wants me to know how to run this business in case something happens to him, and I guess I just don't want to get that involved. It really isn't a real stressful position, but yeah, there is some" (091B).

Although neither of the two passages just quoted indicates that the pressure on a spouse for back-up skill or knowledgeability created the conditions for trouble over who does what, family members with expertise to step into the roles of others obviously have the potential to become part of a troublesome situation. They have the capacity to be powerful critics or to usurp control in the other's area of the business. Thus, drawing on the family system for business system support in the form of back-up help and assurance of business continuity should something happen to the chief officer sets up the possibility of clash over who does what as patterns of relating, rules, roles, and leadership are carried over from family system to business system.

The business operator's own expertise can be a source of tension over who does what. Any business operator will know quite a bit about the jobs of some people in the business, and an operator (perhaps particularly a founder) of a relatively simple or small business may know how to do the job of everybody in the business. Given knowledgeability, a business operator may, for any of a large number of reasons, temporarily move into the work territory of someone else in the business. The motivation for the temporary move into another's work territory may be a goodhearted desire to help out, impatience that a job get done, pleasure in using particular knowledge or ability, concern that a particular task be done very well, or interest in doing something useful when there is nothing else to do that is of higher priority. Moving into the work territory of another person may be no problem; it may even be welcomed and increase the respect and loyalty others in the business have for the operator—but it may create tension. Thus, even with the best of intentions, a business operator may help to create tension over who does what. If the tension involves another family member, then the pattern of resolving tension at the business determines the extent to which tension is likely to carry over into the family. The tension may well affect people more substantially than if no family relationships were involved. So the business may provide additional opportunity for family tension and may tax tension resolution skills.

It also seems that many family businesses are small enough or new enough that a clear division of labor is inefficient or inappropriate. Especially in small businesses, the flow of work and the types of work needed may be variable, so that dividing the work into separate roles may be economically inappropriate. In such businesses, there is value in everybody's being willing and able to do everything.

> "Big businesses have very elaborate job descriptions and are very careful. Being bigger, they

have a wider range of responsibility and, I think, more physical separation. Being a small business, you don't have that much physical separation. Somebody calls in with a problem, you're apt to solve it, and the fellow whose responsibility it was may not be there and may have solved it a little differently. If you've got a thinner skin, it bothers you" (033A, a father working with offspring. A statement by one of his sons, quoted in Chapter Three, suggests that some of the "thin skins" in his business were worn by his sons).

To the extent that family businesses may be overrepresented among new businesses, factors making for unclarity about who does what in new businesses may often operate disproportionately in family businesses. In new businesses, as the following statement indicates, it may be premature to try to work out a division of labor. Until the tasks of a business are clear and until the most effective ways of using the abilities of the people in the business have been established, working out a division of labor may be maladaptive.

"Seeing that this is really our first year in the business, it isn't conflict that we experience over who does what. It's the trying to find out what works out best" (099).

The process of finding out what works best may be a tense one, particularly if there is unclarity about leadership, about who decides what the tasks are and how they will be implemented. Not working out at least a partial division of labor may be worse for family relationships than the struggle to work one out. The tensions in the business as a result of trying to find out what works best or as a result of leaving divisions of labor undefined may carry over from business to family. Unfortunately, there are also carryovers from family to business, particularly in parent/offspring and spouse/spouse relationships, that may create barriers to working out tensions over who does what. These carryovers are discussed in the next section of this chapter.

Parent/Offspring Tensions

Some parents seemed to want to impress offspring and to control them and the business. Lest this statement be read as critical of business-operating parents, it should be pointed out that wanting to impress offspring and to control them and the business can arise from the best of motives. A business operator might want to impress offspring because he or she cares about their good opinion, wants to motivate offspring to learn the important things he or she has to teach, and feels deserving of offspring praise and support. A business operator might want to control offspring because of a concern that they do well and learn how to do jobs the right way. A business operator might well want to control the business out of a concern that the business do well, that hard-won achievements not be undermined, and that his or her expe ise and wisdom be put to good use. Some offspring seemed to fear or respect parents, some to want parental approval and acknowledgment, and some to crave the safety and comfort of having a parent run things, although offspring may also resent and oppose parental attempts to control them and the business.

The following remarks by three business offspring illustrate their perceptions of parental effort to maintain control of the business and the offspring and, to some extent, the resentment and opposition they directed at their parents. The first quotation also suggests how an offspring's respect can help to maintain problems over who does what.

> "At first I was kind of in it as my father's partner, but I had to sit back because he was the domineering type. You know, you respect your father, always brought up that way. And after a while we got a little more tension because I got to the point that I said, 'Well, I think I know this better on this specific thing than you do.' And he's a very stubborn person, and when you tell him something like that, he goes crazy" (031A).

> "My father gave us as long a rein as we wanted, except every so often he'd give it a good

sharp tug to remind us who was in control. And I
think that our biggest battles—he used to fire me,
literally fire me. 'Goddamn it, you're through!' I
can just hear him now. And then he'd come down
to the office first thing in the morning, dictate a
letter: 'To whom it may concern: This is to notify
you that my son is no longer employed by this
company.' And then it would blow over. Eventually, I said to my father, 'You ought to get rid of
your stock. You're just kidding yourself. You
don't have any power. You couldn't run this company for a minute if you had to.' And he finally
did get rid of his stock. It was difficult, though,
very difficult. He no longer had clout over me. He
was always fearful that he would be destitute"
(006).

"The business was sold to me. I insisted on
an ironclad contract, where I controlled 100 percent of the stock. After that happened, it still took
about six years for my mother and father to quit
what I would consider meddling in the business.
They couldn't make me do what they wanted to
make me do" (101A).

In all three quotations, control issues seem important,
control of the business and control of offspring or parent. Issues
of control might have been very much the same had the younger person taking over the business been a nonrelative, but it is
difficult to imagine the respect shown in the first quotation or
the struggles of the second and third ones being present were
the people involved not related as parent and offspring. There
thus seem to be extra barriers in parent/offspring relationships
to working out tensions over who does what as a result of carrying over patterns of interaction, rules, and so on from the family system to the business system.

We do not mean to imply, with the three preceding quotations, that relationships like those are inevitable in family
businesses. Parents and offspring can have relationships with
mutual respect and elbow room to disagree and to be different
from each other, and they can engineer a smooth intergenerational transfer of management and control. But the problem

relationships were ones like the three described by the offspring just quoted. In businesses with strong intergenerational power battles, with tension or confusion over leadership and control, offspring do not always continue to acquiesce. They may, as in the second quotation above, eventually be in a position of de facto control that enables them to move to actual control. Or they may, as in the third quotation, eventually be granted enough power by the older generation so that they can and do win power battles with those elders. However, offspring do not always win battles, even when they seem to have the power to do so. In two businesses run by an offspring, parents seized control.

> "The biggest problem was I opened the business or started it. My father was working with me, and somewhere along the line I lost control of the business. Mother and Dad had virtually stepped in and walked right over the top of me. I was putting in ten, twelve, fourteen hours a day, and we sort of had the duties split up between bookwork and whatever, and all of a sudden it wound up that Dad was taking care of the bookwork and doing the ordering, and it wound up that I was an employee in my own business. I tried for three years to get it back" (061).

> "My son is the general manager, but I think I do more managing than he does. I feel that in business it takes more than two eyes. What one doesn't see, the other one should see. Just because it's not your job doesn't mean you shouldn't partake of doing it when the time arises. My son went away on vacation, to his regret. When he came back, I had turned the small business that he had founded into one of the biggest businesses of its type in the area" (063A).

Both cases of parent takeover illustrate points we have been making in this chapter, that in a family business there is potential for confusion, tension, and stress over who does what, that an older person's expertise can be a source of that tension, and that parents and offspring in business together may adopt stances that create barriers to working out tensions over who does what. Both parental takeovers were matters of genuine tension, even though the parents involved seemed to be doing what they thought was good for the business and for the offspring. Neither offspring moved to sue and neither left the company. The tensions over who did what seemed, in both companies, to exist and to persist partly because of parental interest in impressing offspring and in controlling them and the business and partly because of offspring fear and respect of parents and desire for parental approval and acknowledgment.

Spouse Tensions

From some of the businesses in which spouses worked together or had worked together, there were reports of spouse tension over who did what. In the following comment, an entrepreneur reported his impression that his wife was a source of tension over who did the work of the boss. This quotation picks up an issue of importance in understanding how tensions can arise between spouses in business together. It may be difficult to build a formal structure that neutralizes the imperatives of the spouse role in our society. Spouses of bosses may tend to feel that they deserve something like equal rank in decision making and respect. This entrepreneur's comment is also typical of complaints family members make about one another in that it blames a person, rather than seeing problem behavior as arising from the situation people are in. Blaming a person makes it more difficult to recognize constructive changes that might be possible in a situation.

> "My wife has a tendency to want to be the boss in business always. It doesn't go too well with some of the other employees, with the result that I haven't had her here the last couple or three years. I prefer not to have her around when the other people are here. It causes problems" (032A).

This quotation suggests that people may resolve their tensions over who does what by choosing to have one person involved in the tension stay away from the business. The choice of a person to leave may, as the quotation suggests, involve a unilateral decision by one person. In marital relationships the person chosen to leave the business seems, in our data, typically to be the woman.

The issues underlying spouse tension in business are discussed throughout this book, but as the following excerpts from interviews suggest, they include how to deal with unequal legitimacy to act and with unequal knowledge, with entitlement to a status equal to one's partner's, and with felt need to be respected as an equal. The claims of an entrepreneur to be recognized as a business superior to a spouse and of the entrepreneur's spouse to be his or her coequal both seem to push for tensions over who does what.

> "Someone would be working on a machine. She'd walk through and say, 'That isn't the way to do it.' And she didn't know nothing about it. She should go to me. My ex-wife was quite a mouthy individual" (039).

> "My husband will say, 'I will listen to you,' but he really doesn't like it. He has to listen to me because I'm not quiet. But I want him to do more than listen to me. I guess that's another point I have to make. I want him to act on what I say. Maybe I really do overstep" (096B).

In the first of the remarks just quoted, the wife, one might guess, felt entitled to act like a boss, and the husband felt entitled to be treated like the boss and like a person with greater expertise. The tension in the second remark could also be interpreted as arising from competing claims for entitlement or respect. The woman, who worked in the business some of the time but was clearly not the boss, seemed to want to be on a more equal footing with her husband, and her husband may have wanted to have his entrepreneurial role and his feelings of being the expert insulated from his wife's influence. Both cases are suggestive of a marital dynamic that may push toward tensions over who does what in businesses in which a husband and wife are both involved and in which the husband has more expertise or more executive power than his wife.

Invading Somebody Else's Territory

Loose definition of who should do what seems to create trouble in some family businesses. Working out very clear, tight definitions is no easy matter. Issues can always arise which overlap jurisdictions or which do not fit the system. Some problems seem to need immediate attention, even if the person who should deal with them is not present. When there is a hierarchy, the same problem can be dealt with by persons at several levels, and supervision will at times require a supervisor to intrude into the province of a person being supervised. Thus, either because work roles are loosely defined or because of the normal pressures of messy reality on the neat organization that has been devised, occasionally there will seem to be invasion by one family member of another family member's work territory.

In people's reports of such invasions of territory, it emerged that the apparent invader does not necessarily communicate, in advance of the invasion or while invading, with the person whose territory is invaded. People who think they have the right to do something may not feel that they have to touch base with others who feel they have the same right. However, failures to communicate may increase tensions over who does what. Here are two examples of deficient communication that seemed to be associated with problems of who did what:

> "I don't think there was a jealousy over the duties as much as how you communicated what you were going to do and what your plans were. I think that I was probably too quick to make decisions and not communicate what I was doing with my father. And I think that bothered him" (087).

> "When you are busy all day long, sometimes you don't get a chance to discuss anything" (018, a wife who worked with her husband fifty to sixty hours per week in a family business for which she reported problems over who did what).

One could say that the noncommunication might have arisen because there was not time or opportunity to communicate, but nonrelatives might have been more likely to create the time and opportunity. Although remarks like the two just given might conceivably arise from relationships of nonrelatives in a business, our speculation is that in both cases people felt more free not to communicate because they were relatives. In any family there is likely to be a pattern of noncommunication about many day-to-day activities. People feel free not to communicate about eating a snack, changing clothes, phoning a friend, and so on. That freedom not to communicate, we believe, carries over from family to business and intensifies problems over who does what.

The problems two relatives in business may have over invasion of each other's work territory will affect others, particularly when the relatives both have managerial roles. An undesirable consequence of confusion between managers over who does what is that others in the business can become entangled in conflicting demands. One manager asks for one thing, another for a different thing. Subordinates in the business, as the following passage indicates, may deal with the conflict by ignoring some managerial demands.

"Dad concentrates very much on one thing, and my mother concentrates very much on a lot of different things. If that would happen in an organization that I didn't know them better, it would be a real problem—'cause you get conflicting signals on what you ought to be working on." *Interviewer:* "How do you work that out?" *Respondent:* "You just don't pay attention to one of them" (095B).

Although problems in division of labor and delegation of authority may be difficult to recognize as such (Boswell, 1973, p. 80), members of business-operating families are often painfully aware of personal feelings and business difficulties that result from problems in division of labor and delegation of authority. They experience personal confusion and ambivalence over tasks and decisions. They may perceive in themselves and in the people they work with hurt feelings and anger. They may see confusion among subordinates. They may experience difficulties and personal embarrassments with customers and suppliers over conflicting signals. But whether they recognize these as symptoms of organizational difficulty is unclear. They may instead see the problems as personality matters, often blaming others (people tend not to blame themselves) for the problems that have arisen.

In some family businesses, the problem of who did what was solved by the unilateral action of one family member, with tacit acceptance by other family members. One approach was for a senior person, typically a father and husband, to become authoritarian, to assert a right to gain control in areas where there had been some confusion over who was controlling. The first part of the following quotation was offered at the beginning of this chapter.

> "It's pretty hard to define roles within a family business. Some members see what other members are doing, and they tend to want to do that rather than what they are supposed to do. I usually solve it by being the boss" (119, whose wife and three children worked with him).

The following passage also illustrates an attempt by a father to resolve the confusion over spheres of authority by asserting his own authority. The passage illustrates, as well, one source of problems over who does what—family members sometimes express opinions to other family members that would probably never have been expressed were they not relatives.

> "When we first put in a full-time manager, my daughter who does the bookkeeping was a little touchy about the fact. With an explanation she got over this. Part of the explanation was the fact that it's not her business to run, that she is an employee" (025A).

There were two cases of unilateral takeover of power by a

younger family member, one who had previously not had a clear right to make major decisions or to do the work of the chief executive. In both cases, the takeover was by a son. As with the takeovers by parents mentioned earlier in this chapter, it seems that the fact of the takeovers, the procedures involved in them, and the reactions to them were unlike what they would have been if nonrelatives had engineered the takeovers. The carryover from the family system of patterns of offspring challenge to parent, of parent tolerance of offspring, and of mutual interest in maintaining a relationship may well have provided a foundation for takeovers and the tolerance of them.

"I kind of muscled my father out of the business. He had a great sense of humor, so he was able to laugh at situations that a lot of fathers would have become testy about. When he turned the business over, I knew he was doing it more in name than in function. And he said he was going to take a vacation. While he was gone, I found him another office, moved his office out of the building, and moved his secretary over there. He walked in and his office wasn't there anymore. [Laughs] So we showed him his new office and congratulated him on it. I knew that as long as he was in the same office with me and all the people there, there's no question who they would be reporting to, whether he made me president in title or not. He was startled and shocked, but he got used to it" (044).

A respondent quoted earlier in this chapter whose parents took control of his business dealt with his pain and frustration and with a confusion in the business that led to employees' playing off new boss against old by usurpation. When his father became ill, the son regained control of the business.

"I just very slowly had to watch myself and keep trying to take more and more control of it back, which is a real bear. Questioning a lot of the things he did. Questioning why bills were paid or why bills weren't. Keeping real close tabs on the checkbook and on the dailies, just virtually took

over hiring and firing. About eight months ago,
nine months ago, I went for lunch. We were super
busy. Came back. At that point I had four guys
working for me plus myself, and there wasn't a
damn thing more done when I got back than when
I had left, and I canned the whole goddamn crew.
And that was it. After that I took it myself. He was
a little upset. I suppose I would have been too if he
had done it. The day my father went in the hospital, I took everything that was there. Filing cabi-
nets, the whole works, everything got moved that
day, everything out to my house" (061).

Feelings of upset are among the consequences of confusion over who does what. Many family members reported letting off steam in such situations, being upset overtly, some of
them loudly and in very angry ways. A person quoted earlier
on the tendency for consultation to be poor among family
members in a business when there is tension and stress over who
does what said the following about dealing with the tension.

"It gets resolved, but it takes time to heal
some of those things. I think you resolve it getting
mad at each other, swearing at each other, slamming doors" (087).

For many people, however, swearing or slamming doors is not a
way to resolve tension. It may even be a source of additional
tension. People who find angry encounters punishing and who
find the inefficiency of confusion over who does what costly
may be the people most likely to try to organize themselves so
as to minimize the confusion. One organizational approach is to
work out a division of labor.

Working Out a Division of Labor

By far the most commonly reported solution to the problem of tension and stress over who does what was the working
out of a division of labor. People recognizing the costs of overlap of roles and interchangeability of business activities seemed
often to work out some sort of division of labor.

> *Interviewer:* "How did you solve the prob-
> lems you had over who did what?" *Respondent:*
> "By specializing" (036A).

> "The way we've done, which has helped us
> considerably, is my father is running the plumbing
> company and I'm handling the heating part of the
> company. I'm making the decisions for the heating
> company. Since we've done that, things have been
> a lot better. There were some mornings I didn't
> even want to come to work" (031A).

Both these respondents described division of labor as an adaptation to parent/offspring problems. In the former case, the problems seemed to be primarily over whether the business should
expand; in the latter case, they seemed to be ones of parental
intrusiveness and dominance and offspring deference and lack
of confidence. For some other people, division of labor was a
means of dealing with marital problems. One man explained
why his wife managed two companies, independently of him,
within the family's group of enterprises.

> "I tend to be much more independent when
> my wife's not present, and she tends to be much
> less independent when we are together" (119).

Although the independence mentioned by this respondent
might be a separate issue from the problem of who does what,
lack of independence can be seen as both an entanglement of
responsibilities and a lack of clarity about who has the right
and the willingness to make a decision or take an action. The
following remarks by an entrepreneur (also quoted earlier in
this chapter) concern his relationship with his former wife. The
intrusion of work life into home life seems clear in his remarks,
and it seems clear that he felt that his independence was being
threatened by things his wife did. Like other men whose wives
were quoted earlier in this chapter or who themselves were
quoted, he resented his wife's intrusions into his sphere of operation. The solution he wanted was one of division of labor.

> "If you have a family business, it should be
> very strict as to who's attending to what, and that's

about the only thing we used to lock horns about. A gal can't leave things at the office. So many of them will wake up in the middle of the night, 'Well, what about such-and-such?' " (039).

Division of labor can, of course, solve many problems in addition to the problem of who does what. For example, division of labor helps when people feel they are together too much of the time (see Chapter Six) and when there is too much disagreement in the allocation of blame and praise. Without division of labor, one could not be sure who was at fault when something went wrong and who deserved the credit when something went well. Said one of two sons of a business founder:

> "We split up the business so each person has his category which he's responsible for, and of course, if the thing falls on its face, it's not hard to figure out whose fault it is. This is a very good system because if you do it the other way, where you've got shared responsibility, then you've always got the one person thinking that he's doing more than the other one, or it's hard to measure the degree of success. But if each person has a division he's in charge of, by gosh, the results of division come out at the end of the year in black and white" (036A).

Even when people work out a division of labor, there is no guarantee that it can be maintained. Parents may still feel parental responsibility (or overresponsibility), hunger for control, and fear of being displaced; offspring may still be inclined to defer to parents; spouse may still feel the right to act on a wish to appear equal in status and business wisdom to spouse; and sibling may still find it difficult to defer to sibling. Consequently, it is not surprising that there were reports of violation of agreed-on divisions of tasks. Here are such reports from five family businesses.

> "It's particularly hard for my brother to relieve himself of duties that are not his duties, that are mine or other people's. His memory slips. He

forgets, after being in business for thirty-six years, he forgets we've modernized things, and things are not exactly the way they used to be. I have to go back and try to keep tempers down" (074A).

"I'll ask Dad for a raise, and if he doesn't give it to me, I'll just give it to myself. . . . He finds out at the end of the month 'cause the accountant'll tell him. . . . He's such a cheap sucker. When Dad hired me, he said, 'I'll pay you two hundred dollars a week.' When he was signing paychecks and got to mine, he said, 'This isn't right.' I said, 'What do you mean it isn't right? It's six hundred dollars for three weeks.' He says, 'No, I'm only going to give you one hundred and eighty a week.' And he did, for like a year, till I just said I'm not going to live with this bullshit. I just did it and then told him about it three weeks later. That's how it was going to be, and if he didn't like it, he could find somebody else. He says, 'Yeah, yeah, OK' " (025B).

"I'm unhappy at my mother for her turning around and telling me what I have to do and what I don't. Basically I run the business, but when it comes to the hiring of my cousin, I'm told that he's to work, where he's to work, and a basic area, and how much he's to start at. Whether I like it or not, I have to handle it" (064A, who was president of the family's business, in which his mother was chief shareholder).

"It's probably harder to work for your parents most of the time than to work for somebody else. I would say that people who work for their parents probably are more apt to take a few more little liberties also, like trying to be boss once in a while" (031B).

"My father always had a problem delegating authority. Even when he did delegate it, he took it over. Now his stubbornness is directed specifically at me" (096A).

In some family businesses, the problems arising from confusion over who does what are never dealt with adequately, and either the business goes under or, as the following statement indicates, an outsider must be given substantial control. The statement is by a nonrelative who at one time was stripped of his duties as company vice-president and then left temporarily.

> "At that time I left the company temporarily, and then they had a son, a father, and a daughter as top president, vice-president, secretary. Things just weren't working out. The areas of responsibility weren't defined, and they were crossing each other's paths. The work load wasn't defined, and one was doing a lot bigger share than the other. Since that happened, problems arose financially, and the decision had to be made how to get the business back to where it was, and that was when I was approached again. I was first approached to come back as vice-president and general manager, and I refused. And then I was asked to come back in a different capacity, and I accepted as president and 50 percent owner" (098A).

Conclusion

In this chapter we have shown that tensions arise in family businesses over who does what. These tensions seem to arise from many sources but particularly from the entanglement of the family system and the business system. People who are closely related seem to have a difficult time working out a clearcut division of labor and leadership, being comfortable with what they work out, and sticking to it. Offspring and parents seem to have tensions over who does what in part because they tend to slide back into the offspring and parent roles in relation to each other. Spouses also seem to slide back into spouse roles and to create business roles that make for problems in the area of who does what. Nonetheless, a clear-cut division of labor seems a valuable tool in heading off interpersonal battles, heading off the problems that employees, customers, and suppliers have over mixed signals when it is unclear who does what in a business, and heading off personal confusion and ambivalence over business tasks and decisions when there is unclarity over who does what. To illuminate issues raised in this chapter and to begin to address a broader array of issues, the next chapter examines more closely the dynamics of role carryover from home to business and from business to home.

Chapter Three

Coping with Role Carryover Between Business and Home

Tensions over who does what in a family business often arise when roles are carried from the family system to the business system or vice versa (Beckhard and Dyer, 1981; Kets de Vries, 1977). At times a family member who has a particular role in one system may carry over that role to the other system. Whether the carryover is self-initiated or induced by other family members, its occurrence requires the family members involved to collaborate, intentionally or unintentionally, in how they interact and in what they choose to let happen. A person who is the family patriarch at home may carry that role over into the business. The youngest child in the family may be "babied" by other family members when working in the business, or a person who is the chief executive officer and key decision maker in the business may play that role at home. The patriarch could not, of course, behave that way in the business without some sort of acceptance of patriarchy by other family members in the business. The youngest child could not easily be babied if she or he did not want it to happen and if others did not do it. Similarly, one could scarcely be the chief executive officer at home who did not want the role and who did not receive some sort of support for that role at home.

Such carryovers are often matters of personal and family preference, and the effects can be experienced as both positive

39

and negative. The youngest offspring in the family may, for example, enjoy being helped and working with little pressure. There may, however, be costs as well. The youngest offspring may fear that dropping the dependent role will leave him or her without a role or will leave parents grieving the loss of the parental role and parental identity. The offspring may feel diminished because carrying the dependent role makes it difficult to behave as an adult, with autonomy and confidence. Being "babied" is, in these senses, not necessarily privileged. To be made a family pet may be burdensome. Similarly, the parents may have mixed feelings about the dependent offspring. They may enjoy feeling useful and protective, but they may resent the dependence and be angered by the dependent offspring's not carrying a fair share of the burdens. Thus, the parents too may have problems with having an offspring be so dependent. Yet the system may persist, as may any other carryover system, because it offers something to key persons in it and because change may be frightening and requires the cooperation of others.

Carryover of roles is related to tension and stress over who does what, the issue discussed in the preceding chapter, in that the carryover may underlie tensions over who does what. But the issue of role carryover is different in that the problems it causes may operate primarily on the interpersonal level and not have a clear, predictable projection onto the operation of the business. With confusion over division of labor for a father and son in the business, everyone working in the business and everyone the business deals with may have problems. Employees may not know whose orders to follow or whom to approach with a problem; customers may not know who has the final say about a purchase agreement. In contrast, with a role carryover involving father and son, their own tension may or may not be great, but it does not necessarily have an impact on anyone else. The embarrassments and discomforts, the feelings of being demeaned or overprotected may all occur in their own private interactions. Moreover, there may be situations in which it is clear who is supposed to do what, but the carryover of roles adds a quality (for example, an authoritarian parenting style) that may make somebody feel uncomfortable.

Reports of problems due to carryover of roles were present in twenty-nine interviews, representing twenty-five of the fifty-nine businesses in the sample. Role carryover may not be entirely negative. In particular, offspring may operate in the family business with a sense of safety that a nonrelative would never have. But as the following remark indicates, maintenance of that sense of safety may create problems for the parent and the business.

> "Your own offspring will take advantage of you a lot quicker than the kid that comes in off the street. And it's happened, so it isn't something that I'm guessing at" (027).

Chief executive officers often have a sense that they tend at times to act like chief executives more than is appropriate when they come home, and the members of the family may agree. For example, one company president, when asked whether there was any carryover from business to home, said of himself:

> "I think sometimes you get a little autocratic" (025A).

A son talked about his father, the chief executive at work, trying to be chief executive in the son's family life:

> "As a vice-president for sales, I was being held accountable for the performance of my wife and kids off the scene. But I said that's a separate issue altogether. I guess that created a problem. It hurt my dad. There were a lot of tensions in the beginning, but once we got the rules straight, there have been very little. I was being asked to be two things, an employee and a son" (084A).

The problem of role carryover is also clear in this statement by a man whose youngest brother worked in the family business.

> "We've always had to watch out for him. It's up to your older brother to take care of him.

We don't send him to the funeral because he gets
upset, and you don't tell the folks he's ill because
they get upset. When you're twenty-four, it's time
to quit being babied. My folks just decided that
he's their baby, and evidently that's how it's going
to stay" (005).

One woman found it hard, when at work, to stop acting like a
wife (that is, a coequal whose opinion counted and who deserved to be treated with sensitivity and respect) to her entrepreneur husband.

"Two things I had to learn: that my husband
had the business before he had me, and that there
only can be one boss. Naturally you make a lot of
decisions together. And if you do have a little
hassle about something, a shortage or something,
not to take it personal, not to go weeping away. It
had nothing to do with your marriage. It's strictly
business. It wasn't that really hard to learn. There
was some times it was a kind of bitter pill" (094B).

Role Carryover: Parent and Offspring

The most commonly reported role carryover problems
were in the relationship of offspring and parents. The carryover
problem in that relationship can be understood on several levels.
Consider first what may be thought of as American common sense about families. Many offspring in the families we
studied seem to have grown up with a respect for and dependence on parents. The respect may simply be a matter of taking
parents' opinions seriously or of being inclined to defer to parents. It may represent a fear of parental attacks, a fear of hurting parents, a fear of a break in the relationship, or a fear of
being rejected by parents. It may represent a desire to please
parents or to receive parent approval or a fear of the risks of
acting independently. Respect is not necessarily a "pure" feeling; it may be amalgamated with various fears and anxieties.
Parents may gain respect partly by their expertise and control
of resources, partly because respect of parents is a cultural and

religious norm, partly because parents demand it, expect it, and reward it, and partly because parental anger and aggressiveness may seem fearsome and dangerous. Offspring can get a sense of safety and security from having parents whose authority and protection they can trust, and parents can get a sense of personal power, dominance, control, strength, excellence, and nurturance from offspring respect. Not only may both offspring and parent find the relationship rewarding, but if one of them tries to change it, the other may push to restore it. One force for stability in the parent/offspring relationship is its longevity. Add to that the likelihood that the offspring is moving into a business in which the parent has been in control, and it becomes rather likely that there will be a carryover of offspring deference and respect for parent and of parent control and nurturance of offspring. Here are illustrations from the perspective of offspring in four business families.

> "I always had a lot of respect for my father and knew where the authority was, and even though there were times when I wanted the power, there was never any real question in my mind that he had the gun" (044).

> "It seems that when you work with someone in the family, . . . they expect more of you. It's harder, because you really want to please them; you really do, because it's your dad. You don't want to let him down" (025B, daughter of the chief executive officer).

> "My father is set in his ways. Between he and I, it's a child talking to his parent, and the parent decides he doesn't need to know at the present time. I'm still a child. Some of the stuff I do, I have to talk over with myself and other people before I go in and talk it over with him. I think it's because he's not just the man who owns the building; he's my father. I still have the impression that your father's a little smarter than you are. With my mother, when she's here, she basically works for me. From time to time it's hard to yell at her or to tell her something like you would another employee. The only thing that's changed now is

that we call them by their first name now, instead
of 'Dad' and 'Mom.' On a personal level we still call
them 'Dad' and 'Mom,' but when we get here, it's
first names" (005).

"My father had been in the business so long
and he knew so much more about it at that time
than I did that there was just no question about it.
Just by the mere way he conducted himself on a
day-by-day basis, he was the senior member of the
partnership. It was not only that I accepted it, it
was an advantage to me. He had spent so many
years working in this field; he was so absolutely
knowledgeable about so many things" (097).

Sometimes it is not merely that offspring respect parents
because of their relationship history and their adult awareness
of parental experience and precedence in the business. Some
parents also seem to deal with offspring in a way that says
"Remember that I'm your parent" or "Respect my expertise."
Said one son of his father:

"My father, of course, having fifty-one years
in the business could be a problem, but I let it
bounce off of me. I really don't take it to heart or
serious. My father still has the same attitude he had
fifty-one years ago, that he knows everything in
the world" (096A).

Said one father:

"My youngest son, he's the baby of the family. I find that I want to hold his hand, maybe,
make his job easier, recognize that it's pretty tough
to be in the spot he's in" (084B).

In businesses where an offspring tends to respond to parent as parent and a parent tends to respond to offspring as offspring and where those roles do not allow for substantial autonomy, the offspring may have trouble developing a clear sense of
competent self. Offspring in some businesses thought that they
had trouble being themselves and choosing their own directions
while they worked with a parent. Here are four examples:

"You can't really be independent when your dad's there. But you can, though. He makes me independent. But I sometimes just want to get away from him" (025B).

"I have never really gotten along that well with my mother or my father. For some reason they have embarrassed me. I had enough identity problems and that sort of thing to resolve without having the old man down here. We really went at each other for a period of a few years. But gradually that somewhat got resolved" (006).

"There's always the business of the younger elements of the family wanting to be more expansive because they have more energy and because they don't know anything. Of course we had that too where we pressed our father. He would usually resist that, although not always. He was a very broad-minded person. And then there's always the thought that the older person isn't satisfied with what the younger person does. No matter how it turns out, he still isn't satisfied. And I think that's pretty true of all families, whether you have a business or not" (036A).

"Sons and daughters in a business never measure up to what the parents expect them to do. I definitely didn't do things the way my parents wanted me to. My father and I didn't really get along in a business sense. He had one way of doing it; I had many other ways of doing it" (101A).

A father, recalling what had gone on before his son left the business, also seemed to have a sense of his son's striving for an identity within the business.

"There were times I know that my son felt that he made suggestions that probably weren't received fully at the time, as he felt they should be. Perhaps they were considered or partially implemented at a later date, and he may not have felt that he received proper credit for having made the suggestion initially" (077A).

For some parents, too, there were identity issues. Although some parents and offspring had come to have a relationship as autonomous adults, other parents experienced their off-spring as undermining and threatening. These latter parents could experience an offspring's interest in change or expansion or an offspring's disagreement as personal criticism and a threat to the parental leadership role in the business. Such parents might feel that their competence, the value of their business experience, and the validity of what they had done in the past were being questioned. So at times it was not merely a matter of an offspring feeling overwhelmed or smothered or put down, but of both parent and offspring struggling for recognition. Those struggles at times erupted into interpersonal conflict.

> "Some of the biggest arguments that we had was my father would say, 'Look at all I've given you. I've given you everything.' And then I would fire up and say, 'Look what I've done for you.' And so there was this fight for recognition. And there was a lot of competition between my father and I. I looked at my father as someone who was a deterrent to our growth. He had a lot of rough edges. And he would drink too much, and he would embarrass me in front of our customers. So I resented it" (006).

Coping with Carryover in Parent/Offspring Relationships

Recognizing the problem of dysfunctional role carryover in the parent/offspring relationship, or perhaps simply recognizing that somebody is in pain or that parent and offspring are not getting along, many business-operating families try to adapt to the problem. In some cases in the sample, a son left the business or a parent left or was driven out. In other cases family members stayed together in the business. One approach that family members who stayed together in a business took to the problem of dysfunctional role carryover was to recognize it and to label it for what it was. Even though the carryover persisted, recognizing and labeling it may have made the problem seem more understandable so that people spent less time worrying about it and could begin to solve the problems associated with it.

Many families we studied worked at keeping potential

combatants functionally and physically apart. In many situations separation in terms of roles, space, or time together helps people to get along and to maintain relationships in the face of inherent tensions (Rosenblatt and Titus, 1976; Rosenblatt, Titus, and Cunningham, 1979; Rosenblatt, Titus, Nevaldine, and Cunningham, 1979). In the business-operating families we studied, such separation seemed to be a common adaptation to tensions between offspring and parent. Some of what we learned about separation in dealing with tensions is presented in our discussion of division of labor in Chapter Two, some in chapters that follow this one. An example of the use of spatial separation to deal with carryover was given in Chapter Two, where a son talked about moving his father's office to another building. Similarly, carryover problems were reduced by separation between a son-in-law and his father-in-law:

> "He left me pretty much alone running the business right from the start. He worked in one building, and I worked in another. He just stayed out of it" (078).

Not only may such separation keep potential role carryover problems from emerging, it may provide a rigid boundary that reduces information exchange between the two parties and gives the younger person an opportunity to grow and to get a clear sense of self. Then, when the younger person must come into contact again with the older person or when the younger person assumes a chief officer role, the situation can be dealt with confidently and without a need to revert to a dependent, one-down relationship with the older person.

Sometimes people needed distance only temporarily. A man who worked with his parents said that when he was irritated with a parent,

> "A lot of times you find something to do that's away from people. Maybe five minutes. You then find something else to do. I'll leave a particular job, go for a few minutes or maybe until after lunch, and then come back to do it" (116B).

Separations in conversation topics and in time spent together outside the business were also common for parent and
offspring in our study. Here are three examples:

> "We don't get together so much on week-
> ends or in evenings for a dinner like we did ten
> years ago. I see enough of my father now during
> the day. I don't want to see him at night as much.
> ... We always used to have barbecues over at his
> house. I think he feels right now that I'm kinda
> avoiding him. I pop over there once every four
> months, and before I used to go over there maybe
> at least once a week. It's just that I've got to stay
> away from him. That's the way I feel. I can handle
> it at work; I can't handle it after work. When I'm
> off of work, I try not to talk about work when
> I'm with him" (031A, a son talking about mini-
> mizing role carryover problems with his father).

> "If we hadn't worked together, I'm sure
> we'd be seeing each other more on the evenings
> and weekends. My brother's the same way. His
> wife asks, 'Why don't we go see your folks more?'
> He says, 'I see them every day of the week. Why
> see them on weekends too?' I think it's too bad
> that the business got so much involved with the
> family. We all like working here, and I like the
> business. But the family life suffered in order for
> the business life to stay on an even keel" (005).

> "I don't talk to my dad about business is-
> sues" (084A).

Often the distancing seemed to develop without explicit
discussion. In one case, however, the distancing began when a
son realized that distance was what he needed and confronted
his parent with his need for distance.

> "I went to a psychologist and I got my head
> screwed on right as to where I think I'm supposed
> to be and what my parents' relationship to my life
> is supposed to be. I had to have a big emotional
> showdown with my mother. Almost like 'Hey, I'm
> a big boy. I'm leaving your house; I'm leaving your

control, and I'm going on my own.' It took something like that" (101A, who had gained control of the family business).

Parents, too, realized the risk in not separating, and at least one parent was explicit about the value of separating business roles from familial roles.

> "My dad used to kid around. From eight to five you're working for him in the office, and 'after five you're my son. I'm the father' " (044).

Individuation in Parent/Offspring Relationships

The tensions between parents and offspring can be understood at another level in terms of individuation. "Individuation" (or "differentiation") is a family systems theory concept that refers to independence—not simply opposition, but freedom to agree, to disagree, or just to be different. The independence is one of thought, feeling, and judgment (Woodburn and Barnhill, 1977). The degree of such independence may differ for each family member, so one family member may be more independent in interactions than another. It is not necessarily age-related. A parent, for example, may be less individuated than an offspring (from own parent, from spouse, from sibling, or even from offspring). What we have been calling "role carryover" can usefully be understood in terms of individuation.

One expression of low individuation is to be overinvolved with someone. One may care enormously about what the other is doing, see what the other does as reflecting for better or worse on oneself, be influenced greatly by the other, or try hard to influence the other. Such overinvolvement may be what underlies some parent/offspring tension. It may mean, for example, that the offspring is very strongly governed by what the parent thinks, feels, wants, or approves of.

> "I push myself because I feel that son thing. You're always trying to make your dad proud of you" (084A).

It may mean that the offspring has trouble finding a self because the offspring is so concerned about what the parent
thinks, wants, feels, or approves of or because the parent works
so hard at governing the offspring.

> "The tension that I have felt regarding my
> father or this business or being here or being one of
> the family has been becoming myself and finding
> out who I am and what I can contribute. A lot of
> that has been because my dad is *extremely strong.*
> He's the kind of guy that, when he makes a deci-
> sion, he can live with it for the rest of his life. And
> he believes us young guys aren't tough enough. He
> says that about himself when he says it in relation
> to my grandfather, who was a tough old European.
> And that's why he's been successful, though"
> (033B).

People tend to become more individuated with age, although there are also marked differences in individuation
among people of a given age. Families can be understood as en-
couraging substantial or little individuation. Persons with low
individuation will more often be smothered or smothering in a
family business relationship. Where people have trouble finding
themselves, individuation will be low. When it is recommended
that offspring who might consider succession to the chief officer role in a business get experience in other businesses (see
Chapter Ten), the recommendation may be understood as one
of individuation experiences for both parent and offspring. In
family businesses in which offspring and parents have greater
individuation, there will be more a sense of parent and offspring
as equally professional. There will be more delegation of authority to offspring, more tolerance of difference and what might be
perceived as error, and a clearer definition of leadership.

When a family has individuation problems, a parent may
need to keep an offspring dependent so that the parent can
maintain a superordinate or protective role. In such a situation
the parent, perhaps without self-awareness, undermines the offspring. An offspring can fit in with the system by being compliant, acting unsuited for responsibility, and believing in his or

her own incompetence or inadequacy. This sort of system is frequently accompanied by feelings and beliefs that maintain the system and make it less than pleasant for the persons involved. Offspring and parent may both be angry—the offspring at the pressures to remain dependent, the communication about his or her incompetence, and the control that makes incompetence difficult to overcome; the parent at the offspring's dependency, requests of privilege, and incompetence. At the same time, they may feel they are doing the right thing—the offspring because of questioning personal competence, feeling loyal, fearing loss of privilege, or not wanting to cross or to undermine the parent; the parent genuinely believing that the offspring could not succeed without help.

Another form of low individuation is sometimes called "triangulation" (Bowen, 1971). In families with low levels of individuation, two persons (two parents, a parent and a grandparent, a parent and offspring) may both influence a third person in a way that may seem to overwhelm or somehow trap the third person. For example, a chief officer may be "triangled" by a dependent offspring in the business and a very controlling semiretired parent who is chair of the board, so that the chief officer has little freedom to act independently in dealing with the offspring. Here is an example of a man who was "triangled" by his brother and father:

> "My brother really had it on a downhill pull, because he didn't have to put up with my father. Whenever my father and I got into a battle, my old man always called my brother and said, 'Your no-good brother just did this to me.' And my brother wasn't sharp enough to see what was going on. So then I caught it from the old man, and I'd catch it from my brother. I finally got involved in an encounter group that was the greatest thing for me, because I learned how to deal with two people, my father and my brother. And they didn't get me much after that" (006).

"The greatest thing" this respondent refers to can be understood as individuation, as finding ways not to be bothered so

much or influenced so much by the two persons who were triangling him.

Triangles are often associated with indirect or blocked
communication in interpersonal conflict. Thus, when there are
triangles, some people are in on secrets and others are not, people who feel that they are being caught in competing demands
do not act to resolve the competing demands, and people who
find it difficult to communicate with someone enlist a third
party to help out. Triangling also arises when people form coalitions in opposition to third parties. Such coalitions may arise
when people feel relatively powerless to engage in conflict by
themselves or simply because people need an ally to shore up
feelings of confidence or a sense of reality. In each case, it is
the person not in a coalition who is triangled. A triangle is
often weakened when the triangled person confronts it directly or finds ways to minimize the personal impact of the triangle.

Role Carryover in Marital Relationships

In relationships between spouses the need to get distance
at work or to deal with each other differently at work and at
home was often expressed. Said one entrepreneur, offering an
insight acquired after receiving marriage counseling:

> "One gets used to running a business, and
> you can't run a home in the same way" (025A).

Another respondent had a similar perception of the need for
separating marital relations at home from marital relations in
the business.

> "Sometimes it's hard to separate a boss/em-
> ployee-type thing from a husband/wife relation-
> ship. Every once in a while we might be inclined to
> both of us being the boss, or you resent the other
> one for telling you what to do. You think you're
> the wife, and he's telling you what to do." *Inter-
> viewer:* "How could you head problems off?" *Re-*

spondent: "If I could just always remember that in the business you have to have just one boss. I have a habit of forgetting and trying to take over things myself. You get to the point where you resent your husband or your wife telling you what to do. It can really rub you the wrong way, because at that point you forget that you're boss and employee" (018).

The work and home relationships of spouses seem to be more difficult to keep separate than the work and home relationships of parents and offspring. One reason is undoubtedly that spouses who stay married almost always live together, whereas adult offspring and parents typically live apart. A more important reason may be that the American ideology for marriage gives mixed messages. On the one hand, marriage is less clearly status-differentiated than the parent/offspring relationship. There is a sense that spouses are or should be coequals in decision making, in status, and in other ways. "To share and share alike" was a marriage vow of many Americans. On the other hand, there is also a norm of husband dominance, a norm reflected in the common practice of wife and children taking the man's surname, in the common expectation that wives, even those who work full-time outside the home, will carry far more than 50 percent of the work load at home, and in myriad other ways. This mix of norms makes it difficult for a wife not to feel the right to speak up and to have her opinions valued, but it also may make a husband who is chief officer of the family business feel upset when his wife speaks up critically or in a way that threatens his sense of autonomous control of the enterprise. Many men we interviewed said that it was impossible or uncomfortable to work with a wife. When a wife was present in the business, her businessman husband was characteristically reluctant to have her discuss business matters in any way other than to listen to him respectfully. One man, talking about the ending of his wife's part-time employment with the family firm, mentioned the carryover of home conflicts to the business and emphasized the tension over whether his wife would be autonomous or subordinate in the business.

"I just felt like, you know, I don't think it was a good situation. Well, we're here, we're at home all the time together, and to be at work all the time together—it just didn't seem right. We have our conflicts at home. It's usually carried on at the store. It just wasn't a good situation. It was all minor stuff. I guess she didn't like me being over her all the time, checking things out. The relationship wasn't there as a boss/employee" (098A).

Perhaps part of the problem in spouse relationships is that business decisions are often rather arbitrary or intuitive, not easily justified, not easily differentiated on rational grounds from alternative decisions that might be made. Under the circumstances, anyone who feels equal enough to the decision maker to challenge a decision can be very threatening. Here is one example of a husband sensitive to his wife's challenges to decisions, sensitive enough to want to keep his wife out of the business.

"There's things that go on, like decisions that are made, where a wife don't know nothing about it. And sometimes I've seen where a husband and wife separate on account of that. I feel that it's best to keep your wife out of your affairs at the office" (117).

Another husband also worried about the possibility of his wife's entering the family business:

"It seems to me it would be a potential source of trouble. Especially with her. She's a strong-minded person. We have some differences in nature. I'm introspective. She's just the opposite. Decisions come easily to her. She doesn't worry about why she's decided. I come to a decision very slowly and tortuously. So the two styles don't mesh too well as far as working together" (050A).

Still another husband, who had already had some troubles in discussing business decisions with his wife, said:

> "I hate sitting down and talking to my wife
> about the business stuff, and she gets really upset.
> She wants to be involved, and for some reason I
> put out a hell of a lot of effort to keep her unin-
> volved. I'd love to be able to sit down and talk to
> her about the business, but the biggest problem is
> she starts analyzing shit right away, and it drives
> me up the wall. She questions things" (061).

Another man remembered how his father had dealt with his
mother.

> "When my mother put her two cents in
> about business, my dad would quickly cut her off.
> 'Shut up! This is business we're talking about. You
> stay out of it' " (006).

Does separating home life and business life help spouses
get along better? If spouses work together or discuss business
matters, do they benefit by doing what so many parents and
offspring seem to have done? Do they segregate issues, talking
about business at the business and leaving business issues alone
when away from the business, or do they separate business life
and home life in other ways? As the following three interview
excerpts indicate, some people in business think that it helps to
keep business and marital life separate or to be very clear about
who has ultimate authority. The first of these also discusses the
arbitrariness of decisions.

> "Sometimes it's a hassle because the deci-
> sions that she's critical of, a lot of times I just
> don't want to go through the whole explanation of
> why I made the decision. There are some decisions
> that just feel right to me that I don't have an expla-
> nation for, but I base it on what my experience has
> been and what I feel the consequences of the deci-
> sion are. I can make decisions fairly easy, right or
> wrong, and live with them, you know, don't tear
> myself apart or anything. We've kind of learned to
> separate the home and business. We leave here and
> we don't talk about the business. I have told her I

really don't want to talk about the business when I leave here. If I asked her a question about something, I've asked her to give me an answer, not a sermon about it. I usually don't share the business worries or my concerns a great deal with her outside the business. I try not to" (096A).

"Occasionally my husband will come home and issue orders, and I will remind him that I'm not the secretary" (101B, laughing as she spoke).

"My wife has been my sounding board. My father-in-law was one who said, 'Look, never tell the girls anything.' And I always was just the opposite. I wanted to share with my wife and still do. So she's been involved all the way along the line. But her attitude all the way along the line was 'You do it. It's your deal. I'm not involved'" (078).

This last quotation seems to indicate a relatively high level of individuation, with the two spouses autonomous enough to feel comfortable talking about the business.

Conclusion

The carryover of roles from home to business is a potential problem in both the parent/offspring and the wife/husband relationship, but the way the problem operates is different for the two kinds of relationships. The problem can be understood in both cases as one of individuation, but the content of the tensions seems different in the two cases. When the problem is present for parent and offspring, it is commonly a carryover of parental dominance and offspring disposition to tolerate that. The dominance may involve straightforward authoritarianism, or it may take the form of a kind of passive control, the parent absenting self, not hearing offspring, or disqualifying what the offspring says. Whether the dominance is straightforward or more indirect, the parent and offspring are still relating as parent and offspring. If there is a problem for spouses, it seems likely to be at least partly the mix of marital "shoulds." These "shoulds" give husbands the feeling that they should dominate and wives the feeling that they should somehow go along with that. But other "shoulds" give wives the right to have a say in what goes on and to be coequals.

In both the parent/offspring and the wife/husband relationship, people with the carryover problem often found ways to get some kind of distance (division of labor, physical separation, avoiding talking about sensitive issues) as a way of minimizing tension. This does not mean that tension should always be headed off or that tension reduction through distance is the best policy. Looking at the tensions as a symptom of individuation problems suggests that individuation may be a good solution. However, the tension might be a push to solve problems creatively or to do better. Whatever their way of dealing with the carryover problem, people must recognize and live with the fact that in business-operating families business system and family system are often, perhaps ordinarily or even always, entangled.

Chapter Four

Struggles over Who Makes Decisions

In any business the potential exists for tension over decisions. People are bound to have different goals, different standards, different perceptions of what is true, different judgments about what is necessary, and different styles of problem solving. As one respondent put it, speaking about relationships in his own family business but in a way that can apply to any business:

> "Two people who think for themselves are going to clash once in a while" (031B).

In any business involving more than one person, one person's decision may impinge on the jurisdiction of another person, so if one person makes a decision, another may feel that his or her territory has been invaded. Even if one's jurisdiction is not invaded, one may feel that some decisions others have made are bad ones.

Some decision problems come from factors inherent in decisions. As mentioned in the preceding chapter, there is a substantial amount of arbitrariness and subjectivity in business decisions. ("There are some decisions that just feel right to me"—096A.) More often than not, crucial business decisions are made on the basis of imperfect or selective information and a great deal of experience-based intuition. It may be impossible for a decision maker to justify a decision in a "rational" way. To reject a business decision on entirely rational grounds may also be very difficult. Cold facts must be handled subjectively and weighed against factors that cannot be treated as simple facts.

Beyond the decision problems common to all businesses, family businesses have additional decision problems, problems either with particular decisions or with decision making in general. Twenty-nine respondents, representing twenty-five of the fifty-nine businesses studied, spoke of tension in the decision area.

In business-operating families, the way offspring/parent relationships operate often makes business decisions a source of tension. Contributing to the problem are matters already discussed in previous chapters—confusion over who does what and problems created by the carryover of roles from family life to business life and vice versa. Added to this is, no doubt, the need for offspring to differentiate (individuate) themselves from parents, to know and to show that they can function autonomously, that they are not merely dependent puppies whose business role has been granted purely on a kinship basis. For a parent, the offspring's interest in individuation in the decision area may be threatening. Offspring who individuate by disagreeing with a parent on a decision may seem to the parent to discount the parent's accumulated business sense and previous success. Disagreement may even suggest to the parent that the offspring would like the parent out of the way. Small wonder, then, that intergenerational tensions are fairly common in the decision area!

> "I think, because of the generation difference, my son and I tended to have different standards to evaluate the performance of the people in the company. This was probably the biggest area of problems" (077A).

> "My dad is from the old school and I am from the new. I went out and bought business cards, charging it to the business. He started giving me a stink about it. So I paid it myself" (064B).

> "If it's something that Dad has tried in the
> past and it hasn't worked, he'll tell me, 'It doesn't
> work now, and it never will.' Some of those in-
> stances I just put it off. We'll wait and see what
> happens. When he leaves, when he retires, when he
> dies, we'll try them again" (005).

> *Interviewer:* "Are there any disadvantages to
> having your dad work with you?" *Respondent:*
> "No, other than an arguing here and there [laughs]
> —over the new way of doing it versus the old way
> of doing it" (114B).

The generational difference is not limited to the parent/
offspring relationship. There were also some reports of generational differences when parent-in-law and offspring-in-law
worked together.

> "There were times when I would have pre-
> ferred to do things differently. I wanted to grow a
> little faster. He was always the one trying to hold
> us back. It would have involved borrowing, and he
> just wasn't a borrower" (078).

People may compete not only for decision influence but
also to get the credit for decisions. The clearest example of
competing for such credit came in a sibling relationship.

> "Thirty percent of my time is spent convinc-
> ing my brother that it's his idea for things I would
> like to have done. It's a strain that perhaps many,
> many companies have" (074A).

Cultural norms for marital relationships seem to be in
conflict. As was said previously, one norm is that spouses are
"partners," which makes it appropriate for spouses to want to
have a say in each other's decisions. But there is also the norm
of husband dominance and control. In some marriages, spouses
seemed to have achieved an egalitarian relationship with mutual
respect for autonomy and difference, but that seemed not to be
so in others. For these others, with normative pressures both for
a wife to consider herself a partner (and for husband to some-

how show some adherence to the norm), and for husband to dominate (and for wife somehow to respect his dominance), spouses sometimes had difficulties with each other over business decisions. The following quotation reflects this normative complexity; a man is speaking both to the norm of wife's right to speak up and to the norm (that serves his interests well) of husband dominance.

> "I decided to give the people at our other plant a bonus, and my wife didn't know anything about it or why I arrived at that decision. She thought she should have been consulted." *Interviewer:* "Is there any way you would try to head off that issue in the future?" *Respondent:* "I have tried to discuss as many things as possible to try to lay the groundwork of my thoughts and how the business should be run. I'm trying to precondition her before we do things at least to some extent" (015, who still seemed to believe the decisions should be his but who also recognized his wife's concerns, her right to speak up, and perhaps his own need for her approval).

Some wives seemed not to be taken seriously enough to receive explanations or even basic information about decisions.

> "Our nephew should not be in that business, as far as I can see. He came to work and he was supposed to be the office manager so my husband could go out and sell. It didn't work out. He's not very organized. So now my husband wants him to be out selling and will hire another office manager. In order to have my nephew sell, my husband has to get him a car. To me that's making a whole bunch of expense, and then you have to kill yourself worrying about enough business to cover that expense, and that doesn't make sense to me. This is a recession, and our salesman, who has been in the business for years, is having a tough time. If I make a suggestion about the business, my husband interprets it as my not having confidence in his ability. So he takes it personally. Now I see lots of things

that I know can be improved upon. I'm compelled
to tell him how I feel, what I'm thinking, which
produces our problems. What makes me angry is
that I don't have the right to have an impact"
(096B).

In some cases, a male entrepreneur valued a wife's viewpoint.
But that was not common in the interviews. Only a few interviews yielded statements like the following:

"I really didn't want to hear my wife's input
on a lot of decisions early on. And then after a few
years of marriage I realized she had a totally different perspective than what I had. And more often
than not she was dead accurate and I wasn't. So I
listen a lot more" (006).

The complexity of marital relationships aside, people
who are related may generally feel more right to speak up than
people who are not related.

"Any time you get a family member in the
business, you got to ask them what they think.
You can't tell them 'cause otherwise you got a
problem, you know" (114B).

"There Can Only Be One Boss"

One of the most common statements made by people
who were interviewed is that there can be only one boss in a
business. We are not in a position to say where that comes from.
It may be business-world ideology or a hard-won discovery
based on the trial-and-error experiences of each person who said
that there can be only one boss. It may be an artifact of U.S.
corporation and tax law, the inference people draw about why
they are so often in power battles with each other, or a necessity in businesses where at least one person at the top is inflex-
ible or uncompromising. It may be understood as a necessity in
business families where low levels of individuation mean that
people feel that if they do not control others, the others will

control them. It may have to do with people's seeing leadership as embodied in a person, rather than seeing it as a group (system) function. Whatever the source, it was a common assertion. Said one person, speaking of his opposition to partnerships:

> "There can only be one boss" (100).

Said one woman who was not the boss:

> "There can only be one boss. If there's any decision to be made here, my husband makes the decision. We all kind of abide it. And if I've done something wrong and he tells me that, I don't [pauses]—there's been no tears or any argument about that. At home it might be a whole different thing. At home it's generally a kind of 50/50 thing" (094B).

Here are some other illustrations of the one-boss theme.

> "My wife and I see things in different lights." *Interviewer:* "How do you solve your differences?" *Respondent:* "We don't. I win. She either goes along with me, or she goes away until she understands my position. . . . I am the operating officer in the business. No entity can have two heads and survive, and she understands that. It's just that there are times when she doesn't feel I make the right decisions, and in the long run I make the right decisions, and she admits that. But in the short run sometimes she can't see why I'm doing a certain thing, and I may not take the time to explain all the whole situation to her. She leaves the premises and cools off and comes back when she's realized that I have done the right things, and that usually takes about fifteen or twenty minutes. Or she just goes home and ignores what I'm doing and comes back the next day as though nothing happened" (119).

> "My wife doesn't agree with a lot of the decisions that I make. I shouldn't say that. She doesn't agree with some of the decisions that I

make. She's learned not to argue or hassle about them" (096A).

And to repeat part of a statement quoted in Chapter Three:

> "Two things I had to learn: that my husband had the business before he had me, and that there only can be one boss" (094B).

But Sometimes There Are Several Bosses

Although many respondents said there can be only one boss, a substantial number of businesses in the sample had survived for years with more than one boss. For example, several firms were run jointly by siblings. Despite some obvious indications of tension, the following seems a statement about the viability of a multiboss operation.

> "My brother and I don't argue that much. If we're going to do something, he asks me or I ask him. But he holds back and, well, I'd like to put another addition and get some bigger machines, and he hems and haws. And I said, 'Well, let's each put in a little.' We each got a little money, you know, not a lot. And he won't. He'd rather take it out and sit" (045B).

In some family businesses with multiple headship, major decisions require a vote. For example, in a business in which a son and a parent had equal-sized major shares and two other offspring had minor shares, all major decisions were resolved by vote. In another business, in which two brothers owned equal shares, their equality of ownership seemed to guarantee a certain amount of give-and-take; neither could afford to be intransigent. In addition, the making of major decisions in that business was facilitated by tactful board members who had no vote and by substantial geographical distance between the operations managed by one brother and the operations managed by the other. So the one-boss theme is not a plan that must necessarily be adopted in order for a business to survive, but working out a clear organization for leadership is critical to a business or to any other system.

In some businesses, the one-boss rule was present on the surface but was violated with some frequency. In a surprisingly large number of businesses in the sample, one person found ways to circumvent the authority of a boss.

> "We try to negotiate decisions with my father. If I feel he's wrong, I'll go ahead and do what I want to do anyway" (113B).

> "A lot of times I talk to my mother and tell her, 'You go talk to Dad.' Lots of times I tell her to go in and start badgering him about it. And then I'll go in and hit him a few days later. She's kind of softened him up on it" (005).

Our inclination is to see the one-boss theme not as a necessity of business operation and not even as an effective business policy. Rather, it seems to be a negotiating position in family business power struggles (perhaps in the power struggles of any business and perhaps in power struggles in any relationship). It is put on one side of the scale. On the other side are ideological positions such as "Relatives count," "Spouses must be taken seriously," and "We are all in the same boat economically." It is also possible that the one-boss theme reflects the inability of some bosses to feel effective or to trust their effectiveness in equal-power relationships. The one-boss theme eliminates competition and reduces the threat of disagreement and of negotiation with someone whose arguments may be well founded.

Conclusion

Decision making can be a problem in any business, but we have tried to show that decisions can be special problems in family businesses because the connection of the family system with the business system throws family relationship dynamics into the struggle over business decisions. The salience of the one-boss theme in such businesses may be a symptom of struggles that are present or more difficult because the business is a family one.

When decision problems and other tensions at work involve persons one sees in one's family life, family life must inevitably be affected. Moreover, the business system and the family system operate with different goals, so when the two systems come into contact, they are likely to clash. This does not mean that the systems are somehow separable; their connection means that they exist and evolve together (Kepner, 1983). To understand either, one must understand the overlap and interweaving of each system with the other. The next six chapters extend our discussion of the connection of business system and family system to other areas that seem to be commonly tense in business families and family businesses.

Chapter Five

Fairness of Compensation and Work Load

Many families will go through periods, sometimes for years, during which somebody feels exploited or seems to others to be exploited. A person who feels exploited feels used, feels that expectations of being treated fairly have been violated. Parents, for example, may feel exploited or seem to others to be exploited while meeting the many needs of young children. Family members providing extensive health care for somebody who is chronically ill may also feel or seem exploited. A family member who appears to be exploited may, however, feel fairly compensated. Compensation can take many forms, including feelings of doing the right thing or approval from others. Feelings of being compensated may have led some people not to complain during our interviews about what an outside observer might call exploitation. Our interviews may thus underestimate the frequency of apparent exploitation. Nonetheless, twenty-six of our ninety-two respondents, representing twenty-two of the fifty-nine businesses in the sample, reported tensions over fairness of compensation and work load.

The kinship relationship may keep a person who feels exploited from quitting a family business, but the person may still feel resentful and used. Sometimes the realization or perception that one is being exploited develops late, months or years after the onset of the pattern that one eventually sees as exploitation. A wife, for example, may work for years without pay in the family business and come to resent what has happened only later on, when she finds that her husband and other people give her little or no credit for working in the business, or her husband acts as though the assets were solely the product of his work, or they are divorced and she receives no financial compensation for her work. A wife may realize that she has no independent savings with which to leave the marriage, or she may learn that some other woman who has done similar work in a family business has acquired half ownership of the business.

In matters of exploitation, it is important to realize, as with any other matter in relationships, that perspectives may differ. What appears to be exploitation to one family member may not appear so to another. Or what appears to be exploitation to an outside observer may not seem to be exploitation to anybody in the family. We are not, in a study like this, interested in determining objectively whether exploitation has occurred—if, indeed, it is ever possible to make an objective determination. What we want to do is to write about people's perceptions of what went on.

Feelings of indulgence and the appearance of indulgence are also quite common in families. One family member may apparently indulge another out of feelings of love, because to indulge the other is in some sense to indulge oneself, or because it makes more sense to give a benefit to a family member than to someone else. Indulgence can also, in the relationship of parent with adult offspring, be a carryover of a pattern established when the offspring was young. Family members in a business can be indulged through overpayment, through being granted part ownership without its being earned, through being given a light work load, or through cushioning from the stresses of the business. In some cases, the person indulged may be the person who ostensibly has the greater power in the business. For example, a relative who is a subordinate in the business may protect a superordinate relative from having to work overtime. But typically when people talked about indulgence, they talked about a superordinate indulging a subordinate. Indulgence, like exploitation, is a matter of perception. What looks like indulgence to one person may not look like it to another. A father, for example, may feel that he is indulging a son in the business, whereas the son may feel that he has earned every cent he is paid and may even feel exploited. Or a parent and offspring in the business may both feel that the offspring's compensation and work load are fair, but nonrelatives in the business may feel that the offspring is pampered. With indulgence so much a matter of perception, people in business families often work to assure others that indulgence is not present. This matter is discussed more fully in the section of this chapter dealing with offspring.

Wives

Most of the fifty-nine businesses (rough 95 percent) in the sample were owned and operated primarily by men (see the appendix for more information about the people and businesses studied). Most of those men were married. In fourteen cases a wife never had any direct involvement in the business; in nineteen others the involvement of a wife was temporary or part-time. The pattern of part-time work by wives of male bosses, even in companies in which the woman is an owner, has been observed in other studies of business families (see, for example, Deeks, 1976, p. 92, reporting a study of firms in the furniture and timber industry in Great Britain). In important ways all wives, whether working directly in the business or not, were involved. A founder, perhaps especially during the first five or ten years of an enterprise, puts long hours and typically all the family assets into a business. The long hours mean that the work of the home, everything from shopping to childcare to home repairs, must be attended to disproportionately by someone else, almost always the wife.

> "When the kids were little it was hard, because my husband wasn't home very much" (101B).

At least some husbands knew what they were doing to

their wives (and what their wives were doing to themselves), including the husband of the woman just quoted.

> "When I first took over the business, there was obviously a lot of time spent in reorganizing things. I was never home. I was always working. I just explained to my wife. She understood. She went along with it the best she could. But it made for what you would probably call a difficult marriage. Husband gone all the time, young child at home. During that time, not enough money" (101A).

The income problem mentioned by this respondent is a common problem in family businesses, particularly in new ones. The family assets may be tied up in the business, the dwelling mortgaged to the limit. Any income generated by the business may have to be returned to the business. New clothing, a new car, high-cost food, restaurant meals, vacation travel, and even regular medical examinations may be forgone. A woman not involved directly in the business will be under heavy pressure to contribute through her management of the household budget and her willingness to accept a comparatively low standard of living (Kohl, 1976, writing about farm families). Every cent a woman saves through putting off desired purchases, clothing repair, the purchase of bargain foods, reprocessing leftover food, and so on is a contribution to the business. Some husbands spoke to that point but often in a fashion that gave themselves the credit (and the blame) for the control of household expenditures.

> "We basically have a good understanding of what we want for our family. But on the other hand, the question is 'How much money can we take out of the business?' There's one thing you have to learn in being in business for yourself, and that is you have to plain blow the whistle and say, 'That's it. Right at the present time we're going to pay the house mortgage, and we are going to pay Blue Cross–Blue Shield, and we've got some money

for groceries here, and we just aren't going out and have a big weekend this week. I just paid my suppliers' " (097).

"She'd want things for the house, and I would use the money to further the business here because I'd figure that the business is bringing in the livelihood. A person puts trying to make a living for the family ahead of a lot of other things" (113A; see also a statement later in this chapter concerning his divorce).

"I've been a little tight with the purse strings at home. The children might want a stereo or something like that, and I say we just can't afford it. 'Just hang loose. We'll get it someday' " (015).

Some wives not directly involved in the business seemed to feel neglected. Some had become accustomed to receiving little attention from a husband; others had not. Although feelings of neglect may continue as long as the husband is involved in the business, it is clear that when a business is new, it typically demands more entrepreneurial time, and that is when the wives we studied most commonly reported feeling neglected. A forty-hour work week for an entrepreneur in a new business was rare; even a sixty-hour work week might have been atypically light. In some cases, a low level of attention from the spouse may have hurt because it was interpreted to mean that one was not loved or cared about as much as one hoped. The low level of attention also may have hurt because it may have been interpreted to mean that the expectation of great marital togetherness, an expectation that people typically bring into marriage in the United States (Rosenblatt and Titus, 1976), was being violated. Said one woman:

"In the first years of our marriage I cried. I didn't communicate. I was maybe more apt to keep it inside myself. Then as I became more mature and as this whole consciousness-raising thing came about, I would tell him what I didn't like. I don't think he really understands, but at least he tries" (091B).

At another point in the interview she spoke again about her feelings of being neglected.

> "In the early years of the business, the family did not only not come first, maybe it was eighty-third. I never had to worry about another woman; I just had the business to battle" (091B).

While feeling neglected, a woman in a business family may be less effective at parenting than she would be were she not so burdened. Said the woman just quoted:

> "I know that I used to be very impatient with the little ones and get mad awfully easily, and they maybe thought I was just getting mad at them, not knowing that it was because I was feeling frustrated because I was not getting enough attention" (091B).

The resentment of neglect is not only a wife's. Children in business families may also feel such resentment. Said one daughter:

> "My father won't lock up the doors at night. If you've got something planned, this place comes first. I planned a birthday party for him at six o'clock, and he never did show up. He says the reason he's the biggest dealer and that he's been in business forty years is that he's here if they want a piece of pipe or a compressor part" (113B).

Her story of a family event that foundered because the person operating the business had trouble getting away from his work was echoed by other people interviewed.

> "The family probably comes last. Nothing came before anything in the business for me. I did it the first year I worked. There was a factory man came to demonstrate a new machine, and it was the night of my parents' golden wedding anniversary. I was the only child that didn't show up" (074B).

> "There have been times when we've tried to leave town. One of our earlier trips—I'd been working with a man for a week, and he finally decided to buy. And we were just ready to pull out of town, at about nine o'clock, when he called" (100, who went on to say that the trip had to be delayed).

This last entrepreneur and others who were interviewed recognized the stress that their intense involvement in the business put on the family and the value of what some called "an understanding wife." The man just quoted went on to talk about his recurrent lateness for supper.

> "The stress would be on my wife, expecting me home at six o'clock. Many times you aren't going to make it. Many times you aren't going to be home for supper at all. Being unable to set up regular hours and be available. There are many weekends when I'm involved, but she'd like to be able to do something. We're not going to be able to do it. But we've been taking more and more time off. There is really no way to deal with my unpredictable lateness for supper. The adjustment has to be more or less on her part rather than mine. And no woman likes to have a big dinner prepared and you not show up" (100).

Said another entrepreneur:

> "I wasn't home. Husbands and wives are supposed to be together" (032A).

Another entrepreneur who recognized the stress his work put on the family and who valued what he saw as his wife's capacity to cope told us:

> "I don't see my kids enough. They complain about that. I don't work as much as I used to. I take more time off. If you didn't have a wife like mine that understands as much as she does, or let's say you had a wife that wasn't as independent as my wife is, I could see where it could be a poten-

tial source of a lot of irritation. When you're just
starting a business, you know, during the first
three, four, five years, I think the family really
takes it in the head. I know they do, because I've
been through it. They get shortchanged on everything. A guy like myself would come home. You'd
worked sixteen, eighteen hours, something like
that, things didn't go right, you'd be irritated. You
could be crabby and irritable. During the first three
or four years of that, while you're trying to put
this thing all together and make it work, the family
gets really shortchanged, because rather than going
someplace on a Saturday or a Friday night, there's
always one family member missing, like me. And
that happens a lot of times. And unless the wife of
the guy that's doing this can understand that
there's something better at the other end of this,
a lot of people wouldn't put up with this for very
long" (123).

All the men just quoted seemed to be aware of the feelings of
neglect and the disappointment of expectations their work involvement caused. But there were also men who apparently
were not aware of or were not sympathetic with the difficulties a wife could have in that situation. Some of these men resented the complaints they received from a wife who felt neglected or overburdened (see L'Abate and L'Abate, 1981, for a
discussion of couples in which the husband pursues "the American dream").

"My wife says I never spent enough time at
home, but then that's been that way so long. I
would have to say it hurt my home life. Behind
some successful men there's a nagging wife that
made him want to go to the office and work. I
would say I would fall in that category. It did harm
the home life. It helped the business." *Interviewer:*
"Is there any way you would do it differently if
you had it to do over?" "Maybe got a divorce and
kept right on working" (074A).

"Problems occur if I feel I have to do something on a weekend that would interfere with what

my wife would like to have me be doing on a weekend, and that is usually minor, and after I get it
done, it's usually past. I go my way and she goes
her way, and as soon as I get my stuff done, it's
forgotten." *Interviewer:* "Does she sometimes see
it differently?" "Only from a selfish point of view.
'Let's go do something else. Can't you let somebody else do it? Or can't you let it go until Monday?'" (015).

The differences between spouses on matters of felt neglect and disappointment of expectations may be understood in
terms of the clash of business goals and family goals. The goals
of the business may require very heavy work involvement by
the entrepreneur, whereas the goals of the family may require
substantial interpersonal contact or substantial investments of
time and energy in childcare and in work around the house. In
that sense, wives and husbands are to some extent advocates for
different sets of goals. The tensions of functioning with differing sets of goals seem tolerated in many families but not in all.
In some business families, the entrepreneur's commitment to
the business and his wife's feelings of neglect or overloading
seemed to have contributed to the end of the marriage.

"One of the reasons we got divorced is that
I spent too much time in the business" (113A).

"It's hard to keep a family together and
keep a big business going. You're gone a lot; you
have to put in a lot of hours. If there's anything
wrong, you get calls in the middle of the night.
Some of it has been solved by bringing in an outsider as president of the company. But I'm getting
a divorce" (075B).

Women who have some involvement in the family business may not feel free of neglect, disappointment of expectations, role overload at home, or pressures to minimize household expenditures. As with many women who work outside the
home, there may be little or no diminution of household work
load when a woman works in the family business. One woman

spoke of being under time pressure to do her daily work in the family business and still get home to take care of household responsibilities.

"With myself the only problem that would be is if I got home in time to make a meal or when the children were younger, I would always try and be home so I would be home with them off and on after school" (094B).

Another woman, who thought things had become better, answered a question about whether there were problems over fairness of work load in the following way.

"Only at home. I figure, well, my husband helps a lot more than he used to around home, but not at first. I had housework to do. I have all these things to do. So like on my day off or when I come home, I have to do all the things I normally did all day long" (130).

A wife involved in a family business may find herself burdened, as at home, with business tasks her husband does not want to do. One husband had a clear awareness of doing that to his wife.

"I'll try and dump off some of the callings, have my wife call, because I don't want to deal with this particular person or I'm frustrated with dealing with him. And she doesn't really care to do it either. That would be a slight tension area. It's not earth-shattering" (099).

Clearly there were wives who resented the burdens laid on them in the business.

"My husband doesn't want to hear anything from me. He just wants me to come in and do everything, do more than anybody else would possibly even think of doing or that he would ever ask any other woman in that position to do, and never say anything about how anything could be improved" (096B).

In this case and in some other cases of resentment by wives, the issue seems to be not only the burden but also the lack of appreciation of the wife as a person who might reasonably be expected to have helpful comments. This is, no doubt, partly a reflection of the role entanglement discussed in the previous chapters. The wife may want to be treated as a coequal at work, feeling that it is a treatment fitting for a spouse, whereas the husband may feel that he is the boss and experience her influence attempts as undermining him. The problem may also be seen as a clash of family goals and business goals. The family goals that she emphasizes may include couple intimacy and mutual respect, whereas the business goals that he emphasizes may represent the business as his way of earning a living, by himself, for his family. The problems of wives' feelings of burden and of lack of appreciation from husbands are symbolized and intensified by a fairly common pattern of nonpayment or underpayment of a wife who works in the family business.

> "It helps me, her, and the business out to pay her less" (096A).

Among the women who did not feel exploited at the time of the interview, some reported feeling exploited in the past. A woman who, by the time of the interview, had achieved what seemed to her to be a fair wage reported that things had been different in the past.

> "My husband and I take the identical salary. I didn't even get paid for the first few years. When it comes to setting salaries, he has no problem working with a woman on an equal basis" (095A).

The woman just quoted felt that she was finally receiving what seemed to her to be a fair salary, but at one time she had not even been paid. That pattern of unpaid work by a woman at first and eventually of payment for her work was not uncommon in the interview reports. We do not want to overstate the problem. There were wives working in the family business who seemed not to expect to be paid; they seemed to be comfortable with how they were treated and expressed no resentment at all. The issue of payment was not raised at all by some women, and some who were underpaid in comparison with other people in the business seemed as well satisfied as wives who received substantial compensation. Perhaps monetary compensation is not the issue. In a study of French-bread bakeries, operated typically by married couples, it was reported that many women felt that, despite long hours, little contact with husband, and relatively low income, there were major benefits (Bertaux and Bertaux-Wiame, 1981). The benefits included the freedom of not working for someone else and the freedom to control personal economic fate. Nonetheless, there is a potential ethical issue in the failure to pay a family member for work done in the business. Is it fair to treat a family member in a way one would not and could not treat a nonrelative? Is it unethical to treat someone in a way that person feels is exploitive if the person remains in the situation despite feeling exploited? Of course, payment comes in many forms. A person may be unpaid or apparently underpaid and yet feel well compensated by love, the satisfaction of seeing the business do well, the chance to feel competent, important, and useful. But there are also people who do not feel entitled to compensation or fair treatment who nonetheless deserve much better than they receive.

Another issue to consider is the process of enterprise development. What does it take to develop an enterprise? Individual hard work, cleverness in choice of enterprise, ingenuity at marketing, and wise decisions about financing, purchasing, and choice of workers are obviously important. In addition, there is often, in family businesses, a strengthening of the enterprise that comes with nonpayment or underpayment of family members who work in the business. From a cross-cultural perspective the family enterprises that succeed financially are often ones in which a substantial amount of undercompensated or uncompensated labor can be obtained from relatives. For example, in one study of family businesses run by people from different ethnic groups in the Seychelles (Benedict, 1979), the two ethnic groups in which many family members worked for family enterprises without compensation were less likely to have business failures and more likely to have long-term business growth. The ethnic group with the least unpaid work by family members had the poorest survival and growth of family enterprises. Thus, what could be exploitation in the sample we studied may also be a part of what makes family businesses prosper. Unpaid and underpaid work by family members may make the difference in survival of the business. Moreover, when there is no spare capital, no money at all to pay someone else for work, even very inefficient unpaid labor by a family member may be of great value in the family enterprise (Benedict, 1963). These economic considerations should not, however, obscure the fact that it may seem offensive, demeaning, or damaging to a family member to work without pay or to work while underpaid. Even for those who "do not mind," their nonpayment or underpayment may convey a damaging message about personal value.

Offspring

Like farm families (Anderson and Rosenblatt, 1984; Rosenblatt and Anderson, 1981), business-operating families often press a son or daughter to work in the family business at an early age. For example, three informants had begun working in the family business by age ten, nine more by age fifteen, and another six by age seventeen. Such early business involvement may be character-building and give the offspring some sense of what it takes to generate income for the family, but some offspring seemed to resent it. One woman, when asked whether her fifteen-year-old son ever felt he was being pushed too hard, said:

> "Oh, yeah, but that's because most of his friends don't ever have to do anything, not even carrying out the trash at home. We just think that kids should share in the responsibility of whatever it might be, cutting the grass occasionally or carrying out the trash or whatever. He thinks he should never have to come down here because he should play all the time. He resents that sometimes, thinks we're unfair (018).

In the businesses we studied, most older offspring who were be-

yond doing casual part-time work were male. Older offspring
working full-time in the family business may feel exploited, and
parents may acknowledge that they are in some sense exploiting. Said one parent:

> "We do know that more is expected of a
> relative simply because of the last name, certainly
> by me. They perhaps will get paid less and work
> harder. We don't want them to be a failure. You
> want to convey all your knowledge into them
> sooner than you would someone else, because
> you're going to take the time to do it, and you're
> with them more hours of the month. I wasn't that
> gung ho about having my son in the business, be-
> cause he's not a worker in my opinion. . . . The
> first two months he worked here he was in bed at
> eight o'clock at night, and he wasn't working as
> many hours as I am" (074A).

That pattern of undercompensation and overwork of offspring
was not rare (see Alcorn, 1982, pp. 142–143; Lansberg S.,
1983), and their resentment of it was not rare either. Said one
son who had become the manager of the family enterprise:

> "I was always overworked and underpaid. It
> appeared that I was doing most of the decision
> making and most of the planning, and my parents
> were reaping most of the rewards" (101A).

Some of the offspring with resentments may have felt that there
were compensations or hoped that there would be. A faith in
ultimate reward may have motivated some to continue working
in the family enterprise despite feeling exploited. One young
man said:

> "I always say I want more money. I can't
> get it. I try discussing it with my father, and he
> talks around in circles, and we end up nowhere. I
> know in the end I'll come out ahead in years to
> come" (106B).

He went on to say that his parents did not pay him because he lived at home and that he could not leave home if he did not have an income. He said further, and with resentment, that his parents benefited from his labor and wrote him off as an income tax deduction. It would have been difficult for him to continue in that situation without a feeling that some good would come of it. Similarly, a daughter working for her father said:

> "I get pretty resentful sometimes and feel that I'm being overworked and underpaid, but then when you think about it, I really got it made." Her brother, who was present during the interview (one of the few cases in which another family member was present during an interview), then added, "Yeah, you really do—work when you want" (025B).

Another son who felt exploited yet saw the possibility of eventual indemnification told us:

> "The family doesn't get raises like the rest of the employees. It's upsetting. I mean you feel that you do your job, and it's as important as anything else, and you deserve to get your raises. Truthfully, I love my dad as a father. As a person, I have many dislikes toward him. He is very unfair with his family. Someday the business is probably going to be ours, so you keep trying to do your best" (113B).

Offspring involved in businesses also provided instances of what seemed like indulgence, instances in which somebody (the offspring or a parent) felt the offspring was overcompensated or underqualified for the work he or she was doing. Said one father:

> "We've always compensated the children well. We've paid them more than the going rate" (119).

Often the sense of overcompensation or underqualification of an offspring came out of a comparison of the offspring with nonrelated workers. In the comment just quoted, the employer/ father compared what his offspring received with what a non-relative would receive. Nonrelatives in a family business may often feel that the relatives are getting an easy ride. There may be a grain of truth to that, as the comment just quoted indicates. One of the problems in running a family business is that the nonrelated employees may be sensitive to the advantage relatives have, sensitive in a way that undermines work commitment and cooperation and that may motivate them to find jobs elsewhere (Becker and Tillman, 1978, p. 99; Edison, 1976). One father, aware of that potential sensitivity, had been reluctant to bring his sons into the business, a business that he had taken over from his own father:

> "I felt that bringing my sons on board was not good for the employees. It would give them the impression that no one could advance in this company unless their name was the same as mine. Secondly, I felt that it would give the sons an artificial sense of security" (084B).

Said another father, also aware of the sensitivity of nonrelatives in the business:

> "With an organization like this, probably a family member is looked at a little more closely by peers to see whether or not he is carrying his weight" (077A).

A third entrepreneur, when asked whether he had any relatives in the business, also recognized the problem nonrelatives would have. He chose not to have any relatives in the business.

> "I don't want them. I wouldn't have my wife in the place. I wouldn't have nobody that's related. The other people always figure that you are favoring somebody" (117).

Employees may resent relatives in the business and may leave as a result. One chief executive said:

> "We had an employee leave about a year or two years ago who would have liked to be a partner and I guess would have stayed had he been able to be one. But I'm quite firm on that. To be a non-family-member partner, you'd have to be pretty outstanding" (033A).

Said a woman on the board of directors of her family's business:

> "I guess sometimes there's been a problem on the part of an employee, like when one of my brothers went to work there. There was some jealousy. A couple of them resented my brother coming in. He's younger than they are, and they were afraid that he would get to a position higher than theirs, which he eventually did" (101B).

Many offspring interviewed were sensitive to what others would think, not only others in the business but people in general. Said one son who managed the family business:

> "A son—there's so much more expected of you, and sometimes the idea of 'Well, he's working for his father.' There's a certain downgrading to that" (116B).

And another son working in a junior position in a large firm run by his father said:

> "I've never been at ease with the nepotistic implications. Everyone assumes that I'm working here for one of a couple of reasons. Either it's a family business and I'm eventually going to take it over; or I couldn't get work elsewhere, so I was hired here. In any case it was just the easy choice. I didn't really want to test my mettle elsewhere. It's always there every time I meet somebody. I

always feel defensive. I don't want to take advantage of the fact that I'm the boss's son. I don't
think that's right to my coworkers" (050B).

Concern about what other employees will think is not confined
to offspring. In one of the few three-generation businesses in
the sample, a grandson also expressed concern about what others would think:

> "I would rather be treated as another em-
> ployee than as a relative. The only special privilege
> I've got this year is that I get free Cokes whenever I
> want. But other than that, just so I get along better
> with the other help and so that I feel more com-
> fortable—I feel guilty or I don't feel right when I'm
> treated special" (062B).

Heading off anxieties about what others, especially nonrelated
employees in the business, might think was a concern in a number of the business families. Sometimes a parent/employer
would work at appearing to be unbiased, but the attempt to
appear unbiased may still signal the special status of the off-
spring/employee.

> "If my son is down here with the other em-
> ployees, they figure he gets preferential treatment,
> although he doesn't. So most of the time I might
> bark at my own son louder than I would at the
> other ones just to try and prove that there is no
> favoritism, but I know I was creating some animos-
> ity" (027).

An employer taking a relative into the firm could, in theory, decide from the beginning to be completely unbiased. There were,
however, few instances in which people said that they had tried
to treat a relative as "just another employee" and apparently
succeeded. The few instances usually involved relatives other
than sons or spouses. Some teenage daughters doing temporary
office work seemed to be treated as other employees were. In
one case a brother employed two of his adult sisters.

"When both my sisters came to work, I told them from the beginning that 'You will be an employee. You will be treated the same as the rest of the employees. There will be no favoritism' " (124).

Much more commonly, particularly with the employment of sons, there was bias, an appearance of bias, or concern that there might be the appearance of bias. In response, sons in the business seemed to try hard to prove that they belonged and were not specially favored or that they deserved their favors. Reports of sons putting in long hours of intensely hard work were common. Whatever this may do to the son and his own family life, it may be good for the business. Said one informant:

"Family generally works harder for less money. The kids, for sure, are always trying to prove to the rest of the employees that they are not just the boss's son" (075B).

Another informant, a son of a boss, said in response to a question about tensions in the family over offspring being pushed too hard:

"I went through a lot of that myself earlier in that I think that, any relationship of father and son, you probably have to work much harder to prove yourself capable than any other person who would be involved in the business. You always find those people who are working around the son saying, 'Well, he's got the inside track. He's related, and that's it. That's the only reason. He isn't smart enough to do that' " (070A).

This theme of hard work by sons in the business was echoed by a father:

"I have to say that my sons are the hardest-working men in the company. And this is noted. These people respect them. I think my sons are sensitive to the fact that they do have to prove themselves. It probably places an extra burden on them" (084B).

Another father seemed concerned that if he were indulgent, he might be doing a son a disservice. He spoke, in the following statement, about his son's capacity "to earn it on his own."

> "I have three children, and they have all been employed at times by the company doing technician-type work, helping out on handyman-type jobs. I feel my son is going to earn it on his own. You don't need to give it to him" (050A).

Sons were not alone in the pressure to excel in order to prove that they belonged and deserved. Sons-in-law of the boss also were under strong pressure to excel. Said one son-in-law:

> "Really, you are not accepted by a lot of the employees. And, therefore, you've got to do your job better than anybody else" (080A).

The pressure to excel does not come, however, solely from the need to justify being where one is and receiving what one receives. It also comes from a sense that to be associated with the boss requires outstanding performance. There is a kind of leadership-goes-with-leadership logic underlying comments like

> "We were expected to be so much better than everybody else, because the boss was our father" (031A).

Conclusion

The entanglement of the business system and the family system creates the potential for tensions over fairness of compensation and work load. Most of the businesses in the sample were operated by married men. Wives not directly involved in the business contributed to the business through carrying a heavy work load at home, through tolerating what many experienced as neglect, and through their work at limiting household expenditures. These contributions might not be recognized by the husband (or the wife), but some wives felt overloaded and perhaps also unappreciated and uncompensated for their contributions to the business.

The large majority of wives worked or had worked, either full-time or part-time, in the business. Not infrequently this work was underpaid or unpaid. Although some women seemed not to resent the lack of pay, others did, and their hard feelings carried over into family relationships.

The concerns wives had, whether working in the business or not, about fairness, neglect, unmet expectations for couple and family togetherness, the amount of money available for the household, and other matters can be understood as advocacy of family goals. In a sense the clash of the business system and the family system is personified through a wife's advocacy of family goals and a husband's advocacy of business goals. Couples who find themselves in tense interactions that concern fairness issues might do well to take a step backward, depersonalize the conflict, and ask themselves to what extent they are representing systems in competition.

Offspring often have at least minor roles in a business at a very early age. Although offspring may not, at the time, appreciate the opportunity, the work experience can be seen as potentially advantageous both to them and to the business. Mature offspring with full-time roles in the business generally were males. Some offspring working full-time in the business were, by everyone's standards, indulged. Whether or not they were, the appearance of indulgence was a concern, primarily because of its effect on nonrelatives in the business. Concerns about such appearances led some chief officers to be very reluctant to bring offspring into the business. In other cases, such concerns led chief officers to be "tough" with their offspring and led the offspring to work very hard in order to appear deserving of their apparent privileges. Thus, concerns about apparent indulgence seemed in some cases to lead to very high productivity by offspring. Some offspring were also motivated to work very hard by a kind of leadership-goes-with-leadership logic that made it

seem necessary that anyone associated with the boss do an outstanding job.

The overlap of business system and family system seems
to benefit many businesses by providing unpaid or underpaid
labor, by providing very hard work, by providing home support
for the chief officer's time and financial investments in the
business. But the overlap also leads to tensions over fairness
issues and to a playing out in tense relationships of the clash of
family and business goals.

Chapter Six

Family Togetherness: Too Much and Too Little

Interviewer: "If you were talking to some young person—" *Respondent* [interrupting]: "I know what I'd tell him—spend more time with your family" (113A).

"I prefer not to see the relatives I work with, and that's the way it is. We have no social relations other than family reunions. We rarely have any social contact" (074B).

Americans value high levels of time together and high levels of emotional closeness in family relationships (Rosenblatt and Titus, 1976), but these togetherness values may compete with two other important values, individual autonomy and business success. A high level of family contact may be desired because it can promote family communication. When family members spend considerable time together, they may achieve such desired outcomes as greater expression of love and more satisfaction of needs for touching. Time together may also be desired because it can be understood to be a symbol of family caring and love. Yet a high level of family time together may not be consistent with the work demands of a family business, demands that draw some family members away from others for long periods. Family businesses are consumers of time, especially the time of the person with primary responsibility for the business. Insofar as the family system and the business system are in competition, both systems require time resources, and apparently the business system wins in the competition most of the time.

"I would say that being self-employed takes up a lot more of your time than if you were employed by somebody else. You can't just take a day off" (092B).

"The time you put into the business is always hard. I think that's the biggest thing. Sometimes I'll leave here at 8:30 A.M., and I might not get home until 6:30 P.M. The long hours, that's hard, and it's hard on the kids, I think, more than anything" (037A, a woman entrepreneur with children aged eight and twelve).

"It's hard to get away. In fact, I'd say the first vacation I ever took was ten years ago, five working days. The guys working for me get three weeks. I have a hard time getting away for a week, because when I come back, everything's there" (092A, who had been president of his firm for twenty years).

"The only stress that the business created with my wife was the number of hours I devoted to work. Everybody goes through that, I guess" (077A).

"Certainly my wife has bitched about my long hours from time to time, but she understands we've got a business to run. There are certain things, I don't say they come before the family, that have priorities. She understands that completely" (087, who had been president for five years of a family firm more than thirty years old).

"My father would leave many times on Monday and come back on Friday. We virtually grew up in our very young years without my father. And my brother and I would sometimes, if he called to say he'd be home, we'd sit down at this corner waiting for his car, sometimes for two and three hours, just to get a ride on the running board. But he didn't show a lot of times" (006).

Even when a business was operated from within the home, which was true of two businesses at the time of the interview and several others when they were new, there were concerns about too much time apart from family, about the constant involvement of one family member with the business. In the statement that follows, the apartness referred to seems to have been an apartness of preoccupation and emotional distance, as well as an apartness of physical distance.

> "He was always tired. We'd never get away from it. That's part of what I disliked about having the office in the home. It was unnatural to clean the basement every week, because that's where they were. And the fact that I was never alone. I'm a person that likes to be alone. But more the fact that he never got away from it. When you are downstairs working, you have the demands of your family upstairs, and he couldn't concentrate. And when he was up here, it was 'Oh, I really should go down and do those papers.' I would tend to think that people who started their own companies would tend to be workaholics" (042B).

In each of the businesses we studied, two or more family members were involved in the business at some time. With such shared involvement, people may meet needs for time together and feel satisfied. But working together may aggravate the effect of ordinary relationship tensions; people may feel trapped together or may still have little time for certain forms of intimacy.

Given these and other potential problems of too little and too much physical and emotional togetherness in business-operating families, it is not surprising that thirty-four of the ninety-two respondents in this study reported tensions and stresses in the area of family togetherness and apartness.

The Early Days of Business Involvement

Business executives in large corporations often are absent from the family for substantial periods (Boss, McCubbin, and Lester, 1979; Renshaw, 1976). A corporate executive and the spouse and offspring of the executive may fantasize having the greater togetherness of people with a family business. But in reality at the beginning of involvement in a family business an entrepreneur typically works with few or no other family members. Even when other family members are involved, the entrepreneur may spend far more time on business matters than the others do. Given what the business requires or what the entrepreneur wants to build, the entrepreneur typically must work very long hours in order to get the business organized or reorganized, to establish customers, to accumulate capital, and to pay high start-up expenses. Thus, in the early days of business involvement, the entrepreneur spends many work hours out of contact with most or all other family members, more work hours than most people with salaried jobs would spend out of contact with family. Many entrepreneurs spoke of time away from family members being a substantial difficulty while establishing or reorganizing the business. In each of the following six interview excerpts, an entrepreneur spoke of the difficulty of sustaining a family life while getting a business going. It is possible to read most or all of these quotations as saying that, directly or indirectly, business took priority over family. Some entrepreneurs quoted in the following passages seemed not even to be aware at the height of their business involvement that family life was suffering. Almost all of the six seem to have been saying that they felt comfortable about what they had done, that their choice to work long hours in the business was the necessary choice.

"Tensions within our family? Probably tons. Especially in the beginning, when there was a lot more hours put in. Evening work and the weekend work, which I found very disruptive, which I really resented as far as taking time away from the old 'What good is all the working and all the money going to do when we never get to see you?' type of thing, and not very satisfactory answers except 'I have to do this if we are going to make a go of it' " (042A).

"The "biggest problem up to the last year [the ninth year of business operation] was that it was a whole lot of time away from the family, 'cause we open at seven o'clock in the morning, and I was here until eight-thirty, nine o'clock every night six days a week. And I just finally got fed up with it. So we cut it down. I get here at seven. We shut it down at five" (061).

"It's a stress for the first couple of years until you get going. It's getting over the hump of finances. It seems you've got to put your nose to the grindstone day and night for the first three years, till you get it going" (062A).

"When I took over the business, for a whole summer I worked. I'd go to work at five in the morning and come home ten, eleven, twelve o'clock at night. I wouldn't see my kids from one Sunday to the next for a whole year there. They were sleeping when I go to work, and they'd be sleeping when I got home at night. It didn't really matter to me 'cause I was busy. I never even noticed it" (092A).

"In the past, my ex-partner and I were putting in lots of hours here, and I was on the road and there were some problems, too much time to get the business going. You don't spend enough time at home. I *couldn't* do it any differently, because at that time those jobs had to be done. There's no other way it could have been done" (032A).

"I get home late for supper all the time. When you get home, I have a meeting to go to that night or you have to leave early to go to another meeting in the morning. The time availability with the family and to run a business, it's really hard. You have to be involved in the business if it's going to be a success. You have to stay on top of it. You have to go to these meetings—product knowledge, business knowledge. Job responsibility at home— cut my grass, taking care of my house, taking care of the kids, and upkeep of the place. I end up not having time to do that, or not doing my part, I should say. Or I get told, 'You're not doing this; you're not doing that; you're never home.' It's hard to please the two" (098A, who had been president of his firm less than two years).

In some cases, an entrepreneur or the wife of an entrepreneur expressed concern about the effect of the high level of physical and emotional apartness on the children or on the relationship of father and children.

> "Certainly the older children did not get to know my husband well. The first two years we had the office in our basement at home, so he was there, but yet he really wasn't there, because it was all business. He would work maybe eighteen hours a day. So handy having an office there. He was downstairs most of the time. Certainly I had a problem. I don't think my husband did. In the early years of the business, the family did not only not come first, maybe it was eighty-third. I never had to worry about another woman; I just had the business to battle" (091B).

Some entrepreneurs, realizing that there were potential problems with their children or simply wanting more contact with their children, made schedule adjustments even though they did not reduce their time commitment to the business.

> "When my children were growing up, I would just postpone the work I took home until after nine o'clock or after ten o'clock" (077A).

A common means by which entrepreneurs tried to compensate for the lack of contact with family members was the provision of material goods. Often entrepreneurs who tried this form of compensation came, at some point, to consider it an unsatisfactory solution. By then the business had probably developed to the point that the entrepreneur could spend more time at home, or, like the first person whose comments follow, the entrepreneur decided that the extra work had little effect on the success of the business.

> "I worked eighty-hour weeks. To illustrate: I had been gone for ten days. I came back; my bags were in the door. One of my daughters came bouncing down the stairs with a few of her friends, and she said, 'Oh, Dad, are you going someplace?' And I had been gone ten days. [Laughs] I left before

they got up in the morning, and they were in bed
when I got home at night. I would try to make it
up by buying them things—pool tables and slot ma-
chines, tennis, swimming pool. It helps, but it
doesn't work. I found that a lot of the things I did
to keep me away from home were really not necessary. I found that customers—they did appreciate,
yes, but they didn't know I was down there until
twelve o'clock at night. The importance was in my
own mind, not in the customer's mind" (074B).

"I was thinking if I could supply my wife
and children with the monetary needs and goodies,
then that's doing my job, but in essence it wasn't.
It was hurting more than helping" (042A, on why
he cut back his work hours so that he could spend
more time with his family).

Even when an entrepreneur comes into more substantial
contact with the children who have been neglected, some things
may have been permanently lost. It is impossible to return to
the growing-up years of a child to witness and experience what
one has missed. In some families, the relationship established
with children during the times of high apartness, a relationship
with substantial emotional distance, may never be changed. Relationship issues typically cannot be put on "hold" for very
long without adverse effects.

"My father and I have a problem talking on
a personal level. When I was growing up, he spent
most of his time with his partner trying to build
this place. He spent all his early years, my early
years, down here at the store, nights, weekends, or
whatever. So we didn't do lot of the things that fathers and sons do. What we talk about now is mostly business" (005).

We know of instances, though not in the sample, in which family members considered a problem that a child developed during
years of great apartness from an entrepreneur parent to have
been caused by that apartness. Whether or not a problem such
as alcoholism could have been prevented or cleared up had par-

ent and child been closer, the fact that the problem had occurred at all was considered by some people to be a permanently crippling injury that had resulted from the entrepreneur's choice to have so much business involvement.

Movement toward a higher level of father/offspring contact may reverse some apparently deleterious effects of the years of very high apartness, but some husbands continued to regret, and some wives continued to resent, the heavy burden on the wife/mother.

> "My dad worked for other people and is very proud of the fact that he never missed a day of work. He may be dead, but he goes to work and he comes home and goes to bed and he goes to work the next day. So to me, I'm thinking about my husband, 'Hey, you own this company, and you have to give it your all.' So we have very differing views. When he worked too hard, I felt he was doing what he should, but I resented the time it took from the family. And when he'd take some of the privileges he felt he earned, then he'd get grief from the customers because he wasn't doing his job" (042B).

> "When the kids were little, it was hard, because my husband wasn't home very much" (101B).

Some husband/entrepreneurs talked about the problems they had had with their wives or their wives had had with them during the early days of the business.

> "My wife accuses me of being obsessed by the business, that I spend an awful lot of time at it. It dominates our relationship. Most of my outside activity is somewhat related to the business. Actually, I've been spending lots of time with her on the weekends. You know, I used to work all Saturdays, and Sundays if necessary, and now I seldom do" (122B, reporting a problem that may still be present in his wife's view of things and in his own—see his statement later in this chapter: "I get home about six-fifteen, six-thirty . . .").

"I used to work fifteen to eighteen hours a day a lot of the time. My wife would get mad a little bit. It was either that or pay someone overtime. I'd just let her flame out most of the time. I said very little" (039).

Interviewer: "Was too much time apart from family a problem during the formative years in your business?" *Respondent:* "I think it might have been, but I think my wife can answer it better than I. I just didn't pay that much attention. I paid more attention to the business" (091A).

Wives in that situation seemed often to feel powerless to change things. Even when they felt they had power and exercised it, they still seemed to feel there was too much marital apartness. But, as in the following quotation, it seems that a wife could influence her husband's involvement in the business.

"I'd take the stuff home and be involved in it, almost on a twenty-four-hours basis, because you just are. If it got out of hand, she'd say, 'We've had enough of that. Calm down!' " (078).

There are no easy solutions to the problem of too much apartness when a business is in a stage demanding great amounts of attention. In a sense, a spouse's complaints about too much apartness are part of the solution. Such complaints are a way of saying, "We still care about you and value contact with you." But can more be done to deal with the problem? Here are five suggestions.

1. Segregate home life from work life. Maintaining times and places that work can never intrude on makes it easier to protect home life from work life. Once a place or a time becomes associated with an activity, it is difficult to avoid getting into that activity when in that place or time. For example, a firm adherence to a Sabbath makes it easier not to work on the Sabbath. Similarly, a firm decision never to do work in the living room or bedroom or never to do work before 7:00 A.M. or after 10:00 P.M. makes it easier to insulate those places and times from one's work.

2. Use the available time flexibility. Although people in family businesses often claim that one advantage of being in business for oneself is time flexibility (see Chapter Eleven), that flexibility may be underutilized. Taking a break by telephoning a spouse or child, having lunch or a snack with spouse and children, taking three minutes to drop a greeting card (that will arrive in a day or two) to a spouse or child, taking time off to attend a child's performance at school or to cuddle with one's spouse all may be worth the time investment, both maintaining a good family relationship and renewing one's energy to do work.

3. Make time budgets and stick to them. Any resource that is in high demand must be budgeted. If a chief officer's time is in high demand, that time must be budgeted. To meet family needs, the chief officer's time budget should include family demands as well as business demands. Even an adhered-to weekday budget of, say, ten minutes in the morning and fifteen minutes at night with children and fifteen minutes in the morning and twenty minutes at night with spouse, a total of an hour a day, may make an enormous difference. The time may be as "unproductive" as playing a game, touching, watching TV together, or reading to each other. But the point is actually to spend that time in contact. To do so may delay doing some work activity, but the time may instead be taken from a non-work activity that had been used for relaxation or to ease a transition—for example, reading a newspaper or watching the evening news.

4. Adjust priorities. Say "no" some of the time to the business and "yes" to the family. Perhaps that will mean that the business will grow and expand a little less quickly, but balance sheets are not the only source of information about how well one is doing in life. How one's family is doing and how one gets along with one's family are also important.

5. When possible, pay people to do what you have been doing. That means, when possible, to delegate some of your activities at work and to pay people for services at home such as lawnmowing, as a way of creating time with the family.

We do not want to tell people where to live, but in matters of time budgeting long commutes are worth reviewing. People may commute a long distance between home and work because they need the time to be by themselves or because it guarantees an optimal location for home (considering schools, fresh air, proximity to kin, and so on) and business (considering proximity to transportation, access to low-cost labor, and so on). However, a person whose family life is tense because of too much time away from home and who is spending considerable time commuting may do well to consider changing the location of home or work.

Apartness When the Business Is Well Established

Over a period of roughly three to ten years of involvement in a new business, the pressures on an entrepreneur for great physical apartness from family members often abate. Credit becomes established, products or services are effectively delivered, there are loyal customers, and debts are adequately serviced. In addition, some entrepreneurs seem to become more relaxed about proving themselves, more introspective and family-oriented. Whatever the processes involved, as the following two statements indicate, the entrepreneur tends to take a more relaxed attitude toward the problems of the business.

> "If you let the business run you, it's going to break up a family. If you just jump when everybody hollers, and don't take any free time, you are in trouble. You're not home for the family. It causes hard feelings at home. Let the people who are working for you take care of it the best they know how. If they can't take care of it, then you'd better replace somebody" (117).

> "After being at this for thirty-three years now, I don't worry so much any more. I used to think everything was a crisis. And now I realize it isn't" (036A).

A more relaxed attitude may still involve some tension. The second of the two entrepreneurs just quoted also said:

> "I've never gone on a vacation yet that I didn't leave with the feeling that I shouldn't be going because I should be here, because things aren't really right" (036A).

Even with the reduced pressure of a well-established business, somebody who is involved in the business may remain too
much apart physically from others in the family by the standards of at least one person in the family. Here is how five hus-
band/entrepreneurs spoke of continued physical apartness.

"That sometimes comes up with someone
wanting to go somewhere together, and you have a
customer who wants to do something else. It occurs, but I wouldn't consider it a significant element—irritating more than anything else. Typically
we take care of the customer first. On a summer
vacation with the family, if it's necessary, I just
leave where we are on vacation and come back here
for a few days" (120, who had been president of
his company for six years).

"A lot of guys come home from work four-
thirty or five o'clock and then spend from there
until nine o'clock with the kids hollering at them—
because some guys really don't like kids—or they
spend times with their kids doing constructive
things. I miss out on those hours during the week
that a lot of people have with their kids. And I
think about it now. It was not as much a loss for
my kids as it was for me" (123, a young entrepreneur who had been president of his company for
seven years).

"There are times when my wife will think I
spend too much time at work" (050A, who had
been his firm's president for fourteen years).

"Stresses in family life? I don't really know
of any, other than the fact that you are involved in
business and end up with not having as much time
as probably other people have for home-related
activities" (070A, president of a family business
for fifteen years).

"I get home about six-fifteen, six-thirty.
Some spouses would like you to put in an eight-
hour day, get home four-thirty or five o'clock"
(122B, who had been president of his firm for
seventeen years).

Some entrepreneurs who were well established were able to

maintain a shorter work week than they might have had when their involvement in the business was new, but they still might be drawn into a heavy work schedule at peak seasons.

> "Quite often family businesses are working from sunup to sundown and around the clock. We try to stay away from that as much as possible. Only when the busy season is on—after all, we are like a farmer. When the sun shines, we have to make hay" (116A).

The patterning of togetherness and apartness, in summary, includes very high levels of physical apartness when an entrepreneur first establishes or takes over a business. Later on, if the business survives, there tends to be less physical apartness than at first, but typically more work time is spent away from home than would be true in the average wage-earning or salaried family. Almost always the entrepreneur who is involved in the business and away from home so much is a husband and father. Some entrepreneur/husbands seem less sensitive than their wives to the costs of the apartness. Even when they are aware of problems, entrepreneurs seem to feel that the business must have very high priority. Family businesses, in contrast to stereotypes, do not generally make for great family closeness. The family businesses that do make for greater closeness, as the following section indicates, do not bring an end to problems of family togetherness and apartness. Rather, they seem to change the kind of problem that a family must deal with from one of too little contact to one of too much or too difficult contact.

Together in a Business

The image outsiders may have of a family business is an image of great togetherness: the closeness of wife and husband operating a "Mom and Pop" store or of parent and offspring, where the latter is apprenticed to the former and eventually will succeed to the chief executive role. However, even where several family members have intense business involvement, they may be out of contact with one another most of the time.

"We really don't see that much of each other here. I'm either in here or out in the shop or at our family's other business or out selling, and she's handling her paperwork and receptionist and accounting. There's days when I'll see her in the morning when she comes in, and I'm gone, and she tells me at night, 'Well, I'm leaving,' and we don't see each other in the meantime" (015, who had been chief executive for seven years).

"My brothers I seldom see. One of them works downstairs; the other works in the corner. It's all business with them. We never talk personally. But then we'll get together on the weekend and we'll see each other socially" (084A).

"There is continuous conflict. Let me say that being miles apart takes care of a major part of the conflict. What I figured out four or five years ago in this encounter group takes care of a lot of this conflict. But my brother is a very conservative person, and I'm quite the contrary" (006).

The first and second of these three statements indicate that, in some businesses, family members have so much separation physically and by work functions that they have little opportunity to interact. The third statement just quoted implies that one reason people may be separated in a family business is to minimize tension between equals. To minimize tense interactions, the "conservative" brother and the brother who is not have chosen to be separated by miles (they manage rather independent branches of a single business).

A number of people who work in business with spouse, parents, offspring, or other kin seem to have a sense that being out of contact with those kin while at work is good. Maintenance of some family systems seems to require a certain amount of apartness (Rosenblatt and Titus, 1976). In business families in which people work together, the apartness can be achieved through spatial and functional separation at work. But people may also need, in order to maintain optimal apartness, to see each other less outside work than they otherwise would.

"We don't get together so much on weekends or in evenings for a dinner like we did ten years ago. I see enough of my father now during the day. I don't want to see him at night as much. Right now I think my father feels, see, we always used to have barbecues over at his house. I think he feels right now that I'm kinda avoiding him. I pop over there once every four months, and before I used to go over there maybe at least once a week. It's just that I've got to stay away from him. That's the way I feel. I can handle it at work; I can't handle it after work" (031A).

"One of the problems would be the fact that you get to see your father, my folks, five days a week, eight hours a day. So you don't really relish the fact that you go to see them on the weekend, go to see them on Mother's Day or Christmas. It's just that you see them five days a week anyways. It's not a thrill to go on the weekend and spend some more time with them. If we do go to see them on the weekend, all we usually talk about is business, and I try not to talk business once I leave the place, unless I'm with the people that work here. And from time to time my father and I have differences of opinion. It's a battle. If we hadn't worked together, I'm sure we'd be seeing each other more on the evenings and weekends. My brother's the same way. His wife asks, 'Why don't we go see your folks more?' He says, 'I see them every day of the week. Why see them on weekends too?' I think it's too bad that the business got so much involved with the family. We all like working here, and I like the business. But the family life suffered in order for the business life to stay on an even keel" (005).

"During the summer I notice there's a lot of tension here, lot of static, short tempers, because everybody works here in the summer. My brothers and sisters aren't in school. We all arrive to work together in the morning. Everybody lives at home in the same house. They're there at night for dinner, and they go to work together, and it gets to be a rut" (106B).

For people in family businesses together who do not get apart very much, a common way to cope with satiation from sameness of conversational topic is to have an understanding that family members will not discuss business matters with one another when away from the business.

> "We have tried to quit scheduling so many estimations at night, so that would give us more free time. And we also try not to discuss a lot of business at night, just to turn it off and get into something else" (018, a wife who worked full-time with her husband).

During business hours, people sometimes need to get away from a family member in order to cool off after a conflict. Physical apartness may not necessarily be the most constructive way to deal with anger and disagreements, but if people are unwilling or unable to do something different with their interpersonal problems, getting apart may be one of the few ways available to maintain some sort of relationship.

> "My wife and I see things in different lights."
> *Interviewer:* "How do you solve your differences?"
> *Respondent:* "We don't. I win. She either goes along with me, or she goes away until she understands my position and comes back. I am the operating officer in the business. No entity can have two heads and survive, and she understands that. It's just that there are times when she doesn't feel I make the right decisions, and in the long run I make the right decisions, and she admits that. But in the short run sometimes she can't see why I'm doing a certain thing, and I may not take the time to explain all the whole situation to her. She leaves the premises and cools off and comes back when she's realized that I have done the right things, and that usually takes about fifteen or twenty minutes. Or she just goes home and ignores what I'm doing and comes back the next day as though nothing happened" (119).

For some people, the physical and emotional contact

with a family member in the business is too much, even after they have tried other approaches to minimizing difficulties. Family members (perhaps particularly wives and sons) have left or been asked to leave businesses because of too much family togetherness. The following example came from a man who had ended his wife's part-time employment with his firm.

> "I just felt like, you know, I don't think it was a good situation. Well, we're here, we're at home all the time together, and to be at work all the time together—it just didn't seem right. We have our conflicts at home. It's usually carried on at the store. It just wasn't a good situation. It was all minor stuff. I guess she didn't like me being over her all the time, checking things out. The relationship wasn't there as a boss/employee" (098A).

When a business is run in the home, the opportunities for problems of too much togetherness are great. People risk satiation. There will be trouble segregating home life from work life, so that there is always the possibility that work will intrude into home life. Family members risk getting into territorial disputes, disputes over noise and mess, and disputes about privacy if the business ever brings customers, suppliers, or employees into the house. As the following statements by one couple indicate, another kind of problem is that an entrepreneur's spouse will be in a position to monitor what the entrepreneur is doing and to criticize how the business is being operated. Moving the business out of the home is one way to end a spouse's monitoring and criticism.

> "Not having your wife involved in knowing what's happening in the business, that tension isn't there, other than when I come home and share it. Before she would get the phone calls from the customers that wanted to know where the sub was or where this was, and not having any information at all, it was a stress filling thing because she was wondering whether I was taking care of it. After we

clarified her relationship to the business, she would simply not answer the phone and simply say, 'I don't have any information.' She was able to divorce herself from that end of it" (042A).

"I try as hard as I can to stay uninvolved, which may be different from many family-owned businesses. I find it doesn't work for me. The more I know, the more tense and unhappy we are. I never minded my husband being in the house when the office was here. But if I ever answered the phone, it was someone calling because something was wrong. Somebody wasn't where they were supposed to be. So it was constantly all this negative information. It got to the point where I started to feel, 'Hey, don't you know what you are doing? All I'm hearing was complaints all the time.' And so I would be on his back, as well as the customers would be on his back. So it just didn't work out" (042B).

The foregoing discussion of togetherness seems to imply that togetherness is usually a bad thing in the family business. But some people in the business-operating families we studied felt there were gains from being in business with other family members.

"I probably got to know my children better because they were involved in the business" (011).

"It did give my children a better picture of what the father was doing, what his business consisted of" (050A).

Some people enjoyed sharing experiences and having things to talk about with a family member who was a coworker, having more time together, and having a "family" feeling. Thus, even though family members in business together can have painfully high levels of togetherness, for some people the togetherness seemed, on balance, to be a good thing.

Conclusion

It is important to remember that a majority of respondents reported no problems in the togetherness/apartness area. However, among the respondents who said there were problems, what came out most clearly was that a family business could lead to too much apartness or to too much togetherness. There were businesses, or times in the course of growth of a business, in which one person in the family was deeply involved in the business and others were not. In those cases that person's involvement in and time commitment to the business were the focus of tension over too much apartness. There were also businesses in which two or more family members worked simultaneously. In some of those, the family members involved had very high levels of physical and emotional apartness, but in others they had more physical or emotional togetherness than at least one of them wanted. With too much contact, there were often tensions, but there were also often mechanisms operating to increase physical and emotional apartness.

In family systems an optimum for togetherness and apartness seems to exist. A business system can move a family or a relationship within a family to too little or to too much contact. When there is too little contact, family members complain, and the persons involved may feel strongly motivated to find ways to get increased contact. The problem is not simple when a business operator believes that the business requires enormous amounts of entrepreneurial time, but some entrepreneurs find ways to make more time available to family members, and we suggest other ways that greater contact might be achieved. When there is too much contact, people who feel a need for greater apartness seem often to find it through spatial and functional separation within the business or through greater distance outside the business than they otherwise would have. In some cases, however, the contact in the business remains too great, and business involvement of at least one of the family members is ended.

Matters of time together and time apart are often entangled in issues of emotional closeness and distance, relationship commitment, comfort with intimacy or avoidance of it, and other aspects of kin feeling. Hence, complaints about amount of time together or apart may be complaints, in some sense, about emotional closeness, about commitment of the other or demanded of oneself, and about desired or feared intimacy. Moreover, people who complain about "feelings" issues (such as problems of emotional closeness, commitment, and intimacy) may actually be concerned that they have too much or too little time with someone in the family. Time, in other words, may be, in people's words and thoughts, a surrogate or symbol of kin feelings, but statements about kin feeling may also be surrogates or symbols for concerns about time.

Chapter Seven

Supervising Family Members

"My father is a miserable supervisor. No tact. He's even that way with the employees. He talks to you like you don't have a brain in your head. He puts you down, and in front of other people. There's nothing you can really do, because he will say, 'If you don't like it, there's the door.' He'll think about it for a couple of hours and then he'll come back and feel bad, but the damage is done" (113B).

"I've tried not to be as demanding of my children as my father would have been of me" (070A).

"I need feedback and Dad has trouble giving it to me" (033B).

In this study, supervision was reported as an area of tension by eighteen of the ninety-two informants (from fourteen businesses). Organizations generally involve people linked to people in a hierarchy. In a business, somebody is understood to have the right and duty to tell somebody else what to do. Supervisory control may ordinarily be constructive and helpful, but in any hierarchical relationship there may be too much control or not enough.

When it comes to pushing, as opposed to facilitating, teaching, or helping, some people are uncomfortable or incompetent at using their authority. In some cases aspects of the particular situation or characteristics of the person they are super-

109

vising make it difficult or impossible to push hard. In other cases a person may supervise primarily in a coercive way and push so hard that the supervised feels very upset and demoralized, becomes less effective as a result of feeling anger, embarrassment, humiliation, and so on, or leaves the business. Even apparently positive forms of supervision such as teaching, helping, or praising may be experienced by the person supervised as an unpleasant, perhaps even punishing, push. A push is not necessarily a bad thing, but what is an adequate but not too hard push on one person may debilitate another, block the person's learning, or even drive the person out of the business.

Just as some supervisors have trouble pushing, other supervisors have trouble setting limits. They may not want the responsibility of setting limits, may lack the confidence to stick to limits they set, or may not be competently assertive at expressing limits in the first place. There are, for example, permissive parents who, as bosses of their own offspring, are unwilling or unable to set limits even when necessary. Without limits, a person working in the business may do work that is rarely beneficial to the business and may even do things that undermine the business. Without limits, a person may have a more difficult time learning what his or her job actually is. Without limits, a person may not develop the discipline and conceptual structures needed to do a job adequately. For that reason, when a supervisor fails at setting limits, the person supervised may eventually suffer serious consequences.

Systems require effective leadership, but it is possible in any supervisory relationship for problems to arise. When supervisor and supervised have a kin relationship, there may be more sources of problems, and the ordinary problems of supervision may become more serious.

People may hold back from supervising kin, at least in theory, because the kin can be assumed to be very responsible where the family financial interests are involved or because anything resembling a push risks alienating them or somebody else connected to them (kin who are not directly involved but whose feelings are important to the supervisor). People may hold back in supervising kin out of a sense that the kin need to be protected or a fear that the kin could feel patronized, bullied, or diminished by any kind of supervision. People may also supervise kin more intensely because there is not the usual reserve one has with outsiders, because one expects more from kin, or because kin incompetence or fault is somehow more personally threatening.

Some informants felt that kin have to be supervised in a relatively harsh way in order not to show favoritism. It seems a potential cost of operating a family business that it may be hard to hold nonkin employees who fear that kin are favored (overpaid, allowed unfair influence with the boss, given an easy and undeserved ride to the top). One way people in family businesses try to cope with the danger that competent nonkin employees will feel resentment and will leave the business is to push harder on their kin than they would need to if everybody working in the business was kin or if nobody was. The pushing of kin is an attempt to communicate to nonkin that kin are not favored.

> "A family member, until they're accepted, has to be pushed a little bit hard, because you can't show that favoritism. Then after they're once accepted, that's their job. I think you treat them as any other employee" (080A).

Concerns about possible resentment by nonkin employees were echoed by other informants. (See, for example, comments in Chapter Five by informant 027, "Most of the time I might bark at my own son louder than I would at the other ones just to try and prove that there is no favoritism," and informant 031A, "We were expected to be so much better than everybody else, because the boss was our father.")

Fear of appearing to play favorites is not the only factor that may underlie harsh supervision of relatives. Some people also said that one could be blunt and straightforward with kin, whereas with nonkin one would have to be more circumspect and tactful.

> "You don't treat people that you are very
> familiar with as well as people you are less familiar
> with" (048B, a son).

Some people, however, were more cautious, not less cautious,
with kin. For informants like the following, the need to maintain comfortable relations with family members reduced the
harshness of supervision but may have led to poor work by family members who would have benefited from limit setting and
supervisory correction.

> "If my sons or my wife make mistakes, I let
> it go, because it's not worth fighting over. They'll
> find out it's a mistake by themselves anyway,
> sooner or later. Then you hope they won't do it
> again. With a nonfamily member, you bring them
> into your office and tell them how you want it
> done. You might also tell your son the same thing,
> but he may not want to do it that way. You have
> to live with your family. A nonfamily member,
> you can fire him" (075A).

Other people who talked about holding back in supervision of
kin thought that one had to hold back because kin are more
touchy about supervision. A person who had supervised several
sons in the family business and an array of cousins spoke about
the sensitivity of the men in the family.

> "Polish men are the type that don't like to
> be told things, and no matter if it's a family or
> otherwise, I think that's part of the nature" (063A).

Later the informant compared the sensitivity of family members in the business, both men and women, with the sensitivity
of the unrelated person in the business ("a stranger that you're
paying").

> "It's not like telling a stranger that you're
> paying, 'I'd like this move.' When you tell a rela-
> tive, you've got to think three times and make sure
> it sounds right" (063A).

One of that informant's sons echoed his parent's concerns about possible tensions among family members in the business.

> "If you are going to go to somebody in the family and say, 'Hey, either you're going to shape up or you're going to be gone,' you're going to cause some tension" (063B).

One of the reasons some relatives are more sensitive when supervised is that they may interpret a supervisor's ordinary supervisory distance or a supervisory statement as meaning much more than it would mean to a nonrelative. Emotional distance is common in an ordinary supervisory relationship, yet in a family relationship it may be interpreted as rejection and lack of interest. A statement by a supervisor who is a relative may be interpreted as an attempt to establish or maintain a status difference in the family context. It may be interpreted as criticism reflecting on what one does in family situations outside the business context, or it may be experienced as an attempt to win battles begun in family situations, even battles begun in childhood. Those considerations may be what the following informant was referring to.

> "My two brothers that work there, one is over the other, and the younger brother sometimes takes, not to say an order, directions personally, rather than it should be taken in the context of work, rather than big brother telling little brother what to do" (101B).

The "sensitivity" issue seemed to extend in at least a few families beyond the relationship of supervisor and supervised. Other kin would, in some instances, prevent the supervisor from being very harsh. Perhaps the most striking instance was the following statement by an older brother who was supervising his younger brother:

> "I made him quit one time. The rest of my family told me that I should apologize to him. So I

did apologize to him, and I told him, 'If I fire you again, I won't come back and apologize.' That's when he was twenty-one or twenty-two and we brought him up to be a salesman and he wasn't ready yet. Somebody that is twenty-one or twenty-two and still likes to wear his hair in a knot at the back of his neck is going to have a hard time calling on a lot of redneck customers" (005).

A point implied in this discussion of "holding back" in supervision of kin is that such holding back may be harmful to the person being supervised. Though possibly heading off family tension, a supervisor who holds back may be prolonging the period of ignorance of the person supervised, increasing the person's feelings of frustration, and helping make the person look worse to coworkers. To the extent that supervision involves teaching, encouragement, support, and advice, a supervisor who holds back may be doing the supervised a disservice.

Supervising a Spouse

In supervision of a spouse, the crucial issue seemed not to be harshness versus lenience but, rather, how to blend a supervisory relationship in the business situation with what is ordinarily a nonsupervisory relationship in the home situation. The conflict between the two situations was discussed in Chapter Three, where one informant was quoted as saying:

> "You get to the point where you resent your husband or your wife telling you what to do. It can really rub you the wrong way, because at that point you forget that you're boss and employee" (018).

In a statement also quoted in Chapter Three, another informant said:

> "I guess she didn't like me being over her all the time, checking things out. The relationship wasn't there as a boss/employee" (098A).

A number of couples could not sustain a relationship at work in which husband supervised wife. The wife left the business. The couples who sustained a supervisory relationship typically had a clear division of labor in the business, one that required little contact between the spouses. With supervision requiring little contact, couples seemed better able to sustain the business relationship and perhaps got along more smoothly outside the business.

In some businesses the supervised spouse did not seem to mind being told what to do. She (or, in at least one case, he) seemed to accept the organizational hierarchy and expressed no anger, hurt feelings, or discomfort to us. In at least some of these businesses, the spouse was supervised with enough tact and respect to prevent overt problems. However, in some of the cases with a great deal of tact and respect, the business relationship between spouses had a history of greater abrasiveness. For example, we were told in one case that the tact and respect were achievements obtained with a great deal of hard work and the help of a competent marriage counselor.

Are Offspring Pushed Too Hard?

The most common kinship supervisory relationship in the sample was the parent/offspring one. Seventeen informants (from fifteen businesses) reported that there were tensions over offspring in the family business being pushed too hard or not hard enough. Since the sample contained only thirty-four businesses in which parent/offspring pairs were involved at the same time, parent/offspring tension over supervision can be said to be common where parent supervises offspring. That is, in almost half the businesses in which parent supervised offspring, there was tension over the offspring's being pushed too hard or not hard enough.

Two statements illustrating tension when parent supervised offspring were quoted in Chapter Five. A woman talked about her fifteen-year-old son, who felt he was pushed too hard ("We just think that kids should share in the responsibility"—018), and a son who managed the family business had felt pushed too hard ("A son—there's so much more expected of you"—116B). Here are two other instances.

> "You many times can kill children, you know, kill their spirit" (074A).
>
> "The stresses were probably mostly mine, being concerned that my children would do equally well or perhaps even better than other people in corresponding positions. I think my son really felt the brunt of that" (077A).

Another informant spoke of differing perceptions. He seemed aware that his children felt pushed too hard, but he also seemed sure that his belief that they were not being pushed too hard was the correct one.

> "My children always complain about being pushed too hard. The younger generation is a generation of chronic complainers as far as I'm concerned. Not one of them will ever spend the time or the effort that we have to spend, and they readily admit that they will not. As far as the kids being pushed, we push them less than we do the employees. And, generally speaking, they make a lot more money than the employees" (119, who also had disagreements with his wife; see his statement in Chapter Four: "My wife and I see things in different lights . . .").

There were other parents who felt the offspring were wrong to think they were being pushed too hard, but no offspring said anything like "Dad thinks he's pushing me too hard, but he's not."

In one case a son who was concerned about being pushed too hard seemed to feel that the push resulted in part from his living with his father. The fact that his supervisor had so much contact with him seemed both to intensify how much he was monitored and to reduce the respect that a supervisor might ordinarily have for the individuality and integrity of the supervised.

"I've been sick two times in seven years.
When you live with the boss, you can't just call in
sick. The two days I was sick, I had my wisdom
teeth out. I'm supposed to be here before my dad.
I think if I moved out, he would respect me a lot
more. If I moved out, we'd get along a lot better.
He wants to control my life every minute of the
day" (106B).

He said that his economic dependence on his father gave his father more leverage and increased the extent to which his father
pushed him. Other offspring who were interviewed also talked
about economic dependence as a factor that gave a supervising
relative more power to push on the supervised. Several offspring
and several parents felt that the continuing kinship relationship
made harshness, even extreme harshness, safe. The following
statement seems to refer both to economic dependence and to
continuing kinship as factors allowing harsh criticism.

"Even though you are more critical of fam-
ily members, it's a little safer to be critical of these
people, because the chances of their quitting are a
lot more remote" (116B).

The pressures on the supervised offspring are, in some
cases, indirect. In those instances it is not that the parent is
being excessively critical or that the offspring feels the parent's
wrath. It is that the work of the parent or of other family members sets standards that put pressure on the offspring. Siblings
working in a business may, as in the first of the following quotations, compete in a way that puts the pressure on them that
their parent might if the siblings were not competing with each
other. Alternatively, the parent may work hard, as in the second
of the following quotations, in a way that makes a supervised
offspring who does not work with the intensity and industrious-
ness of the parent feel guilty.

Interviewer: "Any problems over offspring
in the business being pushed too hard?" Respondent: "They take care of that with each other. I

mean sibling rivalry takes care of that. . . . 'What
do you think you're doing?' One son walks out of
here at five-thirty. The other will tell us tomorrow
that he was in here at seven-thirty and he isn't
going to leave until midnight" (095A).

"There's a mountain of work to be done,
and I'm not really told to do it, but yet again my
father will put in a lot of time and work at it, and I
get the feeling that maybe I'm dropping the ball on
him. I should be staying late" (116B).

Pressures can also be self-generated. In a sense, offspring
work that occurs without obvious supervisory push is not appropriately discussed under the heading of supervision. Yet offspring who work hard must somehow get support for that work.
For example, there may be rewards for producing and covert
disapproval of slacking off. So what looks like self-generated
pressure may arise in part from the actions and reactions of others. Recall the discussion in Chapter Five of the pressure that
offspring in a business may feel to justify what would look to
others like indulgence. That pressure may arise because the offspring has been put in a situation in which a nonrelative would
feel resentment if the offspring were not working hard.

"When I was first hired, I took it upon myself to push myself harder just to get along with
the other employees. When I first was brought in
the company, I worked one week with the shipping
man and was promoted above him to my current
position. He was next in line to get the job that I
was started at. So there was a little tension there.
I felt I should work extra hard to prove myself.
But there was no pressure from my stepfather"
(122A).

Similar comments can be found near the end of Chapter
Five, by informants 075B, 070A, 084B, and 080A. One could
say that the motivation reported in the preceding quotation to
work hard to prove oneself was self-generated, yet the informant's motivation came when he was placed by his stepfather in a

situation in which others could feel he was being indulged. The placement of the stepson in a situation in which he felt pressure to "work extra hard" is interpretable as the application of supervisory pressure.

Offspring supervised by parents were generally concerned about the parent/supervisor's opinion. Here is one example.

> "I push myself because I feel that son thing. You're always trying to make your dad proud of you" (084A).

Dad may not, in this example, have applied strong supervisory pressure, but the sensitivity of the son to his father's opinion can be understood to result from socialization to be sensitive to Dad's opinions, a socialization, in a sense, to be receptive to subtle supervision. In addition, the father's pride and his willingness to let his son know about it can be considered supervisory pressure.

Whether or not there is strong pressure on a son or daughter is partly a matter of what he or she perceives, and what is perceived is affected by what the offspring expects. Offspring who expect to be nurtured and to be treated as exceptions with special privileges but who are then treated like ordinary employees may feel pressured too hard. That may have happened in at least two cases in the sample:

> "I think my daughter had some nervous problems when she was trying to learn as much as she could and was a little surprised that I didn't treat her like a family member. I treated her just like an employee. She was a little shook up a couple of times" (011).

> "When you have family working for you, they don't want to take the criticism and directions as outsiders might" (0113A).

The daughter of the first informant just quoted may have felt strongly pressured although other employees in her father's firm may not have thought she was being pressured. The second informant, reflecting on personal experience, said that offspring in his family's business did not expect to be pushed as nonfamily members were. The unexpected pressure might have led the offspring to feel pushed too hard although by the standards of others they were not.

Use of Nonrelatives to Supervise Younger Family Members

Among families that reported no problems with supervision and among those that had eliminated supervision tensions in family relationships, by far the most common solution to problems in supervising offspring and other young family members was to use nonrelatives as supervisors (see Beckhard and Dyer, 1981). When the business was large enough to have nonrelatives in managerial positions, nonrelated supervisors were often used. Many of the following statements were made in response to our questions about tensions over relative supervising relative.

"I would have one of the outside employees supervising my son. I would not have one of the immediate family" (106A).

"My nephews and nieces have department heads they go to, who then answer directly to us. So we have no direct contact with them" (074B).

"My kids don't take direction from me when they are working here. It will be from somebody else" (091A).

"I don't have him working directly for me. He works for another member of the organization. It's a better way to start, certainly. It puts a buffer between he and I. It's a little easier than trying directly to guide your son" (048A).

"Dad was a little uneasy about supervising me. When I started, he put a junior partner in charge of me" (033B).

"I strongly felt that without the unrelated supervisor it would not work. My desire at this age is to be a good father and a good grandfather. Initially, when my older son came on board, I had one very serious situation develop where he felt that maybe I was being challenged by this executive VP. My son felt that maybe I should be in the role of boss man. So I took him to lunch and in no uncertain terms explained to him that he reported to that man" (084B).

In smaller businesses a boss may have to supervise kin directly but may feel that it would be better to have a nonrelative as a supervisor.

"There's only one supervisor in the business, and that's me. My children don't like it, but they have to live with it. They would much rather have an outsider for a supervisor. And I guess I can see their point. On occasion we have done it that way, and it seems to have worked well. I'm a hard man to work for. I expect them to work and not play" (119, whose role as a supervisor may have stemmed from the fact that his business grossed less than $500,000 annually, a comparatively small business income. He could not afford a nonrelated supervisor).

In one business there was such a strong sense that it was better not to have an older relative supervise a younger relative that a prospective marriage into the family altered supervisory relationships.

"When our youngest son and his wife were married . . . she was working close to me, she was already an employee. As soon as we knew they were going to get married, as fast as we could we moved her away from me, geographically, responsibilitywise, everything, because my husband and I both felt that there was a real danger if she was working with me, assisting me, that there was too much possibility of friction which *could* cause a family problem" (095A).

When parent supervises offspring directly, it may help for

both parties to be aware of the complexities discussed in this and other chapters and to be able to talk with each other about difficulties either may be having. Offspring may find supervision by a parent more comfortable when they understand the necessity of supervision and can appreciate how nonrelatives are supervised in the family business. Parents may find it easier to supervise an offspring if they try from the beginning to supervise a son or daughter with the same limit setting, praise, teaching, and so on that they would use with a nonrelative. In the long run, supervision of offspring by parent may be easiest if division of labor is clear and if the offspring, with adequate preparation, has a sphere of managerial responsibility and autonomy.

Conclusion

Supervision of relative by relative is a problem in some business families, and it would be in more if so many of them did not try to avoid family tensions by using nonrelatives to supervise younger family members in the business. Some people said they were more gentle in supervising spouse or offspring, although some of those being supervised may not have believed that was so. Some parents seemed to be harsh with offspring or to be perceived that way by the offspring they supervised. The reasons some parent/supervisors gave for harsh supervision of offspring included fear of appearing to play favorites, a feeling of greater freedom to be critical with relatives, and strong parental desire for offspring to do well. In some cases, the pressure on offspring seemed to be indirect or self-generated, although indirect and self-generated pressure can be understood to be sustained by a supervisory environment.

When offspring felt harshly supervised and parents thought the offspring were wrong, the difference in opinion may, in some cases, have had roots in the offspring's expectation of being treated as they would have been at home. The fact that so many larger businesses used nonkin to supervise younger family members suggests that in many businesses there was a concern that more than perceptual differences could underlie a supervised person's feelings of upset with supervision by a relative. Just as apartness seems to be a common way of minimizing problems of conflicts, hurt feelings over disagreements, and satiation because of too much contact in the business, having no direct contact in a supervisory relationship seems to be one way of coping with the problems that might arise when an older relative supervises a younger one.

In married couples when spouse supervises spouse and in parent/offspring pairs when the parent supervises, a clear division of labor and substantial autonomy (once adequate preparation has occurred) for the relative who is supervised seem helpful. Then supervision requires little contact and little correction, setting of limits, or other things that may become sources of difficulty when relative supervises relative.

Chapter Eight

Boundaries Among Self, Family, and Business

"What's good for the business is good for the family" (099).

Society may be thought of as being crisscrossed by boundaries, with discontinuities between one group and another, between one place in a person's life and another, and between one person and another. A family may be said to have boundaries, both external boundaries that divide the family from people and organizations outside the family and internal boundaries that divide family members from each other. Family boundaries may be understood as easy or difficult to cross. A family with external boundaries that are hard to cross would be relatively closed to different ways of thinking, to informal visitors, to change influences, to people who have values and beliefs different from those now in the family, and to family members leaving. A family with external boundaries that are easy to cross would be open to new information, to informal visitors, to people moving out, to change influences, and to newcomers, even those whose beliefs and values do not match those now in the family.

Boundaries may also be seen as diffuse or definite. When external family boundaries are relatively diffuse, it is not very clear who belongs where or where the family ends and other things begin. The boundaries between work and family are probably relatively clear for most Americans, because the usual geographical separation of work and family allows different roles, different social etiquettes, different goals, even different identities in the two settings. Diffuse external boundaries between the family and the business seem, however, to be a problem in many business-operating families and are the principal focus of the discussion of boundaries in this chapter.

Systems analyses of the effect of boundaries in families (for example, Boss, 1980; Davis and Stern, 1980) suggest that diffuseness of boundaries between home and business can create tensions and stresses, that separation is desirable for many reasons. When family system and business system are blurred together as a result of boundary diffuseness, the problems of competing goals and of inappropriate carryover from one system to the other become greater. Business decisions may be heavily influenced by family considerations (for example, to open a branch office to be managed by a new son-in-law) without any clear sense that the decision may be a mistake from the perspective of the business. Similarly, a family decision may be made (for example, that a daughter major in accounting or that the chief officer not vacation with his family) because of demands of the business, without any clear sense that from a family perspective (the welfare of the daughter or of the chief officer as an individual) the decision may be a mistake. Conflicts involving the goals of the two competing systems (for example, to remodel the house or to hire another salesperson) may be treated as though they were entirely business matters or entirely family matters. Conflicts arising in one situation may be carried over, undiminished, into the other situation. Standards that are appropriate in one situation but not the other may be applied in the other (loyalty and family membership rather than business criteria may, for example, become the only criteria for hiring and promoting). With boundaries diffuse, people can never get away from work, never have a Sabbath, a vacation, a place to refuel or to get distance from work problems. Previous chapters have dealt with such boundary issues as role carryovers and family togetherness and apartness. But the issue of boundary clarity versus diffusion has not been addressed directly. The present chapter addresses that issue and extends the discussion of boundary issues into a number of areas not previously dealt with.

Person/Business Boundaries

"I feel that this company is really almost part of me," said one entrepreneur (006). Many entrepreneurs have feelings like that (McGivern, 1978). Their sense of who they are, what is important, how much interest they have in closeness with family members, the meaning of success and failure in the business, their reactions to others' attempts to change the business, and their willingness to turn over control of the business to someone else could be understood to be affected by what could be called the diffuse boundary between self and business. With that boundary diffuse, all things affecting the business affect the self. With business so entangled with self, the business would have high priority a great deal of the time. Commitments to work and family would be less balanced than they are for most workers. Such uniting of personal identity with the business may be common for people who devote an enormous part of their time and energy to an enterprise (Davis and Stern, 1980). On the positive side, it may mean that the entrepreneur is fully committed to making the business work, as committed to the business as to self. Some management experts see self-identification with the business, at least in one's early years of business involvement, as a strength (Boswell, 1973, p. 82). On the not-so-good side, such self-identification may mean that there is not a clear commitment to the family or an awareness of how family members could be injured by one's commitment to the business. The uniting of personal identity with the business may mean that a business loss, even one that could not be remotely attributed to self, will be felt in an intensely personal and perhaps devastating way. It may also mean that relinquishing control to another family member—for example, by allowing an offspring or a spouse to have some executive control or by moving toward retirement—can feel like a loss of self (Davis and Stern, 1980; McGivern, 1978). With that kind of investment by an entrepreneur, the successful assumption of an executive role by an offspring or a spouse in the business can be not a delight but something for an entrepreneur to grieve, the loss of part of self.

For an entrepreneur to be closely identified with the business may mean that family members are in an unusual situation if they wish to have a close relationship with the entrepreneur. To know and communicate with the entrepreneur, they must have some interest in and caring for the business. Not to be interested or not to care is to reject a substantial part of the entrepreneur's self. Yet many relatives of entrepreneurs may find the business something to be ambivalent about. The business may be resented for the time the entrepreneur devotes to it, resented as competitor, or resented because the entrepreneur has chosen to make it so involving and important. Moreover, the business may not be nearly as interesting to another family member as to the entrepreneur. To the entrepreneur, the life and involvements of a spouse, parent, offspring, or sibling may not be particularly interesting, except as they are related to the business. Family members may resent that the entrepreneur has little interest in their lives and little willingness to place nonbusiness goals at high priority, but the lack of clarity of boundary between entrepreneur and business may mean that family members cannot be clear to themselves or to their entrepreneurial relative about whether resentments are directed at the entrepreneur or at their apparent rival, the business. The lack of boundary clarity means that feelings focused on the entrepreneur may be misperceived or perceived accurately as focused on the business, and feelings focused on the business may similarly be perceived or misperceived as being focused on the entrepreneur. For example, if a son directs at the business his anger over the fact that Dad is interested primarily in the business, Dad may, because of his own sense of boundaries, feel the dislike of the business as a personal attack. Further, if Dad is not clear that family members have important goals that are different from and competing with business goals, Dad may work hard to suppress family members' criticism and anger when they feel shortchanged. It is hard to let Dad know disappointments if, for example, Dad is saying he is working for the family by working for the business and he feels the business is a part of himself.

Mood Carryovers

Entrepreneurs and others in family businesses are not unique in bringing home moods and concerns from work (Renshaw, 1976). But the carryover may often be stronger for entrepreneurs or more predictable because of the heavy investment of time and identity in the family business. As one entrepreneur said,

> "If I'm in a bad mood at work twelve hours out of a day, I'm sure in hell not going to change my mood when I walk into the house" (011).

The carryover of bad mood may simply mean that an entrepreneur is preoccupied and relatively unavailable to others, with the moodiness saying, "Keep away; don't ask me for anything."

> "When you really have serious tensions in the business, such as not being able to finance the business you are doing, I think that they are bound to be reflected. There's a tendency for things to get pretty gloomy around the house" (036A).

Sometimes the carryover means that family members are targets for anger and blaming.

> "If you have a bad day, you'll have a tendency of taking it out on family members" (061).

Although carryover like this from work to home may happen to anyone, entrepreneurs with diffuse boundaries between self and business may carry over moods more intensely and more pervasively. If entrepreneurial self and business are not well differentiated and if family goals and business goals are not well differentiated for the entrepreneur, problems in the business will feel to the entrepreneur like problems with everything.

It's a Twenty-Four-Hour Day

In addition to moods, people may bring home their thoughts, figurings, planning, paperwork, and other aspects of a business in which they are involved.

> "It's hard to leave the business. It's hard to go home at five o'clock and not think about it and discuss it, because really it's a very large part of our lives" (014A).
> "I don't think anybody can go home that owns a business and forget about it" (063B).
> "It never stops. My wife can tell eleven or twelve at night I'm thinking about a particular job, and she'll say, 'Stop it' " (099).

As the "Stop it" in the last comment suggests, bringing work and work concerns home can build a boundary between oneself and other family members. That is, by choosing to have a diffuse boundary between work and oneself, one can create undesirably strong boundaries between oneself and other family members. Family goals unrelated to the business may receive low priority, as may the interests, concerns, joys, and achievements of other family members. The entrepreneur's resources of energy and time may be inappropriately concentrated on matters of work, denying family members a fair share of these resources. Another family member might get inside that boundary by working with the family member who is so heavily involved in the business, but that may mean only that their togetherness will be heavily weighted toward business.

When one works with a relative who continues to make business concerns primary, as we suggested in our discussions of business families with high levels of togetherness, that constant focus on the business risks satiation as well as a kind of narrow confinement.

> "It's more or less twenty-four hours a day
> for both my wife and me, but she has her other
> job" (099).
>
> "The years working here have been closer
> with my father than when I was growing up, but
> it's all business-oriented" (055).

The problem is not always present, of course. Some entrepreneurs, particularly those who are well established and who have interests in things outside the business, can maintain a boundary between business situations and other situations.

> "He took me on a vacation to Colorado, and
> the business wasn't mentioned once. We had a
> wonderful time. Dad's good about that. He can just
> let the business stay at the business" (025B).

However, with entrepreneurs whose interests are largely business-directed, whose personal boundaries are relatively closed to information not related to the business, family members may have to be interested in business matters to maintain more than a modicum of contact. Given that, one way to express hostility, dissatisfaction, and resentment toward a relative who is an entrepreneur is to be uninterested in the business. People who establish their own businesses may have powerful needs for self-respect (Henry, 1965, p. 38) that are connected to being relatively competitive and relatively easily wounded. A challenge to self-feelings as expressed by a lack of interest in the business may therefore be experienced as a very powerful attack. The entrepreneur quoted next expresses his perception that his wife's disinterest in the business represents an intent to communicate disappointment and to aggress, although it is possible that his wife simply found business matters uninteresting, that there was no other motive force behind her disinterest.

> "There are many ways a wife can let her hus-
> band know she's unhappy. Probably one of the big-
> gest ways is her lack of interest in the business it-
> self, whether or not she's responsive to conversations
> around the business" (011).

It has been said that conversations between spouses are crucial in establishing a sense of reality for them (Berger and Kellner, 1964). If one's self-respect is heavily invested in a conversational topic, one's partner may feel pressured to be interested and to be careful, yet the heavy investment also gives one's partner a great deal of power to make one unhappy and to shape one's sense of reality. Perhaps one reason some entrepreneurs do not want spouses to comment on or participate in the business is that they fear the power and the potential to injure that comes when a spouse can help shape the entrepreneur's sense of reality. Perhaps some spouses try to comment on a business (or refuse to talk about it) because of their awareness that the entrepreneur has made it a preeminent priority in his life. To exclude business from marital conversation would be to maintain a relationship with a great deal of estrangement if so much of the entrepreneur's sense of self is invested in the business. Of course, to include the business as a major topic of conversation may be estranging if it means that areas of importance to the spouse are slighted in favor of talking about the business. This line of argument can also be used to explain the dissatisfaction of some wives. If a wife's goals and interests are primarily outside the business—say, the marital relationship and her friendships—that may pressure her entrepreneur husband both to be interested in those topics and to be careful, yet it also gives him a great deal of power to make her unhappy. To exclude the marital relationship and her friendships from the marital conversation would be to maintain a relationship with a great deal of estrangement if so much of the wife's sense of self is invested in those relationships.

People in business may have many reasons for not talking about work when at home. They may want to relax, to focus on family, to pursue other goals, or to get the perspective on business problems that may come from staying away from them for a while.

> "When we are home, the business is not discussed. It feels comfortable that way. Now home is a bastion of sanity and sanctity, back home where

> I'm safe. Now when I'm home, I can go into any
> room and not feel obligated to do anything"
> (042A).

The following two statements, however, both dealing with
wanting to avoid shop talk at home, may be rooted partly or
entirely in the need to keep other family members away from
areas in which they could, simply by speaking, have considerable
power to influence or to offend the entrepreneur.

> "I don't like to bring the business home at
> night and hash over problems with my wife. My
> wife knows very little about what I do" (005).

> "I never talk with my wife at all about busi-
> ness. I try to keep the business out of our personal
> life. She'll know something that's going on but not
> nearly as much as she'd like. That's an area that she
> objects to—that I don't let her know enough about
> what's going on in the business. I don't care to
> have my wife involved with me twenty-four hours
> a day. Her ideas are probably a little bit different
> than mine. I feel that my business judgment is very
> good" (Code number of informant accidentally de-
> leted from transcript).

Being resistant to the influence or possible criticism of
another person may be basically human, but it may also represent an unwillingness to blunder, to be a learner, or to appear
imperfect to others or to self. Being a learner may be easier
when one differentiates self in a clear way from one's errors
and imperfections, when one can say, "I'm OK, even though
what I was doing wasn't so great." In addition, as pointed out
earlier, if an entrepreneur's self is tied up in the business and if
the entrepreneur is easily threatened, the entrepreneur may
have to draw a boundary around self and business to protect
the vulnerable self from the spouse's threats.

Home as a Place of Work

Beginning in elementary school, one may bring work
home. People doing diverse kinds of work may bring some of

that work home. But founders of businesses, more so than most working people, may use the home as the only place of work. When a business is new or money is very scarce, the economic incentives for working at home and avoiding the costs of renting or owning a separate workplace and of furnishing, maintaining, and supplying utilities for that separate workplace may be immense. There may also be comfort incentives for combining home and workplace. One may find it easier to take risks in a place that is comfortable. Working long hours may feel less stressful when one's larder, bed, clothing, and bathroom are nearby. There may also be a dream of family closeness that goes along with having one's place of business within the home. We did not ask respondents systematically about whether the business had ever been located in the dwelling, but several persons volunteered that their business had at one time been in the home, and two of the businesses in the sample were currently being run out of a home.

A key problem when work and home are the same place is that the lack of a physical or temporal boundary means one never gets away from work, that all one's home life is pervaded by work and the possibility of work. That is, if one cannot say, "This place is primarily for work and that place only for family," or "This time is primarily for work and that time only for family," one and one's family will suffer from one's inability to get away from work.

> "I haven't learned to shut off my job yet at a particular time, which would have to be, because I don't have an office. My home's my office. I'll take calls at ten o'clock at night. The mere fact that I have a business phone that I can hear twenty-four hours a day, when I hear it ring, I've got to go pick it up. I should just let it go" (099).

The problems of operating the business from within the home are often so serious that establishing an office away from the home becomes a primary goal, one that may rank in importance with goals crucial to the development of the business as a stable and viable economic enterprise. Even doing bookkeeping at home, while the business is run elsewhere, can be a burden:

"It would really help if I had an office outside the home" (025B).

In the short run, adjustments can be made within the home. A
separate telephone may be installed for the business; a telephone answering device may be installed on that phone; the office space at home may become physically segregated from the
rest of the living space; and there may even be a separate entrance for the office. But it seems that eventually people need
the geographically separate workplace.

"When we first started the business, I had an
overwhelming desire to answer the phone every
time it rang, which was in our home. And Satur-
days and Sundays and evenings and there was just
never any free time. We did some things to correct
that. We moved the office down and put another
phone in the home and eliminated some of that,
because when the business phone rang, we didn't
answer it, even to the point of shutting it off. The
other thing we did was moving into this office several miles from the home, which has only been nine
months ago" (042A).

The stresses of having a business at home are often substantial for family members not directly involved in the business
or at least not intending to be directly involved. An office
phone at home is ringing for them too. They can feel their territory invaded by customers and suppliers, both those who telephone and those who visit. They may feel added responsibility
to keep the home presentable, to be well dressed at home, to
answer the telephone, to be quiet at home, and to be responsive
to the wishes of their entrepreneurial coresident.

"More than likely you relegate your office
to a basement that you fixed up and made nice, or
you're off in a corner of a bedroom. And people
are constantly wandering through the house. Your
wife feels an obligation to be there, make coffee,
welcome the people. That is not her function.
That's not what she should have to do. Also, if she

has to go down and run a load of laundry, that's
happening amongst where the business is happening" (042A).

"We'd never get away from it. That's part of
what I disliked about having the office in the
home. It was unnatural to clean the basement
every week, because that's where they were. And
the fact that I was never alone. I'm a person that
likes to be alone" (042B).

So the absence of a clear boundary between home and
business that can come when the business is run from the home
creates problems for some families, problems with an entrepreneur who can never get away from work and problems with
other family members who have extra demands put on them by
a business within the dwelling.

"What's Good for the Business Is Good for the Family"

In one way or another, many entrepreneurs said that
what was good for the business seemed to them to be good for
the family. Here, as examples, are statements by two company
presidents:

"I don't see how that conflict would arise
between business and family. What's good for the
business is good for the family" (036B).

"What's good for the business is going to be
good for the family eventually—monetary plus
prestige and what have you. If you have a successful business, it carries over to your family. It shows
the things you do, things you have" (098A).

That kind of belief could be understood as a sincere and accurate perception of the crucial role of economics in family well-
being or as an insightful perception of the relation between self-
esteem-supporting aspects of work life and the quality of home
life. From a boundaries perspective, however, a belief that what
is good for the business is good for the family is a belief that
pushes for boundary diffuseness and a blurring of business and

family goals. If two things are seen as distinct entities, it is a simple matter to see that what is good for one may be bad or irrelevant for the other. If they are not seen as distinct, it will be much easier to assume that an outcome for one is likely to be identical for the other (Campbell, 1958).

The ideology that what is good for business is good for family can thus be seen as symptom and cause, as well as effect, of diffuse boundaries between family and business. As symptom, the statement that what is good for the business is good for the family is simply an indication that the person holding the belief lives with unclear boundaries between business and family. As cause, believing that what is good for the business is good for the family may lead one to do things that reduce boundary clarity, such as bringing work home, using home as a workplace, exploiting family members in service of the business, and seeing them as extensions of one's self. Believing that what is good for the business is good for the family also leads to reduced boundary clarity if it means one rationalizes subordination of family priorities to business priorities.

"How Can I Fire a Relative?"

Another symptom of boundary problems is the concern some entrepreneurs have about being able to fire a close relative. If the boundaries were clear between family and business, one might be able to discharge a relative one had hired if the relative's work was substandard. But the lack of willingness to fire a relative, the fear of having to do that, even the inability to do it were common among entrepreneurs.

> "I wasn't very excited about my wife coming into the business. My immediate response was 'How can I ever fire you?' " (052).
> "It isn't so much my brother. It's my nephew. He went to college, and he knows everything. He tells me how to handle myself on everything. For what he does he gets too much salary." *Interviewer:* "Have you ever thought of firing him?" *Respondent:* "How would we do it?" (045B).

"If you got family here, you don't lay them off or get rid of them the way you would other employees" (113A).

"Outside of my immediate family I do not believe in hiring relatives. If your relatives don't perform, what do you do with them? How do you fire a relative? You can break family ties through that" (116A).

Where boundaries between family and business are diffuse, to fire a relative is to risk serious, perhaps irreparable estrangement in the family. But without the power to fire, many entrepreneurs feel that they have lost much of their power to influence a worker or to supervise effectively. Coercion is certainly not the only administrative tool, but for many entrepreneurs it may be a primary or ultimate tool.

Having control over employees who are relatives may seem even more necessary than having control over nonrelatives. As pointed out in an earlier discussion of indulgence in family business, offspring may take advantage of entrepreneurial parents. The threat to fire may be useful when one is trying to control an employee's attempts to take advantage of one, although it could be argued that threats to fire are sometimes poor substitutes for competent limit setting, assertive statements about standards, and a good sense of what people may need to be taught and how they may be taught it.

Another boundary problem that arises, which makes it important to be able to fire kin, is that kin in the business may not respect the internal boundaries of the business. They may, as the following quotation suggests, ignore the chain of command and bring problems, confusions, concerns, or complaints directly to a relative who would be inappropriate to bring these things to if one respected the organizational structure.

"My immediate family are bringing things to me that should be going to their direct supervisor, the plant manager. And I tell them that I'm not going to intervene. 'If you want to get something done, talk to your supervisor.' A lot of it's related

really through my wife" (Code number of informant inadvertently lost in processing of transcripts).

Being able to have leverage on relatives in the business, to have
the power to influence or control, is a matter of genuine concern for many entrepreneurs. An effective threat to fire might
be one way to eliminate deviations from appropriate lines of
communication, but it may be precisely with those persons
most likely to deviate (one's relatives) that one is least able to
use the threat of firing.

The boundary problem can also be seen from the side of
the junior person in the relationship. Somebody hired may feel
forced to stay in the business out of loyalty, may feel that the
ultimate power to influence an employer that comes with being
able to quit (or the ultimate control over personal freedom) is
eliminated by feelings of loyalty or fear of the family consequences of leaving the business.

> "The only thing that has stopped me from
> quitting is that he's my relative" (062B).

A related boundary phenomenon in the hiring and firing
area is that operators of businesses that compete with one's
family's business cannot trust one to be disloyal to one's family
(Donnelly, 1964).

> "It would have been very hard for me to
> work for one of my dad's competitors. They prob-
> ably wouldn't trust me that much, and there was a
> certain loyalty I felt" (050B).

Where offspring cannot be trusted to be disloyal to parent, it is
difficult for a son or daughter who has learned the ropes in the
family business to work in a firm that competes with the family firm. That is another restriction on the power of a younger
family member in the business to quit. To quit the family business may also mean that one might have to leave a field which
one enjoys and in which one is knowledgeable.

One way to head off concern over firing relatives is not

to hire relatives whom one cannot fire or who would be difficult to fire. By not hiring the person one would find difficult or
impossible to fire, one does not clarify boundaries, but at least
one avoids some of the problems that accompany diffuse boundaries. The following two comments, concerning avoidance of hiring relatives, may represent concerns about many problems
(power battles, coalitions, and so on), but they also seem to represent the avoidance of difficult situations that can arise when
diffuse boundary makes hiring difficult or impossible.

> "My partner and I had made an agreement
> when we first started that the families would be
> kept out of the business" (096A).
>
> "I didn't want to have any of my own chil-
> dren or children-in-law involved because I just felt
> that I didn't want to risk that. You have only one
> daughter and then you go ahead and get a son-in-
> law in the business, and if it doesn't work out,
> there is a risk there that you're going to lose the
> daughter" (078).

Although not hiring relatives precludes some problems, it may
make it impossible to pass the business on to kin, and that may
mean the loss of a dear dream for the entrepreneur. Not hiring
relatives may also block one from some kinds of contact with
kin, may prevent one from hiring the best person for a job, and
may create animosity in the family over the business's being
closed to family members.

    Although it is not always easy to accomplish, it seems a
good policy, when there is the prospect of a spouse, parent, offspring, cousin, or some other relative entering the business, for
all parties involved to treat it as an experiment rather than a
lifelong commitment. The tensions resulting from fear of firing
a relative and fear of quitting a family firm can be minimized if
entry of a relative into the firm is understood as tentative, with
freedom on both sides to terminate. The understanding may not
head off all hard feelings if somebody is fired or quits, but it
may make things a lot easier. It might even be a good thing to
agree that reasons need not be given for a firing or quitting.

Whether or not reasons must be given, the agreement should make clear that an end to the business relationship will not be allowed to affect family relationships.

Another part of an agreement that would be useful to make in advance of hiring a relative is that the chain of command in the business should be respected. It should be clear from the beginning whom a relative reports to and what business talk is legitimate and what is not between the hired relative and other family members in the firm. If there is any concern that a family member who is hired may indirectly violate the chain of command, through talking with somebody not in the business who might then talk with somebody in the business, that too might best be dealt with through prior agreement. In general, it is prior to the hiring of a relative that one has leverage, good will, freedom, and the least tense opportunity to work out rules that will allow for boundary clarity. Perhaps one will need some experience before one realizes what rules are necessary, but the more that is worked out beforehand, the easier things may be. Even saying beforehand that rules will be worked out to deal with boundary clarity may help.

Establishing Boundaries

It is hard not to give simplistic and unrealistic advice to people with problems of diffuse boundaries between business and family. If it were easy to establish boundaries, they would be there already. Nonetheless, people in some of the business families we studied had, perhaps painfully and with struggle over a long period, come to some approaches for increasing the clarity of boundaries between business life and family life.

One approach to building clear boundaries that made life easier in some families was to try to segregate business conversations, in both time and place, so that some times and places were havens from the business. It is not as simple a solution to achieve as might first appear, because it requires the collaboration of at least one person beyond oneself and it forces one at times to sit on questions and issues that may be intensely preoccupying. To achieve this kind of boundary, it may be necessary that there be times and places at work where one can deal with business issues. That seemed to be the perception of one woman who worked with her husband fifty to sixty hours a week:

> "If we had a private office all to ourselves, away from everybody, we could meet once or twice a day, close the door, put a Do Not Disturb sign on it, and discuss certain matters. That way it would be easier not to take work problems home" (018).

Another boundary device that some families had found valuable was having a place of work away from the home or having strict controls on use of a home-based office. Economic necessity and personal preference may require that a business begin in an office in the family dwelling, but nobody who had an office in the dwelling, either at the time of the interview or previously (and nobody who lived with somebody who had such an office), said that an office at home was a good thing. If an office must be in a home, boundary problems seem to be less serious when the office space is separated from the living space (with full walls, a separate telephone, and perhaps a separate entrance). But even with substantial separation within the dwelling, people seem to feel that a home office can make life difficult, both in family relationships and in business functioning.

The first two recommendations we have offered for building boundaries are more necessary and more appropriate in the early stages of the business. If the business becomes healthy enough and the entrepreneur becomes confident enough so that the business is out of the home and does not require the entrepreneur to devote enormous amounts of time and attention, the entrepreneur then has opportunity to build boundaries between business and family through developing and strengthening nonbusiness aspects of himself or herself. In building boundaries between business life and family life, cultivating other strong interests, including interests in family members, is desirable. Boundaries come more easily when one chooses to direct attention and conversation to a variety of interests. Just as retirement is eased when one has strong interests alternative to work, so the capacity to sustain a home life not pervaded by work rests in part on having strong interests alternative to work. It is difficult to change abruptly the way one spends large blocks of time, and one cannot quickly come to new, interesting, involving, and sustaining activities. Diversification of self-interests and self-activities may require months or even years of exploring options and trying things out. Those explorations may be interesting and valuable in themselves, or they may seem meaningless and frustrating. We think the diversification of self makes life more interesting and meaningful, strengthens family life, prepares one for retirement, and probably strengthens one's managerial activities in the business (through giving one fresh perspectives and through forcing one to concentrate one's work time on higher-priority issues). Whether it is the cultivation of a few close friendships, spending more time with family members, increased religious involvement, development of some outdoor activities, joining and participating in a community organization, reading, or physical fitness activity, new and intensified involvements outside the business pay off.

A final approach to boundary building that is appropriate only when a business is well established and has attained a certain size is to employ, train, and learn to work with a trusted assistant or manager. A person who can relieve the chief officer of some managerial duties and who can run the business while the entrepreneur is away frees the entrepreneur to separate home life from work life and to leave work behind when with the family. Obviously, many smaller businesses cannot afford such a person, and many entrepreneurs will have to do substantial changing (learning how to delegate authority, learning how to tolerate other people's work styles, standards, and so on in the management area) in order to be able to make use of a manager. Employing a professional manager is by no means simple or without risk, but we think it makes it easier for an entrepreneur to build boundaries between business and family.

Warning signs that there are boundary problems may be spotted by an entrepreneur or pointed out by a family member.

They include finding business decisions inappropriately contaminated by family issues or vice versa, family conversations devoted only to the business, an entrepreneur seeming always to work at or to be preoccupied with the business, the entrepreneur seeming to feel chronically satiated by business matters, and the entrepreneur not being able to identify things that are good for the business but not the family. Boundary problems may have to be lived with. One may decide that what is going on should continue to go on, but even when one chooses to live with boundary problems, the problems may be reduced.

A family member who wants change must believe in herself or himself and assert that things must change in a way that affirms other family members and the business. Such assertions may require a certain amount of repetition and documentation before the message gets through. What may eventually be negotiated will differ from family to family. It could be anything from an agreement not to talk about the business but to talk about other things at least X minutes per day to there being a certain number of nights each week when the entrepreneur brings no work home and gives the family full attention. The agreement could deal with clarifying the priority of family matters such as time with children, help with housework, shared responsibility for sick children and for childcare, and a million other things.

An entrepreneur may blow the whistle on himself or herself or on the family. An entrepreneur may need insulation of the business from family matters (for example, business decisions might have to exclude concerns about the employment of some relative) or self-instruction not to affect the family so much with business matters. An entrepreneur may need to work out a transition process for the end of the workday, to make it easier to leave work behind. The transition might involve a plan to stop thinking about work on the way home, to shower and change clothes once home, to budget a minimum amount of time focused with full attention on the family, to limit home time spent on work to a fixed amount, and to limit the locations at home where work matters will be dealt with. An entrepreneur should be clear that he or she has family priorities and be aware of what they are. And an entrepreneur should know which things are good for the family but not for the business and which are good for the business and not the family.

Conclusion

Boundary problems are present or potentially present for all business families. Having relatively diffuse boundaries between family and business is not inherently desirable or undesirable. Diffuse boundaries may make it possible for family members to know much about an entrepreneur's work life and may make for a business that is relatively effective given the number of people who work in it and the assets invested in it. Yet diffuse boundaries mean that an entrepreneur's life is pervaded by business, that other interests (especially the family) are subordinated, that there are additional tensions both at home and in the business, and that problems arise over attempts to deal with those tensions. We have suggested a number of ways to deal with boundary problems. Even if boundary problems cannot be eliminated, they may be made less disruptive.

Chapter Nine

Money, Status, and Power

It is impossible to understand American businesses without talking about money and power. Money is necessary to establish and to maintain a business. Business growth depends on money. Money is also a symbol of many things, including success in business, personal excellence, importance, and worth (Benedict and Benedict, 1982, chap. 13). In relationships, money can be used to symbolize caring (see our discussion in Chapter Six of the entrepreneur's use of money and material goods to compensate spouse and children for lack of contact). Money is a modern measure of excellence, however much one's own values discredit it as such a measure. With money as a measure of excellence, the concerns many people have about how well they are doing financially and how well they compare with others can be understood as matters of self-esteem and status.

Money and power are interlinked. A person with decision power in a business is typically paid better than one without such power. One is typically paid more the more people over whom one has authority and the more production and sales one controls. Power allows one to influence the course of a business, and it is also, like money, a symbol of excellence, importance, success, and worth relative to other people. The symbolic significance of power seems great no matter how power is defined (a working definition might be "the capability to have happen what one wants to have happen without incurring great cost").

The Importance of Money

If money is a symbol of excellence, success, importance, and worth, business founders typically struggle for the symbol from a position of relative inferiority. The early days of business involvement are usually made tense by a scarcity of money and by having risked most or all family and personal assets. All four of the following statements speak to the shortage of money early in business.

> "When I started in business, I sold my home to go into business. We had two little kids then. Had to make it go, or else" (062A).

> "We went without for a while. You have to build up the store. To make money, you've got to have something to sell" (094B).

> "In order to save, say, a thousand dollars, I didn't go on a fishing trip that I planned, or a hunting trip, because the receivables weren't coming in the way they are supposed to. And you can't just throw money away when you can't pay the bills" (117).

> "It's a new business that started from scratch, and it started with very little money. The business has grown tremendously, and growing businesses require money" (096A).

To the extent that money is a symbol, the shortage of money in a new business means that a founder appears, by that symbol, to be doing poorly. As a consequence, a driving factor in the early business involvement of many founders may be motivation for greater status, to look successful, excellent, important, and worthy in the eyes of self and others.

The blending of money-as-necessity and money-as-symbol is probably out of people's awareness most of the time. The blending may be one reason that entrepreneurs may resent other people's commenting on their business decisions. The entrepreneur may already feel defensive about personal status. Moreover, his or her basis for a business decision may be difficult to talk about because there are status reasons for making the decision that are difficult to recognize or to articulate.

Money can be a problem in a business both because money is often scarce (investments must be made and bills paid while customers are not plentiful or are delinquent in paying) and because the entanglement of status factors means that feelings of self-worth can be at stake. Twenty-five respondents (from twenty-one businesses) said tensions were present over money. Although people most commonly were concerned about whether they could make ends meet, pay debts, finance necessary changes and developments, pay the business bills, and meet family expenses, some people were aware that for them money was a medium of success or of self-esteem. The following statement, for example, refers to pride being threatened when a business was in financial trouble.

> "I always had my dad on a pedestal. It was very stressful to find out, at maybe thirty years old, that my dad wasn't perfect. I was cutting the umbilical cord about fifteen years late. We lost a *lot* of money, and we almost ruined a tremendous father-and-son relationship. Until you lose money in business, unless you've done it, you really don't know what it's like. Your pride is involved, and all the other emotional problems. We were both going through that, and neither one of us really wanting to accept the blame. It took a couple of years and we got our relationship back" (044).

This statement also makes clear that family disputes can arise over who is to blame when there are money problems in the business. Presumably one of the underlying issues then would be whose self-esteem and status should fall and whose should not.

With money so important to the business, to the entrepreneur, to the family, and as a symbol, it is no surprise that business growth is given high priority and that many entrepreneurs and some of their kin think that what is good for the business is, must be, has to be good for the family. As the following quotations make clear, income is for many entrepreneurs the key reason for putting business at highest priority.

> "The business comes first, because basically the business is the one that's throwing off the moneys to take care of the family properly. So if you had to do something tomorrow and it was either the family or the business that had to be done, it would be the business" (106A).
>
> "What's good for the business *has* to be good for the family. If you don't have income, you're not going to be eating" (100).

If people's worth were measured in other ways, for example, by how much joy there was in their family life or by their capacity to live comfortably on little resources, the comparative priority of family and business might be different for many people in business, and there might be fewer people in business reporting tension over money. Although there is no question that to sustain a business and a comfortable standard of living money must be a priority, there seem to be many well-established businesses that could sustain an entrepreneur's family comfortably without the business's receiving as much time and attention as it does.

Why Is Fairness of Compensation So Important?

Twenty-six respondents representing twenty-two businesses said that there were tensions over fairness of compensation or work load. Concerns over fairness result from more factors than can be catalogued here. People in business and in society in general think of earnings as a result of investment of money, effort, and other things. One wants more compensation if one invests more. If one's compensation is too low, given one's investment and one's expectations of return on investment, one becomes upset. Why considerations of compensation are so much considerations of money is not entirely clear. People often seem to think of money as the most important kind of payment, money as opposed to freedom, the opportunity to be creative, pleasant relationships, good health, interest value of the work, the amount one learns on the job, flexibility in time use, convenience of work location, or any of a number of other potential rewards. Money obviously is important because it is what one needs in order to pay for necessities such as housing, food, clothing, and health care. People who are not paid typically have less power to purchase necessities for themselves. Hence, at the extreme, people who are not paid at all may not stay with a business.

> "Our family originally came from Iowa and were farmers. Dad was a very observant man. He noticed that all the kids left the farm because they were expected to work without any remuneration. So his idea was we should get paid and be treated just as if we were strangers" (036B).

The firm that does not pay offspring may not be able to hold them long. However, the issue is usually how much people are paid, not whether they are paid or not. Why is money so important? Why does it seem to be important even for people who are doing well financially? People may so often think primarily or even exclusively in terms of money because money is a symbol of success, excellence, importance, and worth. And by giving people power to control their environment, money increases their feelings of independence and power. Thus, people's concerns about fairness of compensation are rooted in part in feelings about the self.

Fairness is also important because Americans are socialized to value fairness and because people typically cannot evaluate themselves in an absolute sense but must determine how they are doing by comparing themselves with others. Thus, they monitor how well others do as well as how they do themselves; both comparative profits and feelings about comparative entitlements (about how much is deserved by self and others) are important. Fairness then becomes an issue because one's ranking is an issue. To do poorly in comparison with an apparent equal or inferior can threaten how one thinks of oneself and one's sense of how well others think of one. Here are some examples of people's concerns about how they or their offspring rank compared with others.

> "My nephew was just brought into the business by my mother, and he was started with more money than he would be worth to begin with. I was upset about that. It's not proper to start people off with more money than they are worth to the business. My sons are upset. They've been working for many years, and they've been working up to a figure" (064A).

> "Our problems are all caused by my grandmother. Basically they all stem from my grandmother forcing my cousin into the business. My aunt and my cousin are definitely overpaid for what they do" (064B).

> "I have trouble from time to time about the way my brother is paid. I don't like the fact that from time to time my twenty-four-year-old brother makes more money than I do and doesn't work as hard as I do. I've had a couple of talks with my father about the fact that my younger brother is paid more than I. He's paid more than some of the salesmen that work harder than he does. When I was family, I was the lowest-paid salesman in several years and remained there for several years" (005).

One might think that fairness issues would be less significant when family members are involved. After all, the compensation is being kept in the family; it is one's own in-group that is benefiting. But a case can be made that fairness concerns are more intense when relative compares self with relative. One's status in the family may be involved as well as one's status at work. If one is paid unfairly in comparison with a nonrelative, one may be concerned eight hours a day, five days a week that in the work setting one is not being evaluated properly or that one's own sense of self-worth may be mistaken. But if one is being paid unfairly in comparison with a relative, all of one's waking hours may be pervaded by fairness concerns. It is not only at work but also whenever one is in any family setting that one may be aware of the unfairness or be worried about one's own self-estimation. Moreover, if one feels neglected, unloved, unfairly criticized, or otherwise victimized in the family, one may be hypersensitive to how one is treated in the business relative to other family members. Thus, it makes sense that fairness issues should be matters of intense awareness and feelings between close relatives. From this perspective the blurring of family and business goals that was discussed in preceding chapters can also be understood as a blurring of individual goals. From a consideration of fairness, what is good for one person may not be good for another, and of course, what is good for the business may be good for an individual chief executive officer but not for anyone else in the business.

Particularly in sibling or sibling-in-law relationships, people may be concerned about fairness, because there might normally be the most status competition in those relationships. One's status in the family might be most affected if one does poorly or well in comparison with a sibling or sibling-in-law, particularly in comparison with a sibling or sibling-in-law of one's own gender who is close to one in age. Small wonder, then, that there was so much awareness of fairness, so much competition and what some people might call pettiness in sibling and sibling-in-law relationships!

> "My brother looks like a banker, and everybody sort of takes him like that. But he won't call on a customer or anything. He sits. A lot of people tell me that if I left, it wouldn't even last six months. My brother used to sneak money away. He'd make the checks out for more than he'd put on the stub. He was drawing fifty dollars a week more than me. I didn't know about it" (045B).

> "It got so we would send a piece of used equipment up there to my brother's distributorship and say it was just like new, when we knew damn well it was crippled" (006).

> "My father-in-law and I had some knockdown, drag-out things as it related primarily to my brother-in-law, who was no longer related to the business but was drawing a check from the business, which is illegal" (078).

"I know that I work at least 50 percent
harder than my brothers do, but I always have. I
make a lot more money. But if they didn't even
participate in the business, they would get an equal
share of stock" (084A).

In the first of these four quotations, a respondent said that his
brother looked impressive but did not work hard, that the
brother could not sustain the business by himself, and that the
brother had cheated on matters of compensation. All this seems
to say that the respondent considers himself better than his
brother. The second respondent said that his rivalry with his sibling, who had a structurally equal position in the family business, got to the point that in order to feel he was being compensated fairly, he had to create economic deficits for his brother.
The third person said he had fought with his father-in-law over a
brother-in-law's receiving pay without working. The family business in that case may have been so big that whether the brother-
in-law received payment probably had no impact at all on the
respondent's income; the issue seemed to be fairness. The last
respondent said that he was paid fairly and yet in terms of ownership he was or would be receiving unfair compensation, compensation that did not reflect his superior personal involvement
and superior competence. Thus, in all four cases, fairness of
compensation was evaluated in comparison with a status competitor, a sibling or sibling-in-law.

What is fair will often be seen differently by different
people (Titus, Rosenblatt, and Anderson, 1979). Among these
four respondents, for example, two seemed to say that it is fair
to reward work, while another seemed to say it is fair to punish
dishonesty and not to reward appearances. Because of differences in beliefs about what is fair, it may be impossible to treat
everybody fairly by everybody's standards. However, even if
one believes that at times it is impossible to be fair by everyone's standards, family members can benefit from knowing one
another's standards of fairness.

In some families, the competition carries over to the next
generation. That is, the children of siblings who were involved in
fairness-of-compensation tensions take on the concerns of their

parents. The following is one of the strongest examples in our interview material.

> *Interviewer:* "How did it feel for you, knowing that your dad had never been a partner in the business, but your brother ended up owning it?" *Respondent:* "That felt [whispers] like about time we got it. [Laughs] Well, I mean that my uncle had it, and all them years my dad worked for him and never got nothing out of it but his paycheck" (114A).

Power Battles

In any organization, power battles can happen. Power battles have many sources. One of them is that people have different ideas of what is right or what should be done. People have different perspectives on an issue, have different values, try to decide things with information that must be evaluated subjectively. All areas of tension in business families are potential areas for power battles. For example, in the area of decisions, as mentioned in Chapter Four, twenty-nine respondents, representing twenty-five of the fifty-nine families in the sample, reported tensions over decisions in general or over a particular important decision. Respondents often seemed to have their own theories of why power battles happened or would happen. Some cited individual differences in personality, values, or perspective.

> "My father-in-law was a very volatile man, and I'm stubborn. But we'd get through it" (078).
> "I don't think my husband and I look at things the same way as far as the way it could be done in the office. I think he and I would argue" (101B, on what would happen if she took an active role in the business her husband runs).
> "My wife is a stickler for getting things done on time, and I'm a procrastinator, so that's where the tension comes in. She doesn't want to wait. She wants to get it done and off of her desk. If it gets six inches deeper on my desk, it doesn't bother me. So that's where the tension comes in" (015).

However, for some business-operating families, individual differences that were sources of power battles also seemed to help the business. Said the respondent quoted immediately above:

> "I think I suggested she kinda come down
> and help for a while, and I just thought it would be
> on a sporadic basis. She started taking over more
> and finding out that she likes to get things done
> and I like to leave things go. She couldn't stand
> that, so she stayed around to get them done. And
> it worked out real good" (015).

Another theory entertained by some respondents concerning the reason that power battles happen was a developmental one, that as a younger family member matures in the business, self-assertion by the younger family member and perhaps defensiveness by a better-established, more mature family member lead to power battles.

> "As you mature in a family business, you are
> inclined to disagree with the chief. Because you are
> close enough that the wounds will heal tomorrow
> or the next day, you kind of speak your mind.
> Yeah, I think there is a lot of tension in a family
> business in that respect" (087, a son of a boss).

Another theory suggested by some people was that power battles are a normal part of testing where one stands in the business or with family members. Such testing is probably more likely when it is not clear where people stand, either because lines of authority are not clear (a chief officer, for example, might be reluctant to lead or to set limits) or because people are newly in the relationship they have. Here is one example of the testing that might go on in a new relationship system:

> "When I got married, my father-in-law
> would occasionally test whether my wife was loyal
> to him or loyal to me" (078).

Commonly, however, people involved in power battles offered

no theory for why such battles go on. The following statement about one battle, couched in the language of fairness of work load, may reflect a developmental issue, differences in values or perspectives, or some other factor that the participants might have identified. But in this case, no theory was advanced as part of the anecdote.

> "We had an employee here. He was alcoholic and he missed probably a day a week. My dad says to me, 'Hey, don't worry about it; maybe he can work his problems out.' I used to tell the employee that 'when I'm boss, you're out,' because I don't think anybody should have to put up with that. My dad would say, 'It's not of your business. It's my business.' And I would say, 'It's my business more so than yours because I have to work with him every day, and if I come to work and he's not here, I depend on him to do his share. None of us should have to do somebody else's share' " (106B).

If we were to advance our own theories about power battles in business families, one that is supported by some of the interview material is that power battles happen because people do not like to lose battles. That is, once there is a disagreement of any sort, people may dig in and fight for the position they are holding. Such confrontations can polarize a system and lead to rigid, right/wrong, good/bad oppositional and fractionating positions. Such positions tend to invite coalition formation as other people in the business get sucked into the polarization. People who are polarized in this manner may lose sight of organizational goals, so their struggles may be harmful to the business. They may even fight to gain control of the business as a way to win all current and future battles. The most common examples of digging in came in father/son power battles.

> "If ever there was a showdown, Dad would want it his way" (044).
> "I don't enjoy fighting with Dad. In the early years, when I thought I knew everything, we did a lot of fighting" (005).

As the second of these informants implied, power battles are also sustained by the conviction that one knows enough, has the correct goals and rules in mind, or is competent enough to be right, that because of one's knowledge, perspective, and abilities one should not surrender. In that sense one battles to sustain one's self-image and to establish it with one's opponent. Perhaps, too, not to sustain one's position is somehow to be less of a person, to be a "doormat."

> "There's a point where you cannot be a doormat. There was a specific incident where we have an expense account that we charge the customers. And people thought that I should at least exceed the amount that I actually spent. It became a sort of a confrontation with a couple of people and my father. My father said, 'You need a wife and a couple of kids. That will teach you.' And I said, 'Well, I don't have that, so it's not an excuse' " (048B).

Power battles are also assertions of self. One reason people get into power battles is to show others and themselves that they matter, that they know things and are to be taken seriously. Said another son in business with his father:

> "Those kind of things force you to be a little more aggressive or outspoken or value what you are worth. I didn't get enough of that young enough. So the tension I have felt has been learning to be more aggressive as to who I am" (033B).

To the extent that power battles are to establish one's worth, one may lose a battle and yet subsequently feel vindicated because emergent events validate one's position. In the following statement, the winning of a national award seemed to provide some satisfaction in a situation in which battles were not always won.

> "My son would say, 'Why don't we make this a charitable institution? At least we'll get a tax exemption. If you give any more charity to cus-

tomers, we'll have the biggest war they ever had.'
But then we won a national award. And if you had
seen my store, it was really a hole in the wall.
That's all it was. And so then I put it under his
nose. There would be times when my son would
tell people who came in before work hours, 'We're
closed.' And then I'd come in and I'd say, 'No,
we're not. You come in. I'm not quite ready, but
you can have a cup of coffee while I get things
ready.' Then I'd really be mad at my son. I'd say,
'You treat others like they would come to your
house in a business.' Partnership or a corporation
is rough, especially when you're together day in
and day out for decades" (063A).

This statement also suggests that power battles in business may
continue for many years.

Power battles are not necessarily a bad thing. Conflict can
be a source of creativity and necessary change. People in battle
may be motivated to develop ideas and arguments supporting
those ideas that they otherwise would not have come to. Trying
to resolve conflicts may lead to creative approaches to problems, to movement into new ways of thinking, and to compro-
mises that turn out to be more desirable than the uncompro-
mised ways of doing things would have been. Conflict is a way
of dealing with tensions that might be destructive if kept quiet.
Expressing feelings, even when conflicts are not resolved, may
let off enough steam for people to be able to remain in an organization and may give everyone a chance to understand the
differences and disagreements that are present.

To have a power battle is to have a relationship. There is
a kind of closeness or potential for closeness in conflict. People
in conflict with each other may not experience the closeness as
such, but people are in a sense tied together in their conflict.
The conflict makes them in some ways equal (Simmel, 1908/
1955, chap. 1), and in conflict they experience one another's
strong feelings. The tying together, the equality, and the experience of one another's strong feelings are all ways of being close.

Power battles in businesses involving parents and offspring have a certain amount of predictability. Parents often

start out with enormous power, based partly on their positions as parents.

> "That's the way we were raised, you see. Dad was always right. We always did what Dad said right now, right then" (025B).

In a business the seniority and expertise of parents are power bases, not only because of how these things affect their off-spring but also because of how these things affect other people in the business. That is, not only is a son or daughter responsive to a parent's seniority or power, but other employees are too, in a way that makes it difficult for offspring simply to go against parental wishes.

> *Interviewer:* "Who manages the business?" *Respondent:* [Laughs] "Well, as much as we can get away from my father, I do. But he has the over-all; he still pulls all the strings. He may not get his way, but he still has the last say-so" (116B, whose title is "manager").

There is also a residual power that parents in a family business usually have, not only because of their seniority and expertise but because of their financial control of the enterprise. In that sense many family businesses are the parent's business when battles occur, the business of the chief officer and principal shareholder (Hedley, 1981, referring to a parallel perspective on family farms). In intergenerational power battles a parent can often choose to end the battle, at least for the moment, by insisting that ownership controls the situation.

> "If I put my foot down, it goes the way I want it to go" (031B, a father).
>
> "My father had been in business much long-er than ourselves, and I think that we valued his advice. But we didn't always decide that way. And today I've been in the business much longer than my other two partners. I think that it would be obvious that if it was something that was weighty

and was going to make a big difference to us and I disagreed, we'd maybe do it my way. But we don't have many of those kinds of decisions" (033A).

Offspring, nonetheless, have their own power bases. One of them is their currentness. Especially when a parent has been operating a business on the basis of business experience and intuition and the offspring has gone to business school, and perhaps especially if the business has grown quite a bit since the parent became an executive, the offspring's currentness may provide a power base for the offspring.

"The father always knows more than the sons, because he's been there, and the sons are always smarter than the father, because they are hip. They know what's happening" (075B, a son).

Offspring often have power too because the parent wants, even needs, to have the offspring stay in the business and eventually take it over.

Perhaps it is primarily when offspring have a solid power base or when they are not dependent but have the freedom to leave the business and know it that a parent who uses seniority to end battles has to do so carefully and infrequently. Pulling rank rarely endears one to subordinates. The parent who is well thought of by offspring may be the one who uses seniority infrequently or who at least has second thoughts and backs down some of the time.

"He'd think about something after an argument, and sometimes he would come back and say, 'Well, maybe we better do it that way after all.' Dad was a pretty good man" (036A).

In some families, power battles seem to occur not because powerful people push in different directions but because there are no clear pushes and no clear limits. For example, a parent may be so fearful that a son or daughter will leave the business that the parent neither exerts leadership nor sets limits on what the offspring does in the business. Power in those situations comes out of the confusion in the business over what is going on. Confusion gives one room to do almost anything and to avoid taking responsibility for anything that goes wrong. Power is also exercised through the coalitions that form in order to provide some organization and direction. Offspring in such situations may create battles as a way of testing limits and in hopes of getting a parent to be boss. Yet both parent and offspring in such situations stay dependent, in a sense, dependent on coalitions and dependent on the relationship morass that provides the environment for their business life. One symptom of such a power situation is permissiveness, without sanctions for stepping over limits and without clarity to the limits.

Although anybody may use unethical means to win power battles, it may more often be the person who is dependent, feels helpless and one-down, and lacks legitimate ways to win battles who uses unethical ways of winning. Perhaps it is particularly somebody who cannot use seniority or ownership of the business as an ultimate weapon. For example, as mentioned in Chapter Two, some younger people found ways to pay themselves the raises that a senior relative in the firm had denied them. One example of a do-it-yourself raise was the following:

> "I'll ask Dad for a raise, and if he doesn't give it to me, I'll just give it to myself." *Interviewer:* "Does he know that?" *Respondent:* "Sooner or later. He finds out at the end of the month 'cause the accounant'll tell him." *Interviewer:* "Then what would happen?" *Respondent:* "Nothing." *Respondent's brother:* "What can he do? It's too late. How many times have you done that?" *Respondent:* "Just a couple. He's such a cheap sucker." (025B; the respondent's brother was present during part of the interview).

In response to somebody else's great power, people who were in a junior position or who simply could not control some decisions sometimes made decisions covertly, without consulting a powerful coequal or a more powerful relative in the business. Covert circumvention of the recognized decision process is a tactic in power battles. Whether or not such circumvention is a good thing, it can be seen as a self-affirmation, an assertion of one's own worth.

> "Generally I know what might be a disagreement and might not get it to that point. I may go ahead and do it without my brother's consent or his opinion" (074A).

> "Sometimes I thought my father was stupid, that he couldn't see it right away as to why we should do something, but later on I learned that it was his way of justifying in his own mind that it was what he wanted to do. So he would question the simple, the very simple things about a decision. He would start out totally negative, and then you would have to persuade him. I think it was his negative attitude in that area that caused me to make some arbitrary decisions on my own, not counsel with him. But now I'm finding that what he did was the right way to handle a situation" (087).

If secret unethical behavior such as making decisions behind someone else's back is a response to another's power, one might expect such unethical behavior to be shown by junior, less powerful family members. That may be so, but junior family members are often the ones who argue for ethical positions. For example, respondent 048B was quoted earlier in this chapter, "There's a point where you cannot be a doormat . . . ," as refusing to pad his expense account. He also said:

> "I don't *feel* that the other people in the business can turn me into a compulsive liar. It doesn't agree with me. I don't want to do it. It's the crux of their behavior some of the time. They end up saying things that other people want to hear" (048B).

Another young person in a family business also fought what he considered the immorality of his father, who was the company president.

> "When I complain to my father about his
> cheating of customers, he just kind of says, 'Well,
> go ahead; you do it your way, and I'll do it mine.'
> But I think sometimes it has an impact, because
> more and more he's getting away from charging
> when you don't do anything" (062B).

The morality of these younger people could be simply random
variation—in some families it would be an older person who had
a stronger investment in behaving morally, and in some it would
be a younger. It could be a matter of business experience, if one
assumes that business experience leads to a more opportunistic
sense of what is moral. It is also possible that morality is a relatively defensible position from which to deal in a power battle.
Given a shortage of other resources, moral arguments may be
a resource to use in power battles. Thus, morality may become
an issue in part because it is a good position to argue; it is a
position that one can defend, and perhaps also it is a position
that can influence people who are arguing for contrary viewpoints. Taking a moral stance is also, in a sense, joining in a
coalition with moral authority. By saying, explicitly or implic-
itly, that good people, the Bible, God, one's therapist, and so
on support one's position, one in a sense is enlisting allies. This
is not to say that people who take a moral stance are necessarily in need of allies or a coalition, but people who fear asserting themselves and who feel weak and one-down in a system
might well ally themselves in order to feel stronger and safer. It
is also a way of risking less because rejection of one's position
would seem to be rejection of public morality rather than of
one's personal opinion. This is not to take away from people
the worth of arguing a moral position, nor is it to deny that
sometimes everybody's position is the moral one, but it is to say
that there may be good tactical reasons that moral positions are
taken in power battles. There are also self-esteem reasons for
taking a moral position. Even if one loses the power battle, having defended a moral position can be seen by others and by oneself as good and courageous, not selfishly motivated.

    Battle tactics and winning are not, however, the only
considerations for a member of a business family who is in-

volved in a power battle. At times one may feel that losing is necessary in order to maintain family harmony. Although it is often important to make one's feelings known and to battle for what one wants, in a family business, perhaps in any business, one may have to be willing to lose in order to maintain some more general harmony of relationships.

> "I tell one of my sons, 'I think you're Jewish on Saturday 'cause you observe the Sabbath; Sunday you're Catholic—you observe the Sabbath; but after three o'clock during the week I want to know what religion you belong to that you can't be around.' Then he says, 'Well, I work hard.' Sometimes you have to make off you're deaf, dumb, and blind and just patch up and forget it. Money isn't everything. Keeping the family together is more important to me" (063A).

> "My father's being so paternal with me created such a bad issue for me that I went and enlisted in the Marine Corps. I got out of here. I spent four years in the military. I got out a little older, a little wiser. I figured I can handle the situation then. It did us both good, because he realized I was a human being and had my own mind. And I think he matured in that time, too. I did a lot, too. I used to be real quick on the handle. It helped me a lot. More patience involved, try to understand somebody's point of view" (031A).

The Bending of Twigs

Childrearing issues have been discussed throughout this book, particularly in Chapter Five. One aspect of the bringing up of children in business families that is relevant to the discussion of money and power is the anxiety that some people in business-operating families had about the corrupting influence of money. For some it was a fact that offspring can be corrupted by money. Others displayed a more diffuse concern that younger family members who are given so much money as to have an easy time of things may not be well served.

> "We're not sure that our kids should be left
> a lot of money. And we incline to let them know
> that ahead of time" (091A).

> "These kids are casualties of a grandfather
> who gave. It's too bad. You've taken away from
> these kids the desire to work" (078).

The opinion that money corrupts may be held by the majority of people in business families. It is also possible that entrepreneurs who have had to struggle are people who value struggle so much and feel that it has helped them develop their own character to such an extent that they are concerned that anyone who has not struggled may not develop well. For some entrepreneurs there may also be a fairness issue underlying concerns about younger people not having to struggle. Some people may feel that if they had to struggle, it is only fair that others should also.

> "I'm not building this with the idea that I'm
> going to leave my children fat and cushy. No one
> ever gave me anything, but if I can make it easier
> for them, fine" (042A).

Beyond money issues, some entrepreneurs expressed concern over how much or how little they should influence offspring to enter the business. There are certainly entrepreneurs who want offspring in the business and who pressure them to go into the business or to stay there. (See the discussion of succession in the next chapter.) Some entrepreneurs, however, bent over backward not to influence offspring. In at least one case, that meant that a man's children had no idea what their father did for a living:

> "My father was so careful to not—he didn't
> want us to feel pressured to go into the business.
> He was so careful to not say anything that I didn't
> even know what he did" (033B).

In some cases the concerns about influencing offspring arise out of a sense of the undesirability of the family business. The family business may seem undesirable because it is economically marginal (something one can hear relatively often in farm families—Anderson and Rosenblatt, 1984). Or the family business may seem undesirable because it involves excessive filth, excessive hard work, excessive immorality, or excessive unpopularity with the public.

> "I would just as soon that none of my kids ever pick up plumber's tools. I won't push the kids into it. It's a hell of a field to break into. There's a lot of bad feelings about plumbers" (061).

There were entrepreneurs who claimed simple indifference to what offspring decided to do—a sort of do-your-own-thing philosophy.

> "I would never push them to work here. I'm doing what I like and supplying the money, so if they want to do something that they like, they can. I don't give a hoot whether they take over, come down here and work or not. And they know it. So as a consequence they don't come down here [laughs]" (015).

There were also entrepreneurs who, though wanting offspring in the business, feared the consequences for the offspring or for the business of having somebody come into the business whose heart was not there.

> "I know Dad likes it when we have worked here, and I think he likes it when one of us kids has been interested enough to have been in it for a longer time. He's not going to twist our arms to stay" (050B).

In those situations, the fear seems to be either of a poor match of offspring to business or of an undercurrent of offspring resentment at being pushed into a job the offspring actually does not want.

"I don't think I would try to change a son or daughter's mind, if they're leaning toward being a nurse or a doctor or whatever, because they may feel if I ask them, 'Why don't you take an interest in the business?,' that they would be hurting my feelings if they turned me down. So they come into the business. They don't understand; they don't like it. They're doing it for my sake" (027).

Perhaps in many cases, it is not clear to offspring or to parents whether the offspring will fit in the business and enjoy it or not. A son or daughter may try working in the business for a trial period or may be encouraged to go into other firms in the same field. In some cases the offspring is encouraged to go into other lines of work to see whether those things fit better. Some offspring who go away for a while come back to the family business, though not necessarily with the feeling that the family business is the right place to be. However, it is clear that in some instances the early socialization of the offspring, the bending of the twig, makes the family business or one just like it by far the most attractive option for the offspring. Having grown up with the family's bakery business, for example, the offspring continues to value the odors, the creativity, the relationships with loyal customers, and the production of the family's specialties.

Conclusion

Money and power are issues in any business, but in business families they are especially important because of the part they play in the relationship of business system and family system. Because money is an important symbol of worth, when people claim that the business must come first or put enormous amounts of time into the business, part of the motive force for what they are doing may be money-as-symbol. To the extent that is so, a person who battles family members in order to defend business goals may be fighting for feelings of self-worth and a good reputation in the eyes of others. Although that may make somebody very resistant to backing down on commitments to the business, it also means that to the extent the person can turn to other places for feelings of self-worth and for a good reputation, the business can become less preeminent.

Although fairness of compensation may be an issue in any organization, bringing family members into a business may make for more intense concerns about fairness. Two siblings or two siblings-in-law may be strongly disposed to use each other as bases of comparison. That may mean that fairness concerns are more important in a family business and that when people feel unfairly compensated, their feelings may affect their relationships in the family.

Power battles are normal in organizations and are often a good thing. Family businesses may have more sources of power battles than other kinds of businesses. Offspring in the business may battle with parents in part as a development of self-assertion and autonomy. Family members may battle with each other in part as a testing out of where they stand with each other as family members. In any organization, power battles arise partly because people do not want to lose, but the wish not to lose may sometimes be more intense in family situations. For example, a son may not want to lose in battles with his father because he needs his expertise to be acknowledged by his father, and the father may similarly not want to lose because he wants his son to give him credit for his accumulated experience and his investments in the business. However, people in family businesses may, at times, not want to win power battles, for fear of alienating or hurting someone else in the family. To the extent that power battles are assertions of self, family members (more than unrelated people) may engage in power battles, because selfhood has so much significance as a family matter. For example, parents may, at some level, want to see offspring being self-assertive and may want the chance to test their own mettle through self-assertion in dispute with offspring.

For relatives who are rather distant or estranged, conflict is one form of relationship. Through conflict, each can be important to the other, express strong feelings at the other, experience the other's strong feelings, and spend time with the other. Thus, in family businesses, power battles may be sustained in part by people's interests in having some sort of continuing relationship with a family member.

In family businesses, people sometimes use unethical ways to win battles. For example, several persons covertly gave themselves raises they could not have received otherwise. Although unethical tactics may be used in any organization, in family businesses they may be used more, in part because the family relationship may sustain the person's connection with the business even after the unethical behavior is found out. Our impression is that it was relatively powerless people (perhaps particularly offspring) who were more inclined to try to win battles through unethical means, perhaps because they lacked other resources for winning battles. But it was also our impression that relatively powerless people (perhaps particularly offspring) also advocated ethical positions in disputes. People who argue for a moral position may be entirely genuine, but arguing for a moral position is also a useful battle tactic to the extent that one lacks other resources, feels powerless, or wants to give moral rather than personal reasons for advocating a course of action. People are swayed by ethical arguments, ethical arguments put one into a kind of coalition with moral forces and moral authorities, and losing an ethical battle, one can still feel good about oneself.

Money and power are issues in the raising of children in business families. Some parents are concerned that money may corrupt children, that it is better to struggle for what one wants than to be handed it. Similarly, there is concern about what it does to a young person to be handed an executive position in the family business. The concern is partly a matter of worry about corruption but also a matter of worry about whether a person can do good work in the family business and be content there if too strongly influenced to enter that business. Nonetheless, many younger family members do consider entering the family business, and that brings us to the topics of the next chapter, succession and inheritance.

Chapter Ten

Succession and Inheritance

A family business can be a valuable financial asset, to be kept in the family as a source of income. A family business can also be a symbol of the success and accomplishments of family members who have operated it, of the family's power and influence in the community, and of hard work. It is, moreover, a symbol of achievement that can live on after the founder has died. For these reasons some or all family members may value succession to ownership and control of a family business, succession that will maintain the financial assets and the valued symbols. Conceivably any relative might succeed to management or ownership of a business, and in fact there is evidence (for example, Ambrose, 1983, in a study of family businesses in Nebraska) that entrepreneurs who were not founders might consider a wider range of relatives to be candidates for succession to management or ownership. But in the present study (and in the Ambrose study just cited), the actual candidates for succession seemed far more often to be the children of chief officers than to be any other relative. Because parent/offspring succession was the most common type discussed in our interviews, it will be the type of succession emphasized in this chapter.

Parents and offspring can take pride in a successful transition in control of the business.

> "My father was extremely proud of what my
> brother and I did, extremely proud, and even told

us that. And I just think he gradually gained confidence in our ability" (006).

Yet as this chapter unfolds, it will be clear that there are often
problems in the succession process. Perhaps in order to avoid
these problems, some family businesses are designed or eventually become designed to pass out of the family's control.

> "This company isn't set up so that it's a
> father-and-son type of operation. In fact, it was set
> up to be more of a meritocracy" (050B).
> "The troops here sense that we don't have
> an heir apparent here waiting in the wings to swoop
> in at the eleventh hour and displace a whole bunch
> of hard-working people who have loyally served
> the company for all these many years" (120).

It was more common, however, that people who operated substantial, viable businesses and who had potential successors in
the family hoped to have one or more of those potential successors succeed to ownership and control. This was so even
though having a successor in the family had its costs. Often, for
example, having a family successor created problems with the
morale of nonrelated employees and with hiring nonrelated
executives.

> "One of the problems is hiring real quality
> other people, that they are a little reluctant to
> come into a family business, because if they are
> real ambitious and looking for a line job or a top
> job, the gates are kind of barred to them" (032B).
> "I would think we had some employees who
> felt that they should be a partner, nonfamily mem-
> bers that never were encouraged or led to believe
> that they ever could be" (033A).

Identifying and Attracting a Successor

In many businesses in which family succession to ownership and control is desired, children work in the business at an
early age.

> *Interviewer:* "How old were you when you
> first started to work in the business?" *Respondent:*
> "I was about ten when I was employed as a rod-
> man for something like ten cents an hour. It is one
> of your truly unskilled tasks. You just have to hold
> a surveyor rod straight" (050B).

Early experience like that can provide strong interest and motivation to enter the family business. One learns about some aspects of the business; one may become emotionally and symbol-
ically tied to it, may feel committed to that business because of
the work one has already done (Rosenblatt, 1977), and may be
taught to think about the business as though it would someday
be one's own.

Socialization from the teen years or earlier to enter the
family business was reported commonly by sons of entrepreneurs, though not daughters.

> "There was never a doubt in my mind or my
> brother's mind what we were going to do. We had
> been programmed, I guess, by my dad. There's a
> lot of security in knowing what business you're
> going into early on. When we got out of school, we
> both took sales territories" (006).

As the man just quoted said, there can be security in having
one's future plans set so early. However, some people reported
troubles that arose from that early socialization—for example,
goals that were not necessarily well fitted to the underlying personality and needs of the offspring who was socialized so early
to go into the family business.

> "You listen all your life to 'Someday this is
> going to be yours.' I don't think that's healthy.
> You don't really set other goals for yourself"
> (075B).

Commitment to the Business. Beyond early socialization,
people can become committed to the family business because
they expect ownership of the business and desire that ownership, desire it to the extent that they even tolerate low pay or

very difficult relationships with a parent or other relative who is operating the business.

> "All of us kids want more money, but we all know that if we stay with the business, the returns on our investment in the years when we were young is going to be very plentiful. It's just a matter of being patient, and there I hope my patience will pay off" (106B).

> "If my father can't find something, it's always one of us who misplaced it. And the family doesn't get raises like the rest of the employees. Truthfully, I love my dad as a father. As a person, I have many dislikes toward him. Very unfair with his family. Someday the business is probably going to be ours, so you keep trying to do your best. The only problem that has been for me is that I really got to see what my father is like. As a person, I don't like my father" (113B).

Some family businesses were doing so well financially that offspring felt trapped in the business by a standard of living that could be maintained only as long as they stayed with the business. The respondent quoted next was aware of the drawing power of money as well as the drawing power of being involved in a successful operation, although his commitment seems to have arisen from his efforts in moving the business from a precarious position to one of financial safety and viability. The sharing with his father of hard work eventually leading to success may well have solidified his commitment to the family business.

> *Interviewer:* "You can get locked into family businesses." *Respondent:* "Sure, especially if you're overpaid, and especially if the business was successful before you came there, and you just got plugged into it. That was not the case here. This was not successful at all, and I came here and worked with my father to make it successful. I have shared the feelings of real problems, and pushing and working and working and turning it around and making it successful. I have shared that with my father. And

none of my friends have ever done that. My dad
and I were partners, almost, in this venture"
(084A).

For some offspring, power and status came with early entry
into a senior position in a business, and that power and status
made it difficult for them to consider going elsewhere. One respondent talked about his early accession to a business presidency, a presidency which he would not have been given in
any other business and which he could not have performed
competently (at first) without parental help.

> "There's no way I could have been president
> of this company if it wasn't Dad's. And I was presi-
> dent in name more than in function, because he
> was there to help me. He was very generous about
> letting loose" (044).

Overall, potential and actual successors seemed to have a
substantial range of feelings toward succession, many having
mixed feelings and feeling pressured (see Boswell, 1973, chap. 8).

Overlooking Daughters. Typically the male entrepreneurs
who valued family succession to ownership and control of the
business considered sons but not daughters to be appropriate
successors (see Menchik, 1980). Men without sons or without
sons who were interested in the family business often went
through a period of bitterness and grief, a bitterness and grief
that might emerge recurrently (see Rosenblatt, 1983, on the
recurrence of grief).

> "It bothered me tremendously at first. I
> felt very badly that my sons really didn't care
> about coming into the business that much. You al-
> ways have a hope for that. But as you get older and
> you see their point of view . . . I think I'm recon-
> ciled to that" (127A).

Some men without successors worried, as the years went by,
about what would happen to the business when they retired, became seriously ill, or died. Their worries were partly about their

own finances and the finances of their immediate family and perhaps partly about people who depended on the business—employees, customers, suppliers, and shareholders. Some entrepreneurs worried about succession because the business was cherished as a creative achievement, one that they wanted to believe would continue permanently.

> "We are getting to the point in my life right now, especially without sons coming into the business or sons-in-law, that we really don't have any family to build on anymore. And if we're going to look out for the continuation of the business, if something should happen to me, we may merge with somebody or sell to someone in the near future. That's a tough decision for me" (087).

This man mentioned that he also lacked a son-in-law to whom he might pass on control and ownership of the business. The American kinship system values blood relationship. Many Americans do not consider in-laws to be relatives (Schneider, 1980). When a son-in-law enters a business and assumes the role of successor or potential successor to control or ownership, some people consider that to be in some way inappropriate. The son-in-law may be suspected of being avaricious and manipulative, to have violated some cultural rule.

> "Coming in as a son, you are expected to be in the business. I mean that's your inheritance. But coming in as a son-in-law, you're coming in through the back door" (080A).

Yet there were sons-in-law who had taken over control or ownership of businesses in the sample or who seemed likely to do so. In all cases there was no son in the family or none willing and able to move into the chief executive role in the business. Of course, where there was a son-in-law, there was a daughter, but entrepreneurs rarely considered daughters appropriate successors. Even entrepreneurs who were extremely distressed that they had no sons or no sons willing to move into an executive role and who feared that the business would leave the family seemed unwilling to consider daughters. In one business a daughter had succeeded to 50 percent control, the other half going to a nonrelated manager. The only other respondents who seemed to be open to having daughters as successors were a young man whose daughters were still preteens and a man whose daughters had already opted not to enter the family business.

> *Interviewer:* "Are there any tensions over whether a son or daughter should work in the business?" *Respondent:* "Well, we wish we could get some. I have three boys and two girls, but we can't get any of them interested at all. I educated them too well" (036A).

Why are men so reluctant to consider daughters as successors? What leads them so often, even in the face of their own despair at the potential loss of the business as a family one, to ignore their daughters? Some men who spoke to the issue said their daughters were not competent. But then few daughters were given early experiences in family businesses comparable to what sons had. Daughters, if they were involved at all, would typically do secretarial or receptionist work, often part-time or in the summer. So gender differences in competence, one could argue, were usually a result of gender differences in socialization. Some men said that the family business was no place for a woman because the men they dealt with were uncouth or because the company operated in a man's world (for example, trucking, auto repair, or meat packing). But no woman spoke to us about the family business being no place for a woman, and three of the businesses had been inherited by wives.

Perhaps the neglect of daughters as possible successors represents a cultural bias to consider males but not females appropriate in entrepreneurial roles. One can speculate that another reason for the discounting of daughters as potential successors is that in America most daughters change their surname when they marry. Many male entrepreneurs may feel, therefore, that the business would in a sense pass out of the family should a daughter succeed to control or ownership of it. That may be what an entrepreneur had in mind when he said the following about his will.

> "When I kick off down the road, everything
> is going to be divided equally amongst all the kids,
> but the boys will have the business. That way it
> stays in the family" (092A).

Statements like this one seem to say that, for some men, daughters are not family or cannot be counted on to remain in the family. The probable change in surname and the presumed change in loyalty when a daughter marries may lead many male entrepreneurs to consider a daughter not enough a member of the family to be a potential successor to control or ownership of the family business. This viewpoint can lead an entrepreneur to make his daughters-in-law millionaires, through their marriage to his sons, but leave his daughters living on a comparatively modest income. One would think that having the business stay with one's own descendants would be an important value in American business-operating families, but the value of surname succession, the distrust of a daughter's loyalties, and perhaps a view of women as somehow second-class where business issues are involved seem to impel men more strongly. This is so even though there is a sense in which a son, more than a daughter, leaves the family and becomes focused on his own spouse. In America, adult daughters maintain, on the average, more contact with their parents than adult sons do (Cohler and Grunebaum, 1981, pp. 23-24). Although more entrepreneurs nowadays than in the past may be open to having a daughter as a successor, most of the entrepreneurs we interviewed seemed to prefer to have a business pass to nonrelatives rather than to a daughter.

Other factors may also account for the discounting of daughters as potential successors. But, whatever the reasons, what is striking is that daughters were almost never given a chance. Consequently, entrepreneurs lose 50 percent of potential offspring successors, and as the following statement indicates, finding competent and willing successors in a small pool of eligibles is very difficult.

> "It's tough as the dickens to take one busi-
> ness of any size through generation to generation,
> and your chances of finding somebody within your
> own family are just so remote" (078).

The difficulty must be far greater when one ignores half the potential eligibles. It seems not in the best interests of entrepreneurs to ignore their daughters as potential successors. If one
would like to pass a business on to a blood relative, and one
wants to maximize one's chances of finding somebody willing
and competent, it seems self-defeating, even if one has sons, to
fail to consider daughters. For those without sons, the failure to
consider daughters seems possibly to be self-destructive, destructive of the daughter, and destructive of the goal of maintaining the business as a family one. What is maintained in this
situation is a set of rules and beliefs about what is valuable,
what is family, the importance of maleness, and how businesses
can legitimately be transmitted to other family members. The
pride of having a successor in the family and the pride of having
a daughter do well may both be exceedingly important, but
they seem less important than supporting personal and cultural
values about the family, the sexes, and the proper ways of passing on a business to kin.

Tension over How or When a Business Changes Hands

The tangle of family system and business system is commonly expressed in tension over how or when the business
passes from one person to another. Fifteen respondents, representing fourteen businesses, reported tension in this area. In
only eighteen businesses in the sample had a younger family
member succeeded to control or ownership. In an additional
seven businesses, a transition in ownership or control had begun
but was not yet complete. Thus, the fourteen businesses for
which we had reports of tension over succession to ownership
or control constitute a majority of businesses with substantial
potential for that kind of problem.

If a business changes hands in a sale between nonrelatives,
typically the legal transfer is neat and well defined. One person

or group acquires control, with the point of transfer often defined down to the minute. In the transfer of a business within a family, however, the transition is often quite blurred. As in other areas of entanglement of business system and family system, a major cause of tension over transfer of the business is the tendency for parents to continue to parent and for offspring to continue to live with that. A parent who is giving up a business to an offspring may continue to want to tell the offspring how to do things, may continue to want to be helpful to the offspring, and may continue to feel that the offspring is not quite up to running the business independently. An offspring may be reluctant to ignore the parent and may retain some residual feeling that there is a kind of safety in listening to the parent or that the parent is too expert to be dismissed. Tact is also necessary for the offspring dealing with a parent who retains financial control of the business. But even offspring who have worked hard to get a parent out of the way may subsequently feel that the parent's knowledge and abilities are or would be of great value in the business or that the parent's approval is desirable. The following two quotations may merely illustrate what many people come to know in mature adulthood, that parents have more competence than one thought when one was an adolescent or young adult and was trying to separate from them. But it is difficult to imagine a person who had replaced a nonrelative as head of a business saying the following kinds of things about that nonrelative. These quotations seem to say that offspring in family businesses may feel reluctant to replace abruptly a parent who has had the chief officer role.

> "Originally when I was moving more from sales into management, I was kind of eager to have my father go, figuring I knew everything that was going to go on and shouldn't have any problem running the company. But as the years have gone along, I've found out there are certain things that he is doing that I'm not ready to handle on a day-to-day basis. He's like having an adviser around. It's usually a legal problem or a financial problem" (005).

"We were fortunate in that Father voluntarily semiretired. First he'd take a month, and the next year he'd take two months, and the next year we'd find he was gone all winter. It was very good. That's the ideal way to do it, because you can make your mistakes, and your father is still around so that he can come back in from time to time. It would have been really terrible if he would have died suddenly, and we had had no experience in running it at all. I think this is a big mistake that I see in some family businesses, that the old man can't bear the thought that he's going to be on the shelf, and so he tries to keep on doing everything, right up to the end. And of course then the kids come in and make their mistakes" (036A).

Both of the preceding passages indicate that some offspring in family businesses may not desire abrupt replacement of the parent. The second passage also refers to parent reluctance to retire. The interviews turned up many reports of older people reluctant to retire.

"The question of retirement, if and when it's appropriate to an older family member, is a difficult, unresolved question. It's been discussed openly by just my father and me. He is somebody who wants to run a business and doesn't know how to delegate, and the business has outgrown him. But it's hard for him to see himself not being a leader" (068).

"I think men that are mature, that have sons in business, they generally do a kind of turnaround. I think they start relying on the younger generation. The one that laid heavy on my father's mind was when he sold all his common stock. He's no longer running the show, and that bothered him" (087).

Many younger people reported wrestling with parental reluctance to retire. Resistance to retiring may be common in any occupational area in which work is rewarding, provides a sense of self and a worldview, and dominates one's life so that there

is nothing else to do that is as significant as work. But people in
family businesses may be uniquely in a position to put off retiring (Alcorn, 1982, pp. 153–155; Barry, 1975; Boswell, 1973,
chap. 5). Putting off retirement could be harmful if, for example, it meant ignoring a personal need to live a less demanding
life or a family need to allow offspring sufficient autonomy to
function as full adults operating the family business. But some
people saw the freedom not to retire as an advantage of being in
a family business.

> "I've put in time, and I'm committed to
> keep the place going. I don't want to sell it and be-
> come an insurance man or something for some-
> body else. I want to stay in the company. I want to
> be here until I'm my father's age or older. When I
> get to be his age I don't want my kid to come in
> and say, 'Dad, it's time for you to retire.' I won't
> have anything else to do anyway" (005).

> "My husband grew up with the idea that he
> was going to work in the business, that his parents
> told him that the business was for him. So there
> was never any leeway or choice as to what he was
> going to do as an adult. He was going to work
> there. So he did, and the same time that his mother
> had the idea he would run the business, there was
> also the idea that he was taking something away
> from his parents. It was a kind of a confused thing.
> They wanted him to do it, yet they didn't want
> him to do it, because it was taking something away
> from them. They didn't think he could do it. And
> then there was the disagreement with age. Some-
> times a generation will look at running things one
> way where younger people will have different
> ideas, and we had that problem too" (101B, whose
> husband, an only child, is now sole owner of the
> family business. Our informant went on to de-
> scribe, in the following statement, efforts by her
> mother-in-law to retain some sense of significance,
> value, and place in the business).

> "My husband's mother knows she's sup-
> posed to let go. My husband reminds her of that
> when she tries to tell him to do something or not

> to do something, but she can't really let go of the business. She likes to go into the office or she wants to get a financial statement to find out how things are going, and then she'll go through it point by point, questioning different things" (101B).

> "I don't intend to retire unless I absolutely have to" (075A, a board chair at an age at which many people are retired).

> "My dad should be the owner. He's made it what it is. But my grandmother has got this thing of dominance. She wants to hold the reins over the family" (064B).

> "I don't know if I ever would want to retire. I'd just take it a little easier, 'cause I know I'd miss all the friends I've made, all the customers; they're just like friends. I don't plan to retire" (062A).

The process of resisting retirement may be harmful to the business in that it may debilitate or prevent optimum learning by a potential successor or may cut into the resources available to find that successor. If businesses do less well under successors (Savage, 1979), one reason may be the way their predecessors prolong their influence in the business. Hanging onto that influence was quite common in our sample.

One way to keep from retiring is to make it prohibitively expensive for one's offspring to take over the business. In at least one case an offspring and her husband who had tried to buy the family business thought they had been quoted a price that the parent knew was impossible to meet.

> "I really think that my father should have my husband manage this business for him, because there is much, much more money to be made if it was managed in a different way. If my dad would just stay home. We wanted to buy it, and his down payment was so out of sight. He was toying with us" (113B).

However, the parent had a different view, wanting fair compensation and fearing that the business would go bankrupt if it was passed to his son-in-law.

> "I'd like to sell it to my son-in-law if he can come up with some money. That's a big thorn in his side, come up with any money. You don't have money. I've seen a lot of businesses where the father has worked all his life, and he gives it to his son or his family, and in quite a few cases they end up they go broke" (113A).

The father's fear of business bankruptcy was no doubt one reason he wanted substantial payment at the time of transfer of control, rather than gradual payment out of profits obtained after transfer. His fear can be understood to be either a motive not to retire or an excuse not to retire, but it should be pointed out that for many operators of family businesses a substantial part of retirement income will come from the sale or buyout of the business. Their reluctance to sell a business at a low price or with a low down payment is a form of self-protection.

Even when a parent retires, there is the possibility, in at least some family businesses, of keeping some involvement in the business, a luxury usually not available when a nonrelative takes over.

> "I help because I need something to do" (032A, talking about covering for his son in the family business).

> "He's been active all his life. There's no way he would just have gone home and sat down and did nothing. It would have killed him. We've all been working on Dad to slow down, go up to the lake and go fishing or whatever, and he just won't. He won't give up" (061).

In some businesses there had been some planning for letting go. But planned change in ownership and control was quite uncommon in the family businesses studied. Planning for an orderly change of responsibility, training family members to be able to perform new roles with full competence, and making economic arrangements that would minimize the tax and legal costs of a change in control were rare (see Trow, 1961, reporting on data marshaled by Christensen, 1953). The infrequency of planning for a transition in control and ownership is striking, because planning, at least in the larger, well-established firms, was so much a part of the business operations—planning market strategies, planning for peaks and valleys in demand, planning for plant growth, planning for employee vacations, planning for deliveries from suppliers, and so on. Lack of planning for transition is associated with diminished business profitability (Christensen, 1953; Trow, 1961). Nonetheless, the infrequency of planning for a transition in control and ownership is understandable. People who have most of their identity, sense of self-worth, and sources of meaning in life invested in a business will obviously find it difficult to plan to give up the business (Barry, 1975; Boswell, 1973, chap. 5). For them, the first step in planning has to be to change their sense of who they are and to find new interests and sources of gratification. Planning for succession is also difficult to the extent that it will alter family relationships. If the person operating the business derives power in the family from the business role, planning for succession will begin to alter that power base. A business operator and the operator's close relatives may feel insecure and find they have some new relationship tensions as they move forward with an orderly succession. Optimum planning for succession may require more extensive consultation with other family members than other types of business planning. The chief officer may have to consult not only with the potential successor but with a spouse and with others who might have a stake now or might conceivably in the future have a stake in ownership of the business. This is necessary so that those persons will be committed to going along with the succession plan and so that family jealousy and resentment over choice of a successor may at least begin to be dealt with. Thus, it is not merely that the chief officer may be reluctant to plan but that the planning process may require broader discussions than is usual in business planning. Small wonder that planning was so infrequent!

Some people who had gone through a difficult transition recognized the value of planning.

> "The only thing I've thought of is with regard to our kids. I don't want them to grow up with the idea that that's what they're going to do. There

should be some freedom involved. But then with
three kids there is room for freedom, whereas if
you just have one. . . . It would have been easier
for my husband if there was just a planned kind
of breaking in, and maybe there would be the idea
that you want to let go after a while" (101B).

Underlying the last statement is a sense of living with tensions.
The respondent went on to talk about transition tensions.

Interviewer: "How has the transition problem
affected your home life?" *Respondent:* "It was mainly between I being affected by my husband's mother and my husband absenting himself from the problem. He would just leave. When his mother was
here, he would be in the bedroom or something.
She didn't like me or the kids or anything" (101B).

This respondent's husband also regretted that there had been no
planning of transfer of the family business from his parents to
himself. His statement also makes clear that the tensions over
succession to ownership or control can spread to the marriage
of a person experiencing those tensions.

"There are much more orderly ways of
doing things than it was done. The strife that is involved probably in the succession of a family-owned
business like this can be very debilitating. It was
almost disastrous for my marriage" (101A).

Marital problems during transition struggles may be made more
severe when there is dependency by the spouse hoping to succeed to control or ownership of the business, a need to depend
on family elders and the business. With such dependency and
with any kinds of restrictions (actual or perceived) on dealing
with the family elders about succession problems, the potential
successor will bring tension home, where it will show up in
marital arguments, in marital distance, and in other ways. Somebody who was more autonomous might feel more free to deal
with the family elders, would feel less emotionally involved in

how things were going, and would feel free to leave the family business if things were not working out satisfactorily. Emotional dependence on family elders and on the business may be fairly common among younger family members. For them, succession to ownership and control may be important partly because it brings with it a cutting of emotional apron strings.

Transition tensions may develop and be expressed over a substantial period of time.

> "It gets to a certain point where you feel it's your turn to run the business, and your father isn't quite ready to release the reins. That's a big problem. It begins with issues. Should we grow? Father is generally comfortable where he is with the business; the son is not. He wants it to grow" (075B).

In some families, a younger person tried to talk with an older person about the transition, but with no success; the older person put off the discussion.

> "It was a strange thing, and that is that although my father's health failed after my mother's death and I brought the transition matter up to him, not only businesswise but personally several times, this was just something that was not in his nature. He would not accept the fact of failing health, that anything would ever happen to him. It was just a subject that was an absolute stone wall. Nothing had been done. He had not got to the point of admitting that anything would ever happen to him" (097).

In some cases, however, the talking may have made a difference.

> "A couple of years back Father had been ill and was hospitalized, and I mentioned to him that he's a nice guy, he'll live forever, but if something ever happens, I don't want to have to sell the place if I've put in my time and he's put in his time just to give the money to Uncle Sam" (005).

In this latter case, no definite time of transition had been desig-
nated, but there had been estate planning involving a will and
the establishment of a trust.

During a long transition in power, an offspring may have
enough influence to make a business into something a parent
can no longer manage effectively. Innovations in management,
in manufacturing, in product, or in marketing may eventually
leave a parent lagging behind, a figurehead without the capacity
to deal with what is ostensibly under the parent's control. In at
least one case it eventually became clear to the parent that there
was really no alternative to leaving the business.

> "I said to my father, 'You ought to get rid
> of your stock. You're just kidding yourself. You
> don't have any power. You couldn't run this com-
> pany for a minute if you had to.' And he finally
> did get rid of his stock. It was difficult, though,
> very difficult. He no longer had clout over me. He
> was always fearful that he would be destitute"
> (006).

In two businesses in the sample, a son-in-law took over
from a parent-in-law. Those are interesting cases to consider in
that the generational difference is present but the history of
parent/offspring role relationships is not. Although parent-in-law
relationships with offspring-in-law may have their own peculiar
dynamics, it is interesting to note that the two cases of com-
pleted succession involving that kind of relationship tended to
be relatively harmonious. For example, in a passage quoted in
Chapter Three ("He left me pretty much alone. . . . He just
stayed out of it"), a son-in-law (078) said he was given considerable leeway. Still another business established jointly by
father-in-law and son-in-law seems to have run with great
smoothness.

> "There was a *tremendous* rapport between
> my husband and my father. I don't think they ever
> had cross words with each other. They just got
> along beautifully. I always said that my husband
> didn't marry me for my money; he married me for
> my father" (091B).

Despite what has been said here about parent/offspring tension over succession, there were businesses in which things went relatively smoothly.

> "Dad was a very smart man. He just gradually released the business to us. He gradually took longer and longer vacations until finally he wouldn't show up at all" (036B).

The smooth successions seemed most commonly to arise when a parent was able and willing to give up control and there was at least one offspring who had the competence to take over. Giving up control is easier when the business operator does not rely solely on the business for identity, life meaning, and a sense of self-worth (see Bennett, 1976, p. 231, talking about farm and ranch families). To give up control to offspring requires that an entrepreneur has or can find interesting and valued activities outside the family business. We did not ask about retirement planning, but in two cases in the sample an entrepreneur's retirement involved development of a new business, in both cases a kind of "hobby" business, without the scope or ambitions of the business being left.

There is no simple formula for a successful family succession process, but a number of factors seem to be commonly present. One is a business that is in reasonably good economic condition (although even here there was at least one exception in the sample). A business in good condition is economically attractive to a potential successor, can support the training of the successor, can support more than one executive during a succession transition, and can provide reasonable funding of the retirement of the person moving out of the chief executive role. This does not mean that a potential successor is necessarily an economic drain. Bringing in managers with new perspectives may produce substantial business growth (Boswell, 1973). In some cases in the sample, a potential successor brought large increases in income into the business. But there is no guarantee that it will happen or that it will happen soon.

Of course, for succession to occur, there has to be a potential successor. We think that entrepreneurs who want an offspring as successor should consider daughters as well as sons and should provide offspring of both genders with a chance to learn about the business, the chance to say no to the succession role as well as yes, and opportunities to go away from the business for a university or business school education and for experience in other businesses.

An effective succession requires education of the successor but also of the chief officer who will someday step down. The successor needs chances to perform and make mistakes in an executive role, needs supportive supervision, preferably from a nonrelative, needs to be respected as an individual, and does not need to be indulged. Some successful transitions include outside evaluation of the potential successor's managerial skills and knowledge, either as a means of identifying needed training or as a means of deciding whether a potential successor is able to do the work of the chief officer.

The person stepping down often needs to learn a great deal. Stepping down includes genuinely delegating authority, acquiring new or stronger interests in things other than the business, accepting that changes will have to occur and will occur in the business, and being willing to work out a plan for succession with the persons who will be involved. Preparation for succession may well include discussions with other family members who have a stake in the business, working toward shared commitment to financing, and accepting the succession process (Becker and Tillman, 1976). It may also require adding extra incentives for nonrelated personnel to keep them in the business— for example, strong benefit packages (Becker and Tillman, 1976).

There is no guarantee that succession ideals can be met. A chief officer needs to be open to the possibility that a potential successor will lack the interest or ability to do the job, will become estranged and decide to leave the business, or will insist on a course of action that the chief officer cannot accept. We also know of cases, though not in our sample, in which the potential successor died. For these reasons, it helps to have alternative succession plans or to have the flexibility to work them out. Possibilities include having other family members who could also serve as successors groomed for roles in the business and being open to hiring a professional manager, with family members having lesser roles or director positions but not the chief officer role. In some cases, of course, the chief officer must simply sell the business. Even here, planning for this possibility (for example, learning about the market for the business and the best ways to package it; preparing key personnel for the possibility) will make for a more beneficial transition.

The succession processes that seemed to go most smoothly involved clear leadership, flexibility, nondefensiveness, and good communication skills. When the succession process went smoothly, all parties seemed to be able to criticize tactfully and to accept criticism without excessive defensiveness. All parties seemed to be learners, to be patient, and to be nondestructive and noninsulting when upset. All parties seemed accepting of other people's independence and operated with clear boundaries between business and family and between business and self. Dispositions like these can be acquired, if one does not already have them. But it certainly helps to have a succession plan that commits people to a process and a schedule and gives both successor and predecessor meaningful, autonomous roles during the process.

Because life often ends unpredictably and because many people procrastinate in decision making or hold onto ownership (and often onto control as well) as long as possible, in many businesses the point of succession to ownership and control is the death of the chief executive officer. The next section of this chapter deals with what may happen if an owner dies and with problems families have when they try to anticipate or fail to anticipate the owner's death.

Inheritance

Eight respondents, from eight businesses, reported tensions over inheritance. For many people interviewed, inheritance was not an issue. Many businesses in the sample were new and were operated by comparatively young people. In these cases people might not have thought about death of the owner/

operator. In some businesses, transfer of ownership and control took shape and was carried out before the time when a will would have been needed (see Marcus, 1980). Some businesses, especially sole proprietorships, were organized so that succession would be by nonrelatives.

> "When my dad retires, the stock will be divided; it is being sold off to those other principals. Arrangements have been made up so that they will be able to accommodate all of his stock. I think that's fine. I've never felt that it's a family business. I am a firm believer in meritocracy. Also, I have no real interest in business, in conducting it" (050B).

In some families inheritance was never discussed. This noncommunication had several origins. There were business families in which communication on almost any issue rarely occurred. Said one respondent:

> "We just don't communicate a lot, and inheritance is one thing that has never been brought up. I honestly can't tell you what my father's plans are" (116B).

In many families it may have seemed threatening or insulting to talk to somebody about his or her death. Yet failure to talk about inheritance issues may mean that a younger person can remain in the dark and perhaps anxious about a parent's inheritance plans.

> "It's hard to go in and ask your father, 'What are you going to do when you are dead? What's going to happen to me?' It seems too mercenary. I'm able to talk more with my mother on that than I am to him. I don't think anybody likes to talk about the day they're going to die. I think it's kind of mercenary to go in and look someone in the face and say to them, 'What are you going to leave me when you're dead?' If I can find out without having to confront him with it, as far as

> reading the will, it's back here in our safe. Any-
> body in the family can read it. There's a couple
> back there. I've got one back there. My mother's
> got one back there. I just haven't had any interest
> to see what's in the will until he got sick again. He
> does get a little offended if I come in, 'cause for
> many years he's said, 'Don't worry about anything.
> Everything is taken care of. You'll be taken care
> of' " (005).

Although the person just quoted was concerned about being
mercenary, it can be argued that everyone needs to be mercenary. To subordinate one's own wants and needs to other family
members, to the family as a whole, or to the family business
may deny one's individuality and be personally destructive. It
seems preferable to acknowledge an older family member's reluctance to talk about inheritance and succession but also to say
that one has a personal need to discuss the matter. In families in
which that may be sensitive or difficult, it may be helpful to
carry out the discussion in the presence of a neutral third party,
such as an attorney, an outside member of the board of directors of the business, or a neutral family friend.

Some people do not think about inheritance issues, particularly people who are young and have no ambition to take
over the family business.

> *Interviewer:* "Are there any tensions over in-
> heritance issues?" *Respondent:* "I never even
> thought about it" (025B).

> *Interviewer:* "Any tensions around who
> should inherit or the fairness of inheritance?" *Re-
> spondent:* "No, that's entirely—I can't conceive my
> brothers and sister or myself even thinking about
> it. Who are we to, even? It's none of our business"
> (033B).

Nonetheless, for offspring who have invested effort in the business and have hopes of someday succeeding to ownership and
control, there can be substantial anxiety if inheritance issues
are not discussed.

"You ask my father. In case anything would
happen, you'd like to know what goes on. But he
doesn't really give you an answer. Really, it could
go to anybody. We assume the family would get it,
but the way he is, you never know. It's miserable.
He's got savings deposit boxes all over. You don't
know where a will is. You don't know where the
insurance policies are, who they're with, and you
kind of wonder, 'Is this really fair? Is some old
Joe Blow going to get what we've been working
for?' " (113B).

The anxieties may exist because financial stakes are high or because what people will inherit or fail to inherit is not only
something of financial value but also an occupation (Titus,
Rosenblatt, and Anderson, 1979), a status, and a place in the
community (Menchik, 1980). The anxieties may also be justifiable because problems of inheritance occasionally arise at an
entrepreneur's death. Parents may, for example, die without
wills or with wills that have become outdated as a result of
changes in the family or the business. Very substantial problems, both for the family and for the business, may then result.

"He died unexpectedly, and his will was in
bad shape" (044).

"We thought there were inequities and still
think there was. We resented the way it was handled in the will. It wasn't the way he said it was
going to be. We had to assume, even though we
were hurt, that he just didn't know what the hell
he was doing. We have a good relationship now
with his son and wife. But there just isn't the closeness we had before this all took place. His action
divided the family" (078).

"Unfortunately, in my father's situation
there was no will, and I found myself—I won't say
in partnership, but involved with a stepmother that
I barely knew, that had no knowledge of the company whatsoever. And she dragged her feet for five
years, just thinking that she was going to put the
bite to me. It was long and involved. This inheritance situation is a very, very tender spot. Eventu-

ally we hammered out an agreement. It didn't
work out very well. I was so overly generous that it
was a painful situation. Oh, I'm courteous and so
forth seeing my stepmother at Christmastime, but
there is no conversation the rest of the year" (097).

As the last two preceding statements indicate, one of the consequences of not having a will or of having a will that does not fit
the business, the family, or somebody's expectations is that the
survivors may have strained relationships. Open discussion with
all family members about estate plans may head off many potential problems. Openness about one's will and the reworking
of a will as conditions change may also head off problems. Such
discussions seem to us to be a business operator's responsibility
to initiate or at least to join in responsibly if discussion is ini-
tiated by someone else. However, even with the best of planning
and communication, people may be dissatisfied. Family members may differ in their views of what is fair (Anderson and
Rosenblatt, 1984; Rosenblatt, 1983, chap. 10; Titus, Rosenblatt, and Anderson, 1979). In such a situation, the person who
made a will may realize that individuals' views differ and help
the persons involved to see one another's perspective. But often
fairness disputes are not resolvable. In family businesses the tension is often between rewarding offspring who have been more
involved in the business by giving them a bigger share of the
estate and treating all offspring alike. If the former course is followed, offspring who are given less can feel that a parent cared
less for them and favored an offspring who had already been
given a cushy place in the family business and who had taken
the easy route into a noncompetitive situation. If the latter
course is followed, the offspring who worked the most in the
family business may feel that his or her ability to control a business in which he or she has invested considerable time and effort will be diluted because a large share of the assets and perhaps control of the business have been given to other family
members. He or she may also feel that years of working in close
contact with a difficult parent, perhaps at a low wage, have gone
uncompensated. Although these particular patterns of fairness
dispute do not fit all cases, inheritance disputes may arise in vir-

tually any business family and may not be resolvable to the satisfaction of all involved.

Conclusion

When one considers the topics of succession and inheritance, the connection between family system and business system can be seen both as something positive and as something negative. The famly supplies the business with potential successors. The business may supply the family with attractive positions for potential successors and with the possibility of acquiring valuable assets. Problems in succession and inheritance, however, result from the interactions of family system and business system.

In a succession process involving parent and offspring, the parent may be protective in a way that perpetuates offspring dependence and undermines the offspring's learning or autonomy. The parent may fight the offspring for position in the business as a result of a need to maintain a position of family superiority. Many entrepreneurs resist retirement, and having the business be a family one makes it easier to resist retirement in many ways. For example, some chief officers see succession by an offspring as an opportunity to stay in the business, while others encourage a successor to be dependent so that there is a need for the chief officer to remain in the business. The offspring who is succeeding to the role of boss may also undermine the succession process. For example, some may play out autonomy battles within the business or may work at remaining dependent. With family involved, third-party family members may affect the succession process, and of course, there is great opportunity for nonobjectivity, both overestimation and underestimation of family members who are potential successors.

In the areas of inheritance and succession, family communication difficulties make it easy for problems to develop, as people are kept in the dark, fail to plan together, or develop differing understandings of what is going on. In both areas there may be competing standards of fairness, with the possibility that some family members will feel that whatever is going on is unfair. Even if a fair disposition of the assets or a fair succession process is possible by the standards of all involved, what is fair may not be optimal for the business.

Recommendations for a good succession process include counting daughters as possible successors, planning the succession process (in a planning process that involves all family members who may be concerned), giving a potential successor latitude to choose not to be a successor, giving a potential successor appropriate education and opportunity to learn on the job, and educating the chief officer who will be stepping down in how to support the succession process, how to deal with tensions and dissatisfactions that may arise as a result of hard choices he or she has made about succession, and how to prepare for a life of rather different activity and involvements.

Inheritance matters must reflect the realities of tax and inheritance laws and the preferences of the will writer. It is clear that in family businesses the major needs in this area are for wills actually to be written and for the will writer to communicate (both talking and listening) with other family members about what may be written into the will, what it may mean to people, and what influence it will have on the business and the family.

Chapter Eleven

The Advantages of Having a Family Business

At the end of each interview, respondents were asked what they thought were the advantages of having a family business. The question was asked partly because we thought there were advantages and wanted to hear what people actually involved in family businesses would say. We also asked the question to provide some balance for ouselves and our respondents. The interviews had emphasized tensions and stresses, and we wanted to provide an opportunity for our respondents to talk about the advantages.

There are perceptual issues in deciding that one's way of life has advantages. It is easy to come to live with a taken-for-granted view of whatever is going on around one. One's current way of life, standard of living, and relationships become a baseline for whatever is novel in one's life (Rosenblatt, 1977). One may have made a conscious, even rational choice of some way of living, but as one becomes accustomed to it, one may stop evaluating it (if one ever did), even stop paying attention to it. Hence, asking people about the advantages of something that has become familiar to them may be asking them to evaluate something they have not been evaluating. It is a bit like asking a person what the advantages are of being an adult. Many will not have considered the issue seriously for years. Thus, for many people in family businesses, the real answer to a question about the advantages of having a family business might be a shrug and a statement that "I do what I do" or "I don't know; it's how we make a living." In fact, two persons who were interviewed said they did not see any advantages at all to having a family business. Since both these respondents were persons who had been in business for a long time and whose businesses were quite substantial, perhaps they were long past evaluating their business against alternatives and long past stepping back to get some perspective on the way of life they had chosen.

Most respondents made an effort to tell us of advantages. Sometimes, however, the answer came after a substantial pause or came without the forcefulness and enthusiasm that people used when they were saying something which they were confident was correct and about which they had strong feelings. Those pauses may indicate that the question about advantages tapped a taken-for-granted or background area or that the question tapped an area of mixed feelings about being in a family business. Mixed feelings may have been especially salient by the end of interviews that had emphasized the stresses and tensions of being in a family business. That is, for some people who had paused or who had given brief answers to the question about advantages, the first thought when the question was asked may have been something like "I can think only of disadvantages." Nonetheless, people's answers to the question about advantages give additional insight into business-operating families.

Freedom, Independence, Control

Often the advantages people said they saw to having a family business did not seem to us to have any direct relation to the business's being a family business. One of the most commonly mentioned types of advantage was freedom, independence, and the ability to control things oneself. Even though some people complained intensely that government regulations, government paperwork, and taxation cut into their freedom and independence, many of those who complained about the government, as well as many of those who did not, talked about independence and freedom as a gain from having a family business. There may be a paradox here in that family businesses often demand enormous amounts of time as well as investment of virtually all a family's assets, so in some sense there is not much freedom and ability to control things oneself in a family business. Yet self-determination and the liberation that comes from not working for others were seen as advantages that, for many people, counterbalanced the costs in time and in investment of family assets.

It was, as one might expect, primarily entrepreneurs rather than other family members in the business who spoke about independence and freedom. Some entrepreneurs were clear that at first they did not experience the family business as an easy situation, but as the business developed, it was possible to compare the comfort of a self-determined situation with situations in which they had worked for others.

> "I think I'm having less pressures from our business, after we got beyond the first couple of years, than I had from the pressures that were imposed on me by other people with the other companies" (048A).

In a study of executives in twenty-five family firms in Iowa, Dailey, Reuschling, and DeMong (1977) reported similar statements about the greater freedom an executive has who is not working for others. That freedom seems to us to take many forms. Most obviously, there is freedom from supervision. For roughly twenty-five respondents the freedom was simply, as the person just quoted said, a freedom from surveillance by and pressure from others. Then there is the freedom to do things one's own way, a freedom from interference and influence by others. Fifteen of our ninety-two respondents emphasized that kind of freedom.

> "I run my business my way, and that's the way it's run. I own it. I operate it. And we follow generally my ideas" (094A).

Another aspect of freedom mentioned by some people we talked to was that a family business may allow people a great deal of privacy, a freedom not to be seen or judged by others.

> "We're insulated a lot from public opinion in this type of business. You can pretty much shoot from the hip if you want" (087).

Although one might consider such freedom entirely a positive thing, the respondent just quoted said that he felt the need for corrective mechanisms to guard against problems unlikely to develop when others are aware of what goes on. What concerned him was that insulation from the opinion of others might make for management decisions that did not receive adequate scrutiny (see Donnelley, 1964). In a corporation with at least some ownership outside the family, the necessity of accounting to nonrelatives might provide useful protection against poorly thought-out management decisions.

Freedom takes many other forms. Two respondents said that the advantages of having a family business included the freedom to work less hard. One person talked about the freedom not to have to put on a show for someone else, not to have to look good for a boss. That same person said that in a family business one can question things more freely. Although not every respondent would have agreed, in that respondent's experience the family business allowed greater freedom to raise questions. The freedoms mentioned also included the freedom not to be fired or transferred, a kind of security that was especially salient for four respondents. As we said in the previous chapter, the freedom to delay retirement is desired by some entrepreneurs, and one mentioned it as an advantage of having a family business. For still another respondent a salient freedom in a family business was the freedom not to attend many meetings; an entrepreneur can decide whether and when there should be business meetings and has the freedom not to consult with others.

A final area of freedom identified by twenty-one persons was flexibility in using their time. It seemed strange that people who felt that they must work sixty, seventy, or eighty hours a week and who went for years without taking a vacation or even a day off talked about their flexible time use. However, the self-determination these people experienced in a family business seemed to give them the sense that, in an emergency or even on a whim, it would be easier to get away than in a business that was not a family one. Not all respondents seemed to agree. As one pointed out, for example, if all the people in a business were relatives, it might be impossible for all of them to get away to attend a family event such as a graduation or to be present when a family member was seriously ill. But even among people who felt compelled to work far more than forty hours each week, there were many who seemed to feel that they had relatively great control of their own schedules.

Financial Benefit

Another advantage that is not necessarily limited to businesses that are family businesses is financial benefit. This advantage might not be present at first. As one respondent put it, "There aren't a lot of advantages, not until you get the loans paid off" (123). In the view of some respondents, the financial advantage of a family business was simply that it provided an alternative to unemployment. However, for many others (twenty-three of them), financial advantage, in the sense of being able to earn a very substantial income, was a salient advantage. Considering earnings alone, a number of respondents could agree that "it's a comfortable life-style" (042).

A family business is not necessarily more advantageous financially than some other kind of business or some other way of earning money. In fact, starting a family business is quite a gamble. For a person in a family business to claim financial advantage is, in a sense, to claim survival and success against challenging and difficult odds. To say a family business is "a comfortable-life style" is not unlike a circus lion tamer saying "It's an occupation that keeps me healthy." The claim of advantage is, in both cases, a claim of having surmounted dangers that many people could not surmount. Money and assets are, in that sense, symbols of success. (See Chapter Nine for further discussion of this point.)

Not only may financial advantage be a symbol of success and prestige, it may also be a gloss for other gains of having a family business, gains which are hard to admit to oneself or to others or which are not universally recognized as signs of success. In some cases, these other gains may not even be in the awareness of the person who is claiming financial gain. At least for a few people, the gains glossed over by the claim of financial advantage probably include power over others, creative satisfaction, privacy, freedom from the criticism, incompetence, idiosyncrasies, or whims of a supervisor, and freedom to do things that some others might criticize (managing in one's own style, consuming alcohol at work, refusing to negotiate important decisions, and so on).

Even though the claim of financial advantage may be a way of symbolizing or glossing over other things, there are certainly factors that can work to make a family business more advantageous financially. One, discussed in Chapter Five, is that family members may work for little or no wages. As pointed out in that chapter, undercompensated work of family members, even if only marginally useful, may help the business. In addition, as discussed in Chapter Nine, paying family members rather than nonrelatives keeps money in the family. The pay can be written off as a business expense and may allow earnings to be spread in ways that are useful for tax purposes. Perhaps the biggest financial advantage is the accumulation of equity. Working for a salary, it would be virtually impossible, because of income tax, to accumulate wealth as some of the entrepreneurs we interviewed had. Some businesses had gone from zero net worth to millions in a span of two decades or less.

Several respondents argued that some customers may be more loyal to a family-operated enterprise than to one not operated by a family (see Donnelly, 1964). Customer retention guarantees a certain level of business income, may reduce marketing costs, and may enable actions advantageous to people in the business but disadvantageous to customers, such as raising prices or reducing the number of hours that the business is open.

According to another respondent, additional financial advantage comes from being able to use business contacts for the benefit of the family (for example, help with legal work or in buying a home). That same respondent and several others also talked about being able to direct business resources in one form or another for use of the family. For example, a company-owned vacation home, airplane, or car can be used for business purposes at the same time it is being used for the family's benefit. To take one instance in the interview material, a president who enjoyed flying an airplane could fly himself and his family to distant cities for sales conferences that would still leave him with substantial time for recreation with his family.

Another source of financial advantage to a family business, mentioned by a substantial number of respondents, is that family members may be more dedicated to the business than employees would be who were not family. By hiring family members, one may well be hiring more committed workers. The dedication that people talked about seemed most of all to involve hard work, honesty, and trustworthiness. Nineteen respondents (from fifteen businesses) said, for example, that working in a family business one would do better work or more work because one felt a part of the business.

> "Because it is your family's business, you really care about getting the stuff done and getting it done right and making sure he's making money" (025B).

As we pointed out in Chapter Five, not everyone in a family business is seen by others or even by self to be working hard, and one respondent was very clear that a disadvantage of a family business was that people worked less hard than if they worked for nonrelatives. Nonetheless, many people believed that they had witnessed in their own family businesses that members of the family worked harder than nonrelatives, and many found themselves working harder in a family business than they had in other kinds of firms.

Honesty and trustworthiness are also aspects of the dedication that may be advantageous to a family business. Although in four businesses in the sample somebody said that theft by relatives had occurred, a number of respondents thought that in a family business there would be more honesty and trustworthiness than in a nonfamily business.

"You don't have to worry about a relative ripping you off as much as you have to another business partner" (031A).

The theft rate, if it could be studied systematically, may actually be lower in family businesses, but we lack relevant information. What we do know is that fourteen people from eleven businesses said there was more trust, trustworthiness, or honesty in a family business. One of them saw a related advantage of having a family business—that a person with several family members in the business could know that whenever the business was open, there would be a family member watching things.

Respondents were not always clear that having a family business brought financial gains. As mentioned in Chapter Five, for example, family businesses may often carry family members who are unproductive or overpaid. And one respondent complained that for him a cost of having a family business was having to sell the business out, at retirement, at a far lower price than if it had been sold to outsiders. Nonetheless, many respondents felt that, on balance, they gained financially from being involved in a family business.

Prestige and Pride

Eight respondents from eight businesses talked about the prestige and pride involved in having a family business. Being an entrepreneur was seen as a source of pride and prestige, and so was having a business in which several family members, particularly offspring, had a role. Some of the eight were proud of having built a substantial enterprise from modest beginnings or having strengthened an enterprise that may already have been substantial. One of the eight and an additional four respondents said that there was pride in being able to pass a business on to a younger family member. That legacy was, in their eyes, one of the advantages of having a family business.

Many respondents indicated that they valued intergenerational continuity in ownership of a business. They talked in various ways about the advantage of being able to pass something on, the advantage of building something to leave behind, and the pride that people can feel in passing a business on to offspring or perhaps to other relatives. Three persons mentioned the related advantage of having last-name continuity for the owner of a business. To have the business stay "within the family" was of value for them. There is a kind of immortality in that (Cates and Sussman, 1982). However, as pointed out in the previous chapter, the valuing of last-name continuity makes it difficult for entrepreneurs to consider a daughter, who may change her last name when marrying (or presumably a sister, granddaughter, niece, or son-in-law) as a possible successor. A kind of continuity was achieved in some cases by keeping the family name on a business even though somebody with another last name—a son-in-law, for example—was taking control of the business. Nonetheless, as several respondents pointed out, having no son willing to go into the business is a source of tension and stress for some people in business who value continuity. Perhaps there is also a factor of male identification with males; male entrepreneurs may see male, but not female, offspring as extensions of self. Whatever the underlying dynamics, entrepreneurs, as one of them told us, can experience great pleasure and pride in seeing a son make a go of it in the business.

Another way to think about prestige and pride is to think of power over others. There are people for whom prestige lies in being able to tell others what to do and in having nobody above them who can tell them what to do. Two respondents, both presidents of comparatively small firms, talked about that kind of power-over-others prestige as an advantage of having a family business.

Creativity and Ease of Self-Evaluation

An advantage mentioned with some frequency was that having a family business allows one to be creative. Eleven respondents from eleven businesses said that there were rewards in building something and in knowing that the growth of the business was due to one's own efforts. In a large organization or as a junior person in any organization one may not be able to evaluate oneself clearly in that many other people or a few crucial persons are at least in part responsible for the accomplishments of the business. In those cases, one cannot be certain of what one has actually made happen. However, in a business in which one is the chief executive or has a distinctive and central role, one can evaluate one's creative achievements.

For three respondents (none of them among the eleven who talked about creativity and building) evaluation was not an advantage in itself but became an advantage in the face of a challenge such as the need to expand markets or to develop and sell a new product line. For those three, an advantage of having a family business was that one could evaluate oneself against a challenge.

Nurturing Young Family Members

An advantage of a family business mentioned relatively often was being able to bring young, competent kin into the business. Kin who have high potential not only can be brought into the business at a young age but also can be moved into executive roles. However, a man who had entered a family business when young pointed out a negative side to the early entry of family members into the business. He had dropped out of college in order to help his widowed mother with the family business and felt deprived of an education he would like to have continued.

Those who mentioned the gains from early entry into the business talked about the advantage to a person of having such learning opportunities at a young age. One man felt that starting work young was character-building and gave one good work habits. Someone else talked about how work in the family business gave a young person experiences that would help in getting jobs elsewhere. Another person said, however, that work in a family business was hard for outsiders to evaluate. Perhaps one reason was that a young family member might not have enough

work to do in a family business or might have incompetent
work corrected by others without acquiring the necessary competence himself or herself. Four persons said there was an advantage in getting more responsibility or feeling more responsibility at a young age. However, as mentioned in Chapters Five
and Seven, for some young people involvement in the family
business at a young age seems burdensome or jeopardizes the
relationship with a parent. Respondents also talked about family jealousies that arose when some family members were
brought into the business and others were not. Nonetheless,
some people clearly saw an advantage in having a business that
would allow early entry of young family members.

Improving Family Relationships

A final area of advantage mentioned relatively often by
respondents was improvement in family relationships. One aspect of such improvement was the chance for additional sharing and contact. Working together, two respondents said, relatives know more about what is going on in each other's lives.
Nine persons spoke of having business things to talk about as
an advantage. However, others (see Chapters Three and Six)
complained about never being able to get away from work-
related topics.

Four persons, from three businesses, talked about the
satisfaction of working together, and several others talked
about the satisfaction of building together.

"Dad and I turned out to be the greatest of
friends" (055).
"I always have that feeling of being respected, and he enjoyed having me work here,
could always say it was his grandson" (062B).

Some people said that sort of thing even though they had
worked in a high-pressure situation; they felt that sharing pressure and responsibility was an advantage of a family business.
Two other respondents, in talking about family contact in a

business, said that they enjoyed the family feelings, the nestlike quality of the family business. Although there were others who found the contact or the ensuing familiarity a disadvantage, it still seems clear that some people find comfort and security in involvement with the family business. Perhaps the comfort and security lie not so much in reducing conflict as in making the conflict tolerable. Conflict with kin may be very painful, but it also may be more tolerable than conflict with nonkin. The tolerance may come because there is a base for continued contact, because one knows there will be other interactions that will be more civil, and because there may be more forgiveness of kin than of nonkin.

> "I would never go into business with a stranger; I'll tell you that, 'cause when you have your own family, you make allowances 'cause it's yours, and you forgive a little bit. But when you are with a stranger, they wouldn't forgive you, and you wouldn't forgive them. So there's where the advantage is" (063A).

Another aspect of improvement in family relationships was coming to a more respectful or understanding relationship with coworking kin. A man talking about his relationship with another family member in the business said:

> "We've learned mutual respect" (006).

Said another respondent, talking about how her work in the business helped her to understand her husband's behavior in a particular situation in which they once had problems together:

> "There was times that I'd have supper ready, and my husband would be tied up, and then the kids would want to eat, and I'd finally feed them. He'd get home, and I'd heat it over, and then I'd say, 'Hurry up and eat.' And he could never hurry up and eat the minute he got home. He'd say, 'I can't do that. I have to relax a minute.' Then, when I started working in the store, when I had to come

home, I'd have to relax. I got so I knew. That
helped our relationship because I've never done
that to him since. I know that we've got to sit a
minute. You can't just rush into eating" (094B).

One respondent said that working in the business provided an
arena for working out interpersonal problems. Another respondent seemed to be saying that the understanding developed
when working together provided a cushion when relationship
difficulties occurred. As that person put it:

"You're always going to have problems—
day by day, little problems. 'I don't like the way
this is done. I don't like the way that's done.' But
you never have any problem that looms up in anything big that would get a destructive kind of
force, because everybody understands everybody
else. They understand my failings and I understand their failings" (123).

Conclusion

It is striking how often people's answers to the question
about advantages of having a family business were about advantages to the individual. For many entrepreneurs, the family
business is actually understood to be the business of just one
person, the entrepreneur. For many entrepreneurs, the gains
that are salient are gains for self. This finding seems significant
in two regards. First, what we call a "family business" may be
understood by some people involved to be an individual's business. Thus, some people in what we call a "family business"
may not see this book as relevant to their own situation. Conceivably, such people may not be sensitive to family problems
connected to the business because the business is seen as an
individual project. These people may recognize that there are
problems but see them only as clashes of personalities or values,
not as business-connected. Second, the motivation to operate a
family business may be self-relevant, as opposed to family-relevant. Entrepreneurs may be thinking about their own income,

their own status, their own achievements, as opposed to family income, status, and achievements. That may be important in producing the very hard work that so many entrepreneurs have engaged in, and it may be relevant to some family tension—for example, tension over compensation or over credit for the success of a business.

Whether the family business is seen as an individual's enterprise or as a family's, what people had to say about the advantages of having a family business provides, as hoped, a more balanced view of what it means to be in a family business. There are joys for many people in the operation of a family business. However, there were wide individual differences in how much people had to say about advantages and in how much they actually seemed to think there were advantages. Advantages seem generally to be counterbalanced by disadvantages. Those disadvantages may seem especially great in the earlier years of the business, but as the following two statements indicate, making sacrifices for an enterprise of one's own may not seem so bad. For those whose business survives, things may look better in the long run.

> "It was hard on the family. They know when you want a better life, you've got to sacrifice some. You've just got to cut down your expenses an awful lot. You've got to spend minimum. You've got to hold your overhead down. You've got to put a lot of time, most of your years in business. But you enjoy that time more, so it isn't like going to work" (062A).

> "I think that maybe in our earlier years of marriage that perhaps there was some jealousy of the business. But down the road you see what the business does for your family, the opportunity it affords your family. And you see the fruits of your hard work, and it really is, it's *hard* work, but it's your life, really. And I think that the wife and children come to agree that whatever you've devoted to your business, and how hard you've worked at it, was all worth it. I think that what's good for the business is good for the family, and the family is

part of the business and the business is part of the
family in that respect. And they've got to understand that" (087).

As the first of these two statements indicates, for some people
the very hard work of establishing a family business does not
seem so hard, perhaps because the work is for oneself and one's
family rather than for somebody else or perhaps because the
business is seen as an extension of the self (see our discussion of
boundaries in Chapter Eight). But as the first respondent also
said, this does not mean that what the entrepreneur enjoys
makes life easy or pleasant for other family members. As the
second of the two statements just quoted indicates, it is because
the business is one's own, because it is the fruit of personal sacrifice and the sacrifice of members of one's family, that the
struggles are justifiable. Because "it's your life, really," whatever led to it has to be accepted. Yet this last interview excerpt
has a quality that suggests that even though the entrepreneur
may accept sacrifices that were made in building the family
business, other family members are not persuaded. What may
be an advantage for one family member may not be an advantage, or may not be enough of an advantage, for another.

Chapter Twelve

Improving the Management of Family Businesses

The research reported in this book was designed to investigate families, not business management. Yet the findings underscore some important points in the management of family businesses. From the systems perspective taken in this book, it is hazardous to assume that family and business are unconnected when a family is involved, directly or indirectly, in a business. A change in one affects the other. The interaction patterns, division of labor, economics, boundary drawing, tensions, and problem-solving styles of one may influence what can and cannot be done, what should and should not be done in the other. Consequently, this chapter emphasizes that, in contrast to the management of other businesses, there are some special management considerations when a business is a family one.

Goals

A nonfamily business can be managed with business survival and profitability as the primary goals. Decisions can be made to obtain and hold a certain share of a market, to develop new markets, and to meet quality standards in order to promote business survival and to maintain or increase profitability. There are other business goals that may not seem directly related to business survival or profit, such as maintaining a good reputation for the business in the community, having healthy and satisfied workers, and contributing to the general welfare of society. Yet these goals also promote business survival and profit. Working toward these goals may lead to higher worker productivity and to customer and supplier good will. In that sense all goals for a nonfamily business may be seen as related to business survival and profit.

Family businesses also operate with survival and profit as primary goals, but they often operate with an additional set of goals related to the family involvement (Barry, 1975; Davis and Stern, 1980; Lansberg S., 1983; Miller and Rice, 1967). The additional goals typically are to perpetuate the family's operation of the business, to conserve assets for the family, and to maintain family solidarity (Marcus, 1980). Perpetuation of family operation of the business means both to keep the business in family members' control and to pass one's share of the business on to other family members. Conservation of assets for the family means that accumulation of capital in a form that can be controlled and used by family members is important, that asset ownership and control by family members individually and by the family in a corporate sense are valued. Maintenance of family solidarity means that family members will see themselves as in some sense a unit and continue to be loyal to family rules, to one another, and to the family unit.

In some family businesses in our study, the chief officer seemed never to have been interested in perpetuating the family's involvement in the business, conserving assets for the family, or making family solidarity a business goal. In some cases the business was too new, the family too young, or the business too marginal for these goals to be important. In other cases, the owner/operator seemed simply to be uninterested in these goals, possibly because the business was seen as his or her own private interest. But each of the three goals was present and important in some of the businesses we studied.

Beyond the goals that may be present in any business and those that are often present in family businesses, family businesses may have goals that are purely family goals. In our interviews, for example, some businesses seemed to be very strongly influenced by the family goal that family members get along well and with minimal friction, and some seemed very strongly influenced by the family goal of achieving community reputation and respectability. It seems vitally important that family goals, especially when they are impinging on the business, be recognized, articulated, and kept separate from the business goals. A decision may be made that takes a family goal into account, but the business will be in a much safer place if the entrepreneur can recognize when a family goal that may be opposed to a business goal is being served.

The more goals an organization has, the more opportunity there is for conflict both within an individual and between individuals. Conflict among goals may be expressed within an individual, for example, when an entrepreneur struggles to decide between a course that should yield greater profits (for example, business expansion that will require many hours of entrepreneurial time) and one that should promote family solidarity (for example, spending more time with other family members so that a spouse will not be angry and dissatisfied). Goal conflict can also be expressed in tensions between two persons in the business, with one, for example, pushing for the decision that should bring greater profits and the other pushing for family solidarity. When there are more goals in an organization, goal conflict is more likely. There are more situations in which an individual may be pulled in several directions and in which people may have differing but equally legitimate plans, wants, or intentions. Thus, family businesses, operating with family goals as well as business goals, may have more goals/choice conflicts than nonfamily businesses.

One task in the management of any business, but particularly in a family business, is to organize the business to deal with goal conflicts, to maximize the creative and efficient resolution of conflict or at least to insulate individuals and operations from harmful consequences of the conflict (Davis and Stern, 1980). Like any management process, rational management of a family business requires that one articulate the goals that are present. If in a family business one acknowledges only business goals like those of other businesses, overlooking family-relevant goals that are actually present, there may be some serious management problems. Subordinates may receive conflicting or confusing messages. Business decisions may be made that seem irrational in light of the stated goals or are upsetting because they deal only with the stated goals. Decisions may be made that endanger the business or endanger family well-being.

Where goals differ between family businesses and other businesses, the differences necessitate that managerial decisions be based on awareness of the goal complexity. Business goals and family goals must be identified and examined separately. It must be recognized when these two sets of goals pull in different directions, and it is important to realize that choices must at times be made which will oppose one set of goals or the other or which require a balancing that serves both sets of goals but fails to satisfy either set fully. Failure to be clear about the separation of the goals can make for chaotic management and for management decisions that confuse people in the business or the family and seem irrational. We are not saying that the business must always come first or that the family must always come first; we are saying that management considerations must be based on a sense of the difference between family goals and business goals.

There are times, of course, when family goals and business goals seem closer together. For example, the business's need of planning for succession may well be congruent with the family goal of perpetuating family control of the business. Somebody in the family may make a willing and able candidate for succession, and both business and family will be served by grooming the potential successor for a chief officer role. However, to keep clearly in mind that family goals and business goals may differ, it is important for a chief officer to realize when a particular family member would be a poor successor (because of crucial inabilities, lack of motivation, or some other deficiency) and when it would not serve the family to have a family successor (for example, when the only family member who wants the position seems likely to want to own everything and undermine family solidarity). The example of a succession situation is an apt one to consider, because the aging of an entrepreneur and the imminent succession by some relative may be a major theme around which much of the life of a business family (Davis and Stern, 1980) and of a family business is structured.

We believe that even when a chief officer is the only family member with direct involvement in a family business, it is important that family goals be explicitly recognized and the clash of business goals and family goals be addressed. Family matters must be considered when, for example, decisions are made about the allocation of the entrepreneur's personal time and the amount of income to take out of the business. From a systems view, a family business cannot be managed without affecting the family.

Decisions about meeting business goals versus family goals might often involve only the business owner/operator, but a case can be made that family issues cannot be productively considered without some sort of involvement of more than one family member. In a family business, some decisions legitimately require input from family members who may not be directly involved. A decision affecting time together for family members, family finances, or possible business roles of an offspring probably should not be unilateral. We cannot give a concrete recommendation of a course to follow when family and business seem to require different courses of action, but our suspicion is that the best course is not an extreme one, that it is one that sometimes weights business considerations more heavily and sometimes weights family considerations more heavily.

Among the many ways in which one might conceivably involve a spouse or other important family member in the family aspects of business decision making, even when the person is not directly involved in the business, is to structure interactions as though the persons involved were a board of directors for the family "enterprise." Consider the family life at home as the family "enterprise," and consider the resources involved to include everyone's time, the family assets, the good will of friends and kin, and the knowledge and skills of family members in the household. Then the "board" must decide on policies for investing the assets of the "enterprise." This means not that the entrepreneur will have family members intruding into business management activities but that the entrepreneur will be open to hearing family members argue for alternative investments of his time, the family savings, and other family resources, will be open to their requests for information and documentation in support of his preferences, and will be open to a shared decision process on matters of family resource policy. This shared process may lead to the entrepreneur's compromising about personal time expenditure, investments in the business, and other things. We are not thinking here of a legalistic or formal kind of board operation (although that is certainly a possibility) but of an open, communicative negotiating process for setting priorities of direct concern to the family and allocating family resources.

For an entrepreneur to deal with the goal complexity of family business and business family is challenging. Both sets of goals must be taken into account, but the boundaries must be kept clear. The goals of the family and those of the business are different. Dealing with many business matters may be only a matter of considering business goals, but to deal in the business with family goals usually requires more complex thinking and some sort of consultation with family members. All family members will need to feel that their priorities will be respected and their opinions heard. For all involved the boundaries must be clear. Business decisions that may affect the family might often be made with business priorities coming first, but family decisions that impinge on the business may sometimes put family before business. It is a situation that may call for recurrent negotiation and clarification of boundaries and more than a little willingness to hear other people's viewpoints, to deal tactfully with conflicting goals, and to clarify issues that may not at first glance be purely business or purely family ones.

The business and the household are resources for each other, the business providing income for the household and the household providing capital, at least in the form of savings, and time resources for the business. The two are also competitors for resources (Bennett, 1982, pp. 134–147, and Kohl, 1976, chap. 7, both dealing with farm families). There are pressures both for shared management and for competing management. To the extent that household management in the form of food expenditures, allocation of resources for cleaning, and the like is done mainly by one person and business management is done mainly by another, the opportunity exists for a blend of competition and cooperation that may be comfortable, tense, or both for the two "managers." What is crucial in this dual management situation, just as in a business with two managers, is that each manager accept the validity of the other's operation and recognize the boundaries of the two spheres of management.

Management Tactics in Family Businesses

Division of Labor. One conclusion to which our interview findings have led us is that a division of labor is needed and important in family businesses. Most businesses, as they grow, develop clear lines of division of labor. Who does what may be clearly specified at the start or may eventually become clear. But in some family businesses there are factors working against a clear-cut division of labor. A parent may want to supervise offspring in the business in a way that leads to the parent's doing what the offspring could do or could learn to do. Relatives may feel that they have the right and responsibility to cover for one another and to do what one another does. As a consequence, some family businesses may have greater tension over who does what than is typical in the business world. In many of the family businesses in our sample, a division-of-labor strategy was used or was not used but seemed to us to be needed. To head off tensions and to reap other benefits of division of labor, it seems important in managing the family business to be committed to working out a division of labor. With an effectively maintained division of labor, conflicts will occur less frequently, and each person will have clearer incentives for performance through having a clearly defined area of responsibility. With a clear division of labor, it is easier to evaluate performance; a person will have a clearer idea of how well she or he is doing, as will others. Being in a position to evaluate the quality of their work motivates many people, and a manager who knows how well someone is doing is in a better position to make decisions about training, promotion, and other managerial options. With positions clearly defined, if somebody leaves the business, it is easier to know what kind of replacement to hire and easier for that person to know what to do (Becker and Tillman, 1976).

Sometimes a more or less permanent division of labor cannot be worked out. A business may be too new or too small; the demands on a business may be too diverse; key people involved in the business may too often be away from it for a more or less permanent division of tasks to have much meaning. However, even if a division of labor cannot be worked out in the long run, it may be worked out for the week, the day, or the hour. Even temporary clarity about who is doing what can be beneficial.

Barring even temporary clarity about division of labor, people can coordinate their activities only with frequent, understandable communication. Communication takes time, not only because of what needs to be said and heard but also because of the need to clear up confusion and misunderstanding and because human communication often leads into sidetracks, free associations, and other paths not central to what is being dealt with. Such inefficiency can be an incentive to work toward a division of labor, especially where the inefficiency threatens the survival of the business. Not to communicate and not to have a division of labor invites chaos, but we saw no business like that in the sample.

Position Descriptions. A division of labor should be accompanied by a set of position descriptions, each of which is understood and adhered to by all concerned. A position description for a family member might well go beyond a conventional description of responsibilities. It might well touch on matters of what can be said to whom in the business and what boundaries cannot be crossed. That is, position descriptions for family members might well go into details that can help to head off some of the tensions that we found in family businesses as a result of the intrusion of family relationships into the business.

These descriptions may need to be revised rather often, but that does not mean they are of little value. They still may provide a means to avoid some conflicts and to deal with others.

One issue in developing position descriptions that may be more important in family businesses than in other businesses is whether to describe the position as it is now or to describe it as it may change over a career. Is Junior the assistant sales manager, or is he the assistant sales manager in training to be sales manager and eventually general manager? Career descriptions have several advantages. They make clearer to everyone where someone is going, reducing tension and ambiguity about the plans of senior family members in the business. They make it clearer to everyone that positions in the family business are to some extent interlocked. If Junior is going to become general manager, Dad, who is general manager, had also better have some career transformations in mind to mesh with those that Junior will experience. Having career descriptions also makes it clearer what kind of learning a person may have to do. Is it sufficient to learn only about sales if the expectation is that one may have to worry in the future about financing, operations management, and tax issues? Obviously there will be cases in which parents or offspring are ambivalent about an offspring moving into a managerial and ownership role, or an offspring may start in the business before it is at all clear that a managerial or ownership future is a genuine possibility. Offspring in our sample often seemed to start as mere employees and only later on, if at all, came to be candidates for management or ownership. So it may be that the position of offspring of the boss cannot at first be defined in career terms. However, when a career in the business is being planned for an offspring, a career position description may be of value.

Some positions in certain family businesses may not be so clearly present or may not be present at all in other businesses. One such position that we found in many of the businesses in our sample could be called the "utility infielder." The "utility infielder," often a wife or daughter of the chief executive officer, was called in from time to time to help out when a crucial worker was sick, business volume was heavy, or the flow of

work had been interrupted or slowed down by some temporary
bottleneck. Such a worker may come in to help out for a few
weeks or even just a few hours. Perhaps all organizations need
temporary help, and bigger ones either hire such help or can
move workers around within the organization as needs arise.
Our impression is that, in a substantial number of family businesses studied, a wife or daughter would come in to help out
with office work, machine operation, phone answering, bookkeeping, and so on. In some businesses some tension existed
over such a situation. The "utility infielder" might feel exploited or unappreciated, and the entrepreneur might resent
what seemed like extra demands for attention by the family
member doing the temporary work. These tensions might be
reduced were the position to be described explicitly. Then the
"utility infielder" would have a clearer idea of expectations,
and the entrepreneur would be in a better position to say that
this person doing these tasks is what the business needs and to
give appropriate compensation, recognition, and appreciation.

The spouse of the chief executive officer may contribute
to the business whether directly involved or not. Tensions may
arise because of the demands on the spouse of the chief executive in her or his role as spouse; the spouse may resent these demands, while the chief officer may not fully recognize the
spouse's accommodation to them. Tensions might be less for
both chief executive and spouse if the position of the spouse
were formally described. A mutually agreeable position description might specify anything from entertaining customers to
being in reserve as a temporary worker for the business. With
such a position description would come some idea of the "pay"
that comes to the position; pay might include anything from
attention, time, and appreciation to an independently controlled share of the business income. When the spouse role is
made explicit, there is room to contract for rewards. The position description for a spouse might also recognize the role the
spouse would play in the event that she or he inherited control
of the business (Beckhard and Dyer, 1983a). The inheritance-
contingent role should be coordinated with the roles of offspring and others who might someday expect to have a leader-

ship or ownership role. It would certainly head off family problems if inheritance-contingent roles were a matter of mutual discussion and agreement and were associated with appropriate preparation for those roles.

Pay. In profit-making organizations it is difficult not to think in terms of financial remuneration, but payments other than money are important for everybody. Particularly in family businesses, it may be important that those other payments not be forgotten. Everyone needs appreciation, a chance to do things that seem worthwhile, and treatment that seems fair. Family members directly or indirectly involved in the business need such pay, and in "managing" them one should know or learn how to give praise sincerely, to recognize their effort and the quality of their work, to help them to see value in their work, and to show how they are being compensated fairly. Failure to recognize the need for such pay was, in some of the business families we studied, a source of difficulty both in the family and in the business.

Supervising Relatives. Some people hesitate to criticize or set limits for a relative, perhaps even hesitate to give any evaluation to a relative, while others may find it hard not to be very critical of a relative. In our interviews the most common difficulties of this sort were in parent/offspring relationships. To avoid such difficulties, we recommend several management tactics.

A corrective to many problems in family businesses but perhaps particularly to problems in the supervision area is that senior persons be open to constructive criticism, legitimating the process of criticism, modeling the receipt of criticism, and being open to the possibility that change may be valuable. Senior persons in family businesses should also learn how to criticize in nondestructive, constructive ways. By "criticism" we mean a nonhostile, even supportive evaluation that points to alternative actions. We do not include in the category of "criticism" blaming, shaming, aggressive attack, severe rebuke, or questioning another's competence, legitimacy, or worth. For example, in criticizing a younger family member whose clothing seems inappropriate for the sales work he or she is doing, one may say something like "I think you aren't dressed right for this kind of sales work. I'd like you to try wearing a business suit." We do not mean by "criticism" "You blankety-blank idiot! What gives you the idea that you know anything at all about sales?" In addition, family members who manage in family businesses must be sure they follow the good managerial practice of balancing criticisms with praise and appreciation. If a manager does not feel free to criticize a relative working under her or him, that person should be working under someone else. Similarly, if a manager feels that somebody working under her or him need not or should not be praised or receive appreciation, that person should be supervised by somebody else.

Many people manage poorly or choose not to be in management positions because they are uncomfortable at leadership or inept at motivating others, particularly when leadership and motivating require making decisions, setting limits, enforcing limits, pushing, or criticism. Judging by what some respondents told us, problems in managing people are more common when the people being managed are relatives. As we said earlier in this book, one way many families we studied found to get around such problems was to use nonkin to supervise kin in the business. Another way around the problem that some respondents recommended was to discuss concerns with the family member to be supervised, making it clear to that person that pushing, limit setting, criticism, and so on are job-specific, that saying, "You botched that contract. It might have worked better if you had tried X," or "I want to see you making more progress on that job. You need to do more Y and Z," are comments only about specific work, not about the person or the relationship in general.

Conflict Management. Conflict management is a key to leading in any organization, particularly a family business. One useful tactic for minimizing destructive conflict is to manage with an openness to dissent and a willingness to consider change. This is so in part because disagreement and difference are often easier to live with if they are in the open, and they are more likely to be in the open if the chief officers in the business welcome dissent. To have someone say that a decision was poor or that someone is being unfairly treated may help a manager to see things in a different and productive way and may help a dissenter to let off steam, to be helpful, and to feel appreciated. Openness to dissent does not mean an end to managerial autonomy. A manager may, for example, feel that a decision that has been criticized is the right one or that a person who seems to someone else to be treated unfairly is being treated fairly. A manager can encourage and support dissent in such a situation without backing down from what seems to be the best managerial choice. Saying something like "I hear you, but I disagree with you" is better than not hearing dissent and better than trying to bully the dissenter into agreement. The model of an open relationship for people in business, as for people in families, is one of autonomous, mutually respecting individuals.

A second tactic for managing conflict in the family business is to communicate, being both a good listener and a good talker. Disagreements should be understood, in family businesses and business families, as normal and OK, not as disasters. People will have different opinions, different ways of doing things. To live with the disagreements and to tolerate the differences, one must give others a fair hearing and be clear about one's own viewpoint. To be sure that good communication actually occurs, it is desirable to schedule time to air disagreements and differences, particularly when feelings are running strong. Avoidance of conflict by avoiding communication is only a last-ditch coping mechanism and often exacerbates tensions through coalitions, triangles, secret keeping, and festering resentments. In the management of difference and conflict about difference, it is also important to keep interactions nonviolent and focused on the issues, not to make issues into matters of personalities. Of course, the issues may be different for different persons, and one must be accepting enough of that to understand and communicate adequately. The point is to expect differences and to air them in a respecting way.

Another aspect of conflict management that is important in the family business is to prevent conflicts from spreading to other relationships. If one wants to ensure viable family relationships and a viable family business, it is important to keep

conflicts from spreading to family members not initially involved in the conflict. One should avoid enlisting other family
members as allies in a conflict, avoid jumping into conflicts between other family members, and avoid combat with family
members other than the person with whom one is in conflict.
Said one man in businss with his brother:

> "My wife and my brother's wife have made
> a pact never to get involved. He and I can really bat
> each other, and they'll stay out of it" (006).

Had their wives become involved in the conflict, it would have
made the wives targets, polarized the brothers, and made family relationships outside the business more tense than they already were. The principle of encapsulating conflict should also
be understood to apply to nonrelatives in the business. Family
conflicts in a business should not be extended through recruit-
ment of nonrelatives as allies or through targeting of nonrelatives (Davis and Stern, 1980).

If one is not oneself a combatant but is working in a situation where others are in combat, the most appropriate thing
might be to keep out of the battles. Joining in may catch one in
the cross-fire, spread the conflict, lead one to disrupt a relationship that is in some ways beneficial and desired by the persons
involved, and prevent the combatants from working out their
differences and learning conflict resolution skills. However, people may want a mediator, someone who can help them get past
a stuck place. Being a mediator is risky, particularly when one
mediates between persons one will work with in the future or
mediates the conflict of someone who has more power than
oneself. If one does mediate, one's basic goals are to avoid taking sides but to help people see each other's viewpoint and to
work toward a mutually satisfactory resolution of the difficulty. It is not particularly helpful to listen to one person in a
controversy complain about the other, although it may help
that person let off steam in a way that allows the person to
function in a less disrupted fashion. Hearing one person's side of
things, one may help, if help is desired, by pointing out alterna-

tive ways of understanding what is going on and alternative resolutions of the conflict. However, it is important to remember that, hearing one person's side of things, one really has no balance to what one hears. The various sides of the story are almost always discrepant. Often the best thing to do with a person's complaints about a boss, coworker, or subordinate is to ask whether the person has talked to the other and to encourage that the two talk out their difficulty together.

In business families in which conflict is powerful and in which family members are not achieving resolution, the business may benefit if it can be organized to keep combatants apart. In such businesses people accept their differences, agree to disagree, and structure the business to minimize friction resulting from the differences. For example, at least four businesses in the sample seemed to be organized so that people who might be at odds with each other managed relatively autonomous divisions. Such decoupling of units (Davis and Stern, 1980) makes sense in some businesses, although it is impossible or very harmful in others. There are more possibilities for coping with unresolved family conflict through organized apartness in businesses with divisible activities, especially if not much contact is needed between divisions, if the business is large, and if the business operates in a large or protected market. Even if family members in serious conflict cannot achieve adequate apartness and even if their conflict is debilitating to business operations, the business may survive. As Davis and Stern (1980) point out, businesses in well-established markets may be in a good position to survive and profit even though the management structure is hampered in day-to-day operations or in innovation by family conflict or the employment of relatively incompetent family members in key roles.

Selection and Training of a Successor

In family businesses, selecting and training a successor requires considerable management expertise. As a transition develops, it is important for a chief officer to allow a potential successor autonomous managerial experience (Alcorn, 1982, pp.

138–140). Many successors acquire managerial experience and fresh perspectives in organizations other than the family firm. But even with such experience, a potential successor who has entered the family business may require quite a bit of latitude and room to learn from mistakes. Consequently, training for succession may require the potential successor to have an area (say, a branch operation) of control. In some cases, as mentioned in Chapter Ten, a chief officer seemed to help the growth of successors by going on extended vacations.

From a family systems point of view, it is important to realize that the training of a successor requires the training of several family members. Most important of all, a chief officer who expects or aspires to be replaced by a younger family member must do a great deal of self-education. The chief officer must learn to manage so as to allow the junior person to acquire on-the-job management experience and must acquire interests and abilities that will allow a gratifying life during and after the transition in power.

As we said in our discussion of succession in Chapter Ten, planning for retirement or for the untimely death of the chief officer was uncommon in our sample. This was so even though management is almost by definition a planful activity. We believe that effective managerial planning for succession requires both organizational and personal preparation. The obvious gains from such planning include continuity of operations throughout the succession process, a minimum of conflict over how the transition will occur and who will occupy what role, and survival of the business.

In planning for succession, it may be useful to provide for outside evaluation of family successors. People may be biased both for (Trow, 1961) and against their own kin. Nonrelated, professional evaluators and advisers may determine whether a potential successor has requisite abilities and dispositions, has learned what is necessary, and is ready for the next step (McGivern, 1978). The incompetence of a potential successor may delay succession (Trow, 1961). The incompetent or slow-learning potential successor may need additional training or may need to be shunted into a role other than that of potential successor.

Knowing When to Call In a Business Consultant

Family businesses, more often than other businesses, may benefit from calling in a consultant (Christensen, 1953). Being stuck in a conflict or suspecting that business problems originate in or are magnified by family problems may be clues that a business consultant is needed. The problems in planning and executing intergenerational succession so common in the businesses we studied and in those studied by others (for example, Christensen, 1953) often can be reduced by calling in outsiders, either consultants or members of the board of directors who are not family members.

Another sign that a consultant may be needed is that there seem to be many business problems entangled in a relatively undifferentated mess—for example, tensions over succession seem to be linked to problems in knowing who can decide what, tensions over money, disagreements over hiring and firing, and family members' sabotaging one another's business decisions. A failure to encapsulate specific issues incapacitates people as problem solvers (Davis and Stern, 1980) and signals a need for change and perhaps a need to hire an expert change agent.

People may be reluctant to call in a consultant and may believe that a consultant would be excessively expensive. We certainly would not say that every consultant or every consultation by every consultant will pay off, but some of the people we interviewed felt that consultation had been beneficial.

> "If the kids are forced into the business, which we were not, sometimes I think there's a tendency for them to think they're doing more work than the other family members. We solved that years ago by . . . we had a counselor in here, a business counselor. We really hired the business counselor because this was about the time when our father was pretty well out of the business, and we were looking around and we were saying maybe we *had* better be a little careful about how we expand. We thought, at the time, the business counselor was very expensive. It was the best money we ever spent, of course. It cost us about $5,000 for a three-week consultation" (036A).

Consultants can provide a wide range of services, from helping
to evaluate sales strategies to providing an overview of organizational structure, from assessing competences of individual
managers to defusing long-term conflict. The consultant sought
and the questions asked of the consultant presumably arise
from the concerns of the persons seeking consultation, but a
good consultant often finds that it is important to redefine the
issues, to point out that there are other ways of understanding
what is going on (see Chapter Fourteen). These alternative views
of reality are part of the consultant's problem-solving reper-
toire. Once a situation is redefined, new solutions to problems
may appear. One must have some understanding of what is
needed in order to call in a consultant, but a good consultant
may transform one's understandings by providing an alternative
view of reality.

Conclusion

Throughout this book, suggestions are made about management in the area of parent/offspring and husband/wife relationships. There are also suggestions about management when a
business is operated at home, about dealing with personnel in
the business who are not family members, about the value of
obtaining others' opinions, and about self-management of the
entrepreneur's own motivation. The present chapter reviewed
and extended the discussion of the management implications of
the linkage of business system and family. Tactics for managing
a family business were outlined, issues in and approaches to selection and training of a successor were discussed, and suggestions were made about when a management consultant should
be called in.

On the basis of our interview material, we have presented
in this chapter a number of specific recommendations for managing the family business. These recommendations—to have an
explicit division of labor, to prepare for management succession,
and so on—are important, but we think the overriding issue to
keep track of is that family businesses involve the family, including those family members not actively involved in the busi-

ness. In any business, management decisions are more than simply economic choices, but especially in a business connected to a family, more than economics must be considered. Attending to family relationships inevitably makes managing the family business a challenging task, but doing things "right" may have a big payoff for the business and for the family.

Chapter Thirteen

Therapy for People in Business Families

This chapter provides an overview for therapists who work with members of business-operating families. Therapy is, of course, not the only route to insight and change. People from business-operating families may find perspective and stimulus to change outside therapy—for example, through participation in local or national organizations such as the National Family Business Council or the Young Presidents Organization. They may also find perspective and stimulus to change through reading books like this one. But for many business families in serious difficulty, therapy may be the most effective source of help, and this chapter addresses major therapeutic considerations in working with such families.

The symptoms that bring members of business families to therapy are not necessarily different from those that bring other families. They include marital conflict, anxiety, eating disorders, sexual problems, depression, and stress-related physical symptoms such as high blood pressure. Some problems that members of business families bring to a therapist may exist only because of the family's involvement with the business, but perhaps most would have been present even without the business involvement. However, business involvement may aggravate or magnify many problems, may shape the form and content of

230

problems, may affect how people try to deal with their problems, and will certainly provide the therapist with added challenge in helping a family deal with its problems.

A therapist may build rapport with members of business-
operating families, may join members of business families,
through showing awareness of the tensions and stresses that are
common in such families. This book offers such an awareness,
as well as help in identifying and diagnosing the family's situation. An understanding of the symptoms will help the therapist
to see how the business may be affecting the family and to see
that any change a therapist tries to facilitate may have an impact on the business or be resisted because of the business.
Therapy with members of business-operating families must be
done with an awareness of the influence of the business on family relationships. It is for this reason that some therapists who
work with people in business-operating families bring in business consultants or themselves learn how to do business consulting, addressing issues of ownership, organization, management,
tax law, and so on. Similarly, organizational consultants working with family businesses often bring in therapists or find that
their organizational intervention seems to have a therapeutic
effect.

One expression of the interweaving and overlap of family
system and business system is that, with the same personnel involved in both systems, patterns that occur in one system will
occur in the other. For example, the management of family
members in the family-owned business, particularly when such
management is carried out by a parent or grandparent, can be
expected to parallel the "management" of family members in
the family. Thus, similarities in rules and style related to system management tasks (role allocation, communication, individuation, goal setting, and so on) can be expected in the two
systems. In multigeneration businesses these may be found to
represent patterns that have persisted across the generations,
and a therapist may usefully guide a family to explore such family "management" patterns as a way of providing a perspective
on what family members are experiencing.

This chapter is not a comprehensive statement about

therapy with any family. It is written to emphasize therapeutic issues that seem to us to arise again and again in dealing with members of business families. The emphasis in this chapter is on boundary maintenance and on individuation, two processes that overlap but allow different perspectives on what is needed for most business families to function adequately. The two processes are important in business families because the linking of family system and business system, the intense commitment of some members of business families to the business, and the continued contact of kin, particularly parents and offspring, make boundary and individuation issues especially important.

This chapter also addresses issues of sexism and of money. Sexism is important in that patterns involving gender differences in rights, privileges, compensation, and so on seem to make trouble for many business families and seem to rest on cultural assumptions that many people do not think to question. Money is important because in many business families it is a key locus of meaning and of problems.

Boundaries

Boundaries are a major issue for members of business-operating families. Tension in individual family members or in relationships between family members may arise in part because boundaries between business life and home life or between family members involved in the business may be diffuse or poorly developed. This is not to say that boundary tension is necessarily bad. Boundary tension seems inherent in all social systems. It may reflect the normal dynamics of people with differing views, needs, wants, and standards. It may reflect ordinary goal conflict within the business, ordinary decision-making processes, or ordinary efforts to develop or maintain boundaries. But people may be debilitated by their boundary problems and be in a position to benefit from work on those problems.

Role Confusion. In business-operating families, one of the more common boundary problems is role confusion. People may inappropriately carry over roles from one place to another. A dominating father may try to be a dominating boss to a family member in the business; a person who has difficulty making decisions in the family may resist making decisions at work; a dependent offspring at home may try to be a dependent employee. Where such role carryovers impede the achievement of individual or system goals, or where individual or system well-being seems undermined by a role carryover, it may be important to help clients to separate the roles and to negotiate mutually acceptable terms for carrying them out.

Here is an example of one approach to treatment of role confusion in a business family. A couple worked together in a business in which the husband's services were in high demand from customers. The wife served as the bookkeeper for the business and also filled in, along with a paid employee, as receptionist and as an assistant to her husband. She was referred for therapy by a physician who considered her physical symptoms to have arisen from the stress of the situation she was in. Her husband was willing to participate with her in therapy and to work at making changes. One of the issues that emerged in the therapy was that the power differential in the business kept her feeling one-down and inadequate. His expertise, experience, and community reputation meant that he was in a position to tell her what to do, and she could not bring things back into a balance. Moreover, the pattern of his telling her what to do at work carried subtly into their home life. In this case, the therapy produced efforts toward substantial change without much effort by the therapist. Simply making the issues of power differential at work and carryover to home life salient helped immensely. The husband seemed not to have realized what he had been doing, and he was willing to work at changing. At the same time, the therapy helped the wife gain self-confidence to express her own reality, needs, opinions, and wants directly. Once she could do this, they were able to deal with other issues and together to redefine her responsibilities at work so that she had more autonomy in certain decision areas and so that he would less often have to tell her what to do there.

In couples or families in which individuals are relatively well differentiated from each other and from the business, therapy often takes the form of help with problem solving. In couples and families in which differentiation is not so clear, therapy ordinarily must be more extensive. Not only must problems be solved, but a groundwork must be laid that enables the problems to be solved. In some cases, the groundwork cannot be achieved satisfactorily, and then the best that can be accomplished may be a makeshift or partial problem solution or perhaps a break in relationship of person with person or of person with business.

Togetherness and Apartness. Persons who are involved together in a business may have a problem in obtaining sufficient apartness, or the way they go about obtaining sufficient apartness may be problem-creating. A parent and an adult offspring working together or siblings or spouses working together may need greater independence, both within the business and outside. It may be important for the persons involved to recognize the need for separateness, not to feel threatened or insulted by expressions of this need, and to develop ways of getting such separateness that are easy to live with.

Maintaining sufficient contact is a problem in some business-operating families, a problem that may be related to the entrepreneur's immersion in the business. Somebody who is away at the business or preoccupied with it most waking hours may not be sufficiently available to other family members. For an entrepreneur whose business seems on the margin of survival or profitability, it may be difficult to devote time to family matters, yet it is important that the losses in not attending to the family be understood and the profits from increased contact with family members be appreciated. For spouse and children, a spouse/parent who is away or preoccupied most waking hours may not be sufficiently available to meet family goals and needs. One key to dealing with the situation is to help family members to realize that seeing things as a matter of one commitment versus the other, all or nothing, either/or, can be a source of difficulty. The entrepreneur may be helped to find and to gain new appreciation for family goals.

In one example of therapy with a couple where too much togetherness and too much apartness were both problems, a couple owned and together operated a business with great seasonal variations in work load. The therapy had arisen out of a physician's referral of the wife for help with stress-related symptoms, and the husband's cooperation in the therapy was fueled by his concern about his wife's symptoms. The woman had been very afraid to disagree about anything with her husband, and the therapy dealt with a number of conflict issues besides the ones of togetherness and apartness. The therapy worked on developing communication skills in both partners and on legitimating negotiation. The couple eventually negotiated both greater time together during the heavy work season and greater time apart during the light work season. The husband had been very reluctant to get away from the business during the heavy season, and he thought the negotiated togetherness away from the business was somehow artificial and game-playing. But after the couple had tried it out a few times, he seemed to enjoy the time together and to become committed to it. His gains seemed to include increased trust for the employees he left in charge of the business and a genuine appreciation of how much of a difference the time together made for his wife. For apartness during light work seasons, the couple had to develop separate interests and friendships. They were both at first somewhat fearful of doing so, but they both seemed to value the apartness once they saw that their relationship would survive and at times benefit from their separateness.

Boundaries Between Entrepreneur and Business. Related to the need for boundaries between people is the need for boundaries between entrepreneur and business. In a sense the preceding therapeutic example is one of boundaries between entrepreneur and business. One point to be emphasized here is that, in doing therapy with members of business families, a key issue may be that the entrepreneur lacks sufficient distance from the business, that he or she is overidentified with the business. Without that separation, the entrepreneur may perceive issues in home life as so significant for the business as to be very resistant to persuasion or compromise. The entrepreneur may have difficulty balancing his or her business role with his or her relatively ignored family and social roles. In addition, the entrepreneur who experiences the business as an extension of self may also see family members as extensions of self. It may then be difficult to grasp or to validate the legitimacy of individual family members' varying interests, values, goals, and needs. The entrepreneur may expect that family members will want to direct their energies in service of the business and may experience family members with little commitment to or interest in the business as disloyal or ungrateful. The entrepreneur who does not see that what is good for the business and for him or her may not be good for other family members may not perceive, accept, or tolerate other family members who feel little or no commitment to the business.

Differentiation of family members is much easier when it is legitimate for individuals to differ in their commitment to the business, in their perspectives and opinions, and in anything else, whether connected to the business or not. In some cases therapy may, however, succeed more in differentiating other family members from the entrepreneur and the business than in differentiating the entrepreneur from the business. For example, consider a couple who jointly owned and operated a business in which the husband spent virtually every waking moment. The business seemed well established and not in danger of failure were he to spend less time there. The wife came for therapy both depressed and angry. Her husband's unwillingness to be a companion to her away from the business, to participate in parenting of the children, to help out with household chores, or to take her seriously was upsetting her. He was willing to join his wife in the therapist's office, but despite many attempts to negotiate differences he did not seem to take his wife's interests seriously. He seemed to think that things were as they had to be and that his wife's concerns were not matters in which she would continue to have strong feelings. However, she was uncompromising in her desire to have her husband be more available in the ways that were important to her, and her anger about their differences persisted. In this example it may be that long-existing relationship issues came to a head through "symptoms" centering on the family business. She decided to get a divorce. Even though one's ideal for therapy with a couple like that might be to resolve differences and to develop a strong marital relationship, the divorce did lead to an ending of the wife's anger and depression, while the husband continued to have the business involvement he seemed to want. In the divorce property settlement, the business was divided, and each ex-spouse received and became sole proprietor of a viable, separate business; his absorbed all his waking hours and hers received substantially less time commitment.

Another issue of boundary between business and family is mood carryover. As discussed in Chapter Eight, entrepreneurs sometimes bring bad moods from business to home. The carryover may mean both that the entrepreneur is relatively unavailable emotionally to the family and that family members may be targets for anger and blaming arising from business issues. The therapist may help the family to see that when feelings arise at the business, it is ineffective for both business and family goals to direct the feelings to people who are at home, and that direct communication of feelings to persons with whom the difficulty occurred in the business is more likely to help resolve an issue. A person may legitimately be angry with members of the family, but venting anger at people who are not the primary source of distress is destructive and unhelpful. Clarifying that it is inappropriate to carry over anger from work to home may require some differentiation of roles in the home setting from roles in the work setting and of entrepreneurial self from business. That is, minimizing the carryover of bad mood from work to home may require the entrepreneur to learn how to leave work at work and to see business roles and family roles as separate. Therapeutic help might also include helping the family members to identify more effective methods of directing their feelings as a way of achieving their goals and to understand that the form in which feelings are communicated is a choice.

One therapeutic approach to achieving boundaries is to question the belief that what is good for the business is good for the family. Family sessions may be an arena in which therapist support of family members' self-disclosure may help all family members to see that it may not be good for the family to promote the business through working at home, through preoccupation with the business while at home, through devoting enormous amounts of time to the business, or through minimizing household expenditures in favor of investing in the business. Family sessions may help to illuminate the costs of seeing family members as extensions of the entrepreneur's self. In a family session, members may air resentments over exploitation—for example, being expected to work without pay or with inappropriately low pay in the business or being expected to cover for the entrepreneur at home when he or she is not there to do an appropriate amount of childcare or household maintenance. The therapist may highlight family rules in regard to availability and nurturance. Such rules take various forms, ranging from an active, explicit statement of expectation to a passive assumption that one's needs for help and one's unavailability will be understood without one's having to ask. Although a business may need a great deal of attention in order to provide an adequate or satisfactory income to a family, one clue that an entrepreneur has not worked toward relatively clear boundaries between self and others or self and business is a constant, often explicitly rationalized subordination of family priorities to business priorities. In family sessions the entrepreneur's denial can be challenged when family members are able to identify and represent their own feelings and needs.

It is important to point out that an entrepreneur cannot make the business preeminent in the family and cannot exploit other family members if they are unwilling to go along. To challenge the system, the therapist must avoid "ganging up" with family members who have covertly or overtly made it seem as though the entrepreneur were the sole source of troubles. Family members who have gone along with diffuse boundaries between the business and the family but who are now seeking some kind of change will need to be encouraged to consider their own part and their potential gains and losses from giving up those diffuse boundaries. For example, offspring who want Dad to change but who want to maintain the right to be protected by him may need to be confronted with their wanting to have it both ways. They may need coaching to accept adult responsibility and to grieve for the loss of youthful privileges. Offspring who see their own ability to operate as full adults in the business as dependent on the entrepreneurial parent's acceptance of and response to them as adults may need to be directed to choices and alternatives available to them that are not connected to waiting for the entrepreneur/parent to change.

The therapist's work may also be focused on differentiation of individual boundaries and goals within the family, differentiation of business goals from family goals, and some sort of joint work toward seeing that not all goals are subordinated to the goals of one person or one place. Of course, if everyone in the family likes the situation the way it is, it would be inappropriate for the therapist to push for a change, but presumably the therapist has been engaged to help produce some sort of change. Nonetheless, many business families may function in a way that seems satisfactory to their members without differentiation of goals and without clarifying boundaries or addressing other difficulties that are the source of tensions in some business families.

Triangulation. The continued close contact of people in some business families makes such families ripe for triangulation problems. Triangulation arises when people ally against somebody. Such alliances are common where people feel powerless, where they avoid direct communication and confrontation, where they cannot tolerate perceptions and beliefs that differ from their own, where secret keeping is the rule, or where some people "protect" others. Triangulation also arises where somebody caught in conflicting demands of others in the family chooses not to do something to resolve the problem. In general, triangulation occurs where internal boundaries are formed in the family such that some people are allied against others or where people put conflicting demands on somebody who is not disposed to say "Stop." Triangulation can thus be understood as a boundary issue.

In what may be the most common triangle in business families, in a system of three persons related as parent/supervisor, offspring/husband/supervised, and daughter-in-law/wife, there is ample opportunity for any two of them to behave in a way that leads the third to feel entrapped in conflicting demands. Because women are often symptom bearers, family

members who react with the strongest expressed tension in the
system, perhaps in triangle relationships it is most often the
daughter-in-law/wife who appears for therapy (just as it is often
the wife who appears for therapy in corporate families; see Gullotta and Donohue, 1981). In such cases the therapist must be
alert to tensions that may be involved in the relationship between the husband and father-in-law. The triangulating may be
intensified by scapegoating patterns that develop as tension is
projected onto the identified patient, who is cast as the family
problem.

Individuation

Therapy with business-operating families will often con-
front issues of individuation, of failures to grant and achieve
sufficient autonomy and separateness from other family members. These issues may be confronted in the family first or in
the business first, but in either case successful confrontation
will probably have an impact in both places.

In our interviews we most often heard of sons trying to
separate from parents, but there were also instances of brothers
trying to separate from brothers, daughters trying to separate
from parents, and perhaps wives trying to separate from husbands. In the family, the issues of individuation may be played
out through trying to be different from somebody else, trying
to break away from somebody else's control, trying to have
more privacy, or choosing goals different from what another
would endorse. Development of individuation proceeds through
several stages. At the first stage a person who is trying to individuate is locked into a pattern of complying with and defying
the values, ideas, and goals from which he or she is trying to
break away. Both a compliant "yes" and a defiant "no" are
within the pattern. The "yes" and the "no" are both connected
to seeking approval or permission from the other, who has been
an important figure to depend on. The "dependency" figure is,
in this first stage of individuating, empowered and complied
with but also defied. In stage one, togetherness/apartness energies seem directed to getting more from the other or to protect-

ing oneself from the other. Energy in such systems tends to be focused on the relationship. Often this focus diverts energy from other important tasks and goals. Nonetheless, the movement away from simple compliance while still within the original system seems often to be an important step. That may have been what was going on with one respondent who had benefited from individual therapy.

> "I went to a psychologist and I got my head screwed on right as to where I think I'm supposed to be and what my parents' relationship to my life is supposed to be. I had to have a big emotional showdown with my mother. Almost like 'Hey, I'm a big boy. I'm leaving your house; I'm leaving your control, and I'm going on my own.' It took something like that" (101A).

At a more individuated stage, one accepts and negotiates personal differences in goals, values, and standards, and also the implications of such differences, without defying and without seeking permission, affirmation, and approval as primary goals. Energies are freed to make decisions and to attend to various ideas, tasks, and goals.

The stages of individuation are also played out in the realm of geographical and psychic distance. At an initial stage one may remain close to those from whom one is individuating. At a next stage, one may have to move very far away, because with closeness one is still too strongly influenced. Although this step in individuating is common in families, it may occur less frequently in business-operating families. Many offspring in business families never move far, physically or psychologically, from kin. Consequently, some of them may have difficulty reaching the next stage of individuation, in which one can be close and still be differentiated. An individuated offspring may or may not choose to enter or to continue in the family business but will not simply take it for granted that the business is the right place for him or her and will not enter or stay in order to gain a parent's approval or to make a parent proud. Therapy that promotes individuation may support an offspring who is trying to decide whether to be in the business to be clear about personal needs and dispositions.

In an example in which autonomy and individuation were at issue, a man in his thirties who had succeeded to the role of chief officer in the family business was referred for therapy by a physician who believed the young man's physical problems were stress-related. Although the man's father had, on paper, given control of the business to his son, the father was, according to the son, interfering, extremely critical, and frequently undermining of the son's efforts. Although the father refused to join in the therapy, the client's mother and sister did, and they confirmed the client's view of what was going on. The therapeutic process strengthened the son's bonds with his sister, and in the end the son took a stand with his father, saying that he would leave if the interference did not end. That confrontation seemed to be a turning point. Previously he had been afraid to take such a stand or even to tell his father how he felt, although he felt furious. The son's self-esteem had been quite low, and he seemed to have been very dependent on his father. The therapy had led the son to the realization that he could survive even if he left the business, and the successful confrontation communicated to his father things his father might not have realized. The confrontation led to higher self-esteem for the son and to a firm control of the business.

If individuation occurs for all adults in a family, they may feel close or not, but they will be tolerant and respecting of their differences and not be battling over whose right it is to do something, want something, believe something, or plan something. This does not mean they will not experience anger and disappointment. Family members may disagree and may express strong feelings about their differences. The bottom line, however, is that each person's right to disagree will be accepted without rancor or judgmental rejection. In a family that has achieved individuation, or among family members who have done so, working together in the business would allow them freedom to differ from one another and even freedom to go their separate ways without punishment, retaliation, or an end to interaction. They would not be tied to the business. However, where individuation has not been achieved or is still an issue in family struggles, relations in the business may be tense in several ways. A sort of dictatorship may exist, in which the boss tells others what to do and they simply do it, or there may be recurrent struggles over control, goals, rights, duties, credit, and other issues, with arguments and feelings running at several levels. On a surface level, the issue is who knows best, who is competent, who has the right to do what, or who deserves what. At another level, one more likely to be below the surface and not discussed directly, the issue may be gratitude (are you grateful to me or not), loyalty (are you loyal to me or selfish, loyal to the family or selfish), freedom, or the right to be seen as a grownup (however one defines *grownup*).

Therapy designed to support the individuation process that will help get past family struggles may not succeed in producing individuation but may lead to some sort of disengagement that will preserve the family relationship. In one example of therapy where individuation was an issue, a couple came for therapy with the husband's physical abuse of the wife as the presenting problem. At that time it seemed quite likely that she would seek a divorce. They jointly owned and operated a business. Previously she had done managerial work in a very different kind of business, and one of the sources of tension in their relationship was that he felt that, through her managerial efforts, she was taking over things in his province. The therapy was associated with a number of individual and couple changes but not with an individuation that would enable them to work out their differences with regard to business roles. However, she left the business and returned to her own line of work. She subsequently said that "it was the smartest thing I ever did." That change, along with two other important changes, seemed responsible for the continuing survival of their marriage and an improved relationship. The therapy did not lead to great individuation but it did lead to enough to allow her to leave the business, and her departure insulated the marriage from some of the effects of their comparatively low level of individuation.

Relations in business families where individuation has not been achieved may also be tense because offspring and other family members in the business may be giving mixed messages to the entrepreneur or to other senior family members in the business. They may be saying, in effect, "Tell me what to do, but treat me like an adult and let me make my own decisions." Or they may be saying, "fix things if they go wrong and accept the blame if there is trouble, but accept me as I am and acknowledge that I am entitled to adult financial benefits and adult social independence. Treat me as an adult when it's to my advantage, but don't expect me to take adult responsibility when it's painful." Such ambivalence about dependence and independence may well be rooted in how the family member who is a business subordinate has been treated, but the mixed message may well enhance tensions for a family member who is senior in the business and create no-win situations for all involved.

Whether a therapist takes on the individuation issues at the level of home life or at the level of the business, there is likely to be an impact at both places. In the United States, a moderate level of individuation seems to be valued, and movement toward greater individuation is more common than movement toward less. With such cultural support for individuation, the therapeutic task may be to facilitate movement toward greater individuation without denigrating family members who resist it and while helping people to see what all family members could gain and lose from the individuation. The gains may well include the comfort of contact with other full adults and relief from the pressures of having to carry a lot or too little. An entrepreneur will be closer to having an autonomous offspring (or perhaps spouse) who could take over the business or will know that family succession is unlikely and that plans should be made accordingly. For the offspring, sibling, or spouse who is trying to individuate or at least has some interest in it, what there is to gain includes responsibility, freedom, self-respect, and a chance for a more adult relationship with the person from whom she or he is individuating. An offspring may lose the privileges of the child status, and parents may lose desired control and assurance of contact through being needed. The therapist can help family members to find new ways to be connected as well as individuated, realizing that people may resist the individuation because the pattern of dependence can be rewarding and comfortable.

People working for a relative with whom differentiation is limited have the opportunity to remain dependent and perhaps are under substantial systemic pressure to remain so. Even in a culture that seems to value independence, people can find substantial rewards in dependency. The rewards include freedom from major responsibilities and from making choices about important things when there is a risk of mistake. Some people, both younger family members involved in a business and more senior ones, may find having someone else to blame an advantage. So it seems not unlikely that both the older and the younger members of a business-operating family may have substantial conflict over matters of dependence and independence. Therapy that puts such matters on the table may be helpful in reframing and resolving the conflict. The therapist may need to struggle with the subordinate's feelings of entitlement "to be taken care of," and all family members may benefit from being shown that age-appropriate "care" may involve promoting the development of autonomy and responsibility.

We are not saying here that individuation is unambiguously desirable. There may be costs all around as a family member becomes individuated. Individuation becomes critically important, however, if a person's self-esteem is reduced by dependence, if the person's marital relationship is undermined because of dependence on spouse or parent, or if a person is crippled in making adult decisions about personal or business matters.

Sexism

For those doing therapy with people connected to a family business, issues of sexism may become salient. Women may seem to be discounted. For example, a woman's role in the business may be only to provide her name, as a convenience in the legal process of incorporation. She may be used only in support roles. She may be expected to be available to the business at the pleasure of the man or men who manage it, and her work may

be undercompensated or even uncompensated. Female offspring may not receive encouragement, opportunity, and education that would qualify them to move toward an executive or
ownership role in the business, whereas male offspring may well
be given such help. As a business becomes more successful, its
success is likely to be credited to men, in part perhaps because
the women are devalued financially or not given credit for organizational contributions. That success, along with the financial and managerial power the men acquire, may help to keep
women in the family in a one-down relationship with those
men. Daughters may be "bought off" with support stipends
while sons acquire business expertise and control and achieve
wealth through the business. Whatever clients' understandings
of the business world, it may be important to emphasize the
family costs of sexism, that it prevents the family from being
one of autonomous, mutually respectful, egalitarian adults.
It may be important, too, to recognize the issue as one of dou-
ble standards for individuals. The family can gain much from
treating the interests, values, opinions, abilities, and needs of
its female members at a high level and equal to the level for
men. However, in the short run, the men and perhaps the wom-
en of a family moving to egalitarian relationships may experience the move as an unpleasant loss of privilege and a threat to
the ego, to the family, and to the business. They may need help
and recurrent assurance of eventual gains to continue working
toward reducing and ending sexism.

Money

A final issue to be aware of in doing therapy with business-operating families is money. As the stakes rise, as the possibility for substantial wealth becomes greater, relationships become more complicated (Marcus, 1980, 1983). Concerns about
capital and income create motives that affect an individual's as-
pirations, hopes, and concerns and complicate the individual's
relationships with other family members. A therapist would do
well to make money issues salient in therapy with anyone from
a business family. It is important to probe for such issues as a

younger person's money-connected unwillingness to differentiate from parents and grandparents, jealousies and suspicions that are money-connected, use of financial incentives and threats, bribes paid in exchange for loyalty or to buy off anger, and misuse of money as a way to "punish" another family member. Money is a major source of secrets in business families, and family rules about talking about money help to maintain secrets and make therapy that touches on money issues more challenging.

A key money-connected problem common in business-operating families is the failure to discuss succession and inheritance. At one level, such a failure can be understood as a neglect of responsibility by entrepreneurial parents and spouses. At another level, it can be understood as a matter of family secrets, with all the destructive power of such secrets (Karpel, 1980). The destructiveness occurs in a number of ways. Some people may be in on the secret or partly in on it, so that coalitions are created within the family, dividing sibling from sibling or parent from offspring. Another route to destructiveness when there are secrets is that they leave people guessing about what the facts are, often with anxiety and with fantasies that may be harmfully misleading, misleading in a way that sets people up for disappointment and leaves them ill prepared to cope with what actually eventuates. Secrets are also understandable as power maneuvers. To have a big secret is to control others or to foster their dependence. It is a cancerous kind of control of dependence, because it creates distance and distrust between the secret holder and those who want to know the secret; in that sense, secrets are divisive. An entrepreneur may say, "I don't want people to know what my plans or my will are because I might change them," but it is certainly legitimate to tell others that such-and-such are one's plans and one's will but that they are subject to change. Once one is open with others about succession and inheritance, it is possible to interact about the issues and perhaps to do necessary planning together for the eventual changes. The entrepreneur may then learn that there is more to be considered than was initially realized—for example, that different family members have different ideas about what division of the estate is fair or about who should succeed to the chief officer role. To learn these things is not so much a problem as an opportunity to work toward mutual understanding and to search for problem solutions that may be acceptable to all.

Many entrepreneurs seem conflict-avoidant or seem to avoid thinking about or dealing with issues of retiring or dying. By not discussing succession and inheritance with family members, by not working out a succession plan or an estate plan, one may avoid conflict with family members and ego threats associated with mortality and giving up a way of life. As with other avoidance issues, a therapist with sufficient rapport may challenge and push. A therapist with less rapport may finesse the issues by broaching threatening topics in diluted form. One might, for example, talk about five-year plans or about a review of business and personal tax situations. The therapist may focus discussion mainly on what is appropriate for any well-run business, steering the discussion toward business-world norms. The talk would then focus on plans and papers that are appropriate for any business, long-range plans, key executive insurance, back-up contingencies if key persons leave the business, and so on.

Conclusion

It is often useful in counseling to reframe or redefine people's concerns, anxieties, and upsets. For business-operating families, this book may be helpful in showing how common certain business-connected problems are. It may help therapists and clients to know that the family is not unusual if there is tension between parent and adult offspring in the business. (In fact, tension may be a good sign.) It may help therapists and clients to know that the family is not unusual if the wife finds herself feeling isolated and unappreciated by a husband who puts all his waking energy into the business. It may help to know that problems are in part situationally connected, and it may be helpful to point out that a resentful wife's anger is a systemic response to her husband's absenteeism and to an expectation that she agree to accommodate to his assumption that his needs are more valid than hers. Both may be helped to see their joint contribution to polarization of goals, his needs and goals being blurred with those of the business, her needs and goals being blurred with those of the family, and perhaps neither person's needs and goals being met. Framing the problem as a common family/business system disorder may free people to work toward a system that benefits the family and the business. Work with such couples may, however, require additional therapeutic efforts. To the extent that the couple can be understood as narcissistically vulnerable, the entrepreneur perhaps wanting a spouse who is always approving and who never disagrees and the spouse wanting attention at all times, both may need work on empathy, at recognizing narcissistic and cognitive distortions, at dealing with narcissistic rage, and at solving problems constructively (Feldman, 1982).

What brings members of business-operating families into therapy is typically what brings people from any family into therapy. Almost never are business issues the presenting problems or the only problems presented. Even when business issues are presented or have emerged, they often rest on a substratum of problems like those found in any family. A therapist knowledgeable about business families, however, may be more effective in joining clients in a business family and may be in a much better position to address important business issues. Business issues quite often become increasingly important as therapy with members of business-operating families progresses. Family changes may be resisted because of business concerns, and any family change that is engineered may have an impact on the business.

Two key issues emerge recurrently in therapy with members of business families because of the connection of business system and family system: boundary issues and individuation. For families with clear boundaries, adequate individuation, and adequate communication skills, therapy will have the quality of problem solving. For other families, however, therapy must work to provide boundaries, individuation, and communication skills that will enable subsequent problem solving.

Therapy with business families may be less often success-

ful than work with other families. The business involvements reduce people's felt freedom to change. We have given examples
of successful therapeutic interventions with business families,
but we certainly can also provide examples of failed therapy, of
entrepreneurs' wives who remained chronically depressed, of
parents and offspring who remained estranged, and of siblings
who continued not to be on speaking terms. Nonetheless, we
hope that this book will make it easier for therapists to help
business families deal with their problems.

Chapter Fourteen

Consulting with Family Businesses

"We had a counselor in here, a business counselor. We split up the business so each person has his category which he's responsible for, and of course if the thing falls on its face, it's not hard to figure out whose fault it is. We really hired him because this was about the time when our father was pretty well out of the business, and we were looking around and we were saying maybe we *had* better be a little careful about how we expand. We thought, at the time, he was very expensive. It was the best money we ever spent, of course. It cost us about $5,000 for a three-week consultation" (036A).

Organizational consultants are not often called into smaller family businesses. In addition to the possible stigma of calling in outside help (Steele, 1975, p. 1) and perhaps consultants' lack of interest in a business with a small income, there may be a great deal of conservatism in family-owned businesses, particularly those operated by an entrepreneur/founder (Cohn and Lindberg, 1974, p. 2). Even when someone in a family business contacts a consultant, the consultation is rarely carried through to completion. Levinson (1983) estimates that only 10 percent of such contacts lead to a consummated consultation. Often the

251

person who contacts the consultant is a younger family member, perhaps most often a son or younger brother of the chief executive officer. The contact may be motivated by the person's pain and anxiety resulting from feeling one-down, from ambiguities in the succession process, or from feeling undermined in managerial activities. At another level, contacting a consultant may be understood as a tactical act in a power battle (see Baizerman and Hall, 1977, on consultation as a political process). If the consultant has not been called in by the chief executive officer, it may be difficult to interest the chief officer in consultation. The chief officer is unlikely to be feeling as much pain as the person who called in the consultant (Kets de Vries and Miller, 1984, p. 209; Levinson, 1983), does not need help to neutralize a more powerful other, and may not even want to work with a consultant who has heard another person's definition of the organizational difficulty. Even when the chief officer is involved in calling in a consultant, the involvement may be more a symbolic expression of concern about the feelings, possible resignation, or possible family estrangement of the younger family member, not an expression of strong interest in change.

Consultation issues in many organizations, not merely in family businesses, are made more difficult because conflicts and problems are often defined in terms of personalities. People tend to blame others and to try to avoid blaming themselves. So to be called in by one member of a family business may make the consultant appear to others in the family to have been persuaded that the person who called in the consultant is blame-free and that others are to be blamed. Although a consultant may, from the beginning of a consultation, make clear that blame is not an issue, emphasizing that situations are the source of problems and that situations can be changed, it may be very difficult to convince people who themselves are thinking in terms of guilt and innocence that one is not thinking in the same terms.

The frequent failure to get beyond the family member who has called one in means that a consultant to family businesses may have to be able to switch to the level of individual advising and referral. Advising an individual may help the individual in the short run but is unlikely to benefit the organization or to lead to organizational change (see Hirschhorn and Gilmore, 1980).

Because family business problems are often entangled in family problems, a business consultant needs to have good therapists to refer clients to, just as a consultant may need good accountants, good computer systems people, good people in the area of managerial evaluation and training, good tax lawyers, and other experts for work on particular problems of clients. Therapeutic referrals are also necessary because it would not be ethical to do therapy with an individual connected to an organization in which one has made organizational interventions or in which one may do so in the future. There is bound to be conflict of interest between what would benefit an individual and what would benefit an organization with which that individual is associated.

Typically a consultant is called in by an individual. The consultant and the client should negotiate, in the initial laying out of consultation ground rules, who the client is. Although the consultant may all along report to the individual who made the initial contact, a consultation with a family business, as with any organization, works best if the client is the organization. For example, trying to help a younger family member displace his or her parent will not be as helpful as trying to help a business come to terms with the problems of succession. Trying to help a brother in a power battle with a sibling is not as helpful as trying to help the business come to terms with the power battle. In the long run, business survival, profitability, and growth are promoted by consulting designed to benefit the whole business, and in the long run organizational change is facilitated when the client is the business. However, with family businesses the issue of defining the client may be complicated not only by the interests of the individual who contacted the consultant but also by the interests of the family. A business consultant can help a business meet such common business goals as profit, growth, and survival of the business. Yet business families often have a competing set (or even several sets) of family goals. Consultation is much more difficult when these family goals are taken into account. Indeed, some consultants would consider consultation that works toward family, as opposed to business, goals to be inappropriate or even illegitimate. We think it neither inappropriate nor illegitimate to take those other goals into account. Those other goals (for example, trying to keep the business in the family) are present and are being acted on in some way. Family members, we think, may legitimately want and receive help toward meeting family goals, but to try to help a family business achieve both business and family goals or to balance the two sets of goals makes the consultation task more demanding.

Challenges in Family Business Consultation

Consultation is more difficult with family businesses than with other businesses because of the entanglement of family and business. An organization constrained by the goals, limitations, demands, and so on of a business may have very little latitude for change. If consultation is an uphill battle when one is consulting with a nonfamily business (see Hirschhorn and Gilmore, 1980), how much more difficult it must be when the processes of change resistance within an organization are reinforced by resistances to change within the family! It is not merely that the business has some organizational patterns that will be difficult to change because they are connected, for example, to jealousies among executives, how the business is financed, and the architecture of the plant. It is also that the relationship of the chief officer's spouse, parents, children, cousins, grandparents, and in-laws with the business may push toward a status quo and away from solutions that might be obvious and rational were the business not a family one. For example, in one of the businesses we studied, a divorced father may have had more difficulty allowing his son autonomy in the business because of feelings that he had to prove to himself, his son, and his ex-wife that he was a good father. By his standards, a good father gave a son close supervision and considerable advice. Eventually the son was given managerial latitude, but achievement of that latitude might have come sooner had the son been unrelated. That may be another reason that consultation is comparatively rare with family businesses.

The entanglement of family and business also means that a consultant may be caught, from the very beginning, in the hostilities, alliances, and jealousies of the business family. Even to have an initial phone conversation with one person in the family may mean that one will be seen as having taken sides. Working free of the disabling aspects of being identified with one side or another in a dispute—avoiding being sucked into hostilities, jealousies, and alliances—adds to the work of consultation with a family-owned business.

When one consults with a nonfamily business, the cast of characters is usually defined by positions on the organizational chart. But with family-owned businesses, crucial characters may not appear on the chart. Thus, the task of the consultant may be complicated by the need to discover and perhaps to call in, certainly to address issues centering on, persons who have no direct relationship to or involvement in the business. Two brothers, for example, may find it difficult to resolve tensions in their business relationship that handcuff the organization because of their mother's concern that they remain connected in a certain way.

Some of the common problems of family businesses make the process of consultation more difficult. Family businesses have been alleged to have, more often than other businesses, managers whose ability is limited but who have been kept on because of their position in the family, because they are nonrelatives willing to accept a position without much opportunity to get to the top, or because of their ownership. Under such circumstances, a consultant may have to push to make education and outside, objective evaluation important (see Greiner and Metzger, 1983, pp. 302–303). This is not to take sides in personality conflicts or even to argue that managers of family businesses are less able than managers of other businesses. But it is to argue that rational evaluation and training of executives may be an important element in consulting with a business that needs some help.

Although the point may be overstated, it is often said that chief officers in family firms tend to behave conservatively and autocratically. They are, the stereotype has it, resistant to change and no longer interested in risk taking; they have power they enjoy using and wish to retain. To the extent that the stereotype is true, a consultant may have trouble promoting change. People who do not like change and have power they do not want to give up will limit the extent to which an intervention can produce anything other than more of the status quo, yet the very concentration of power is also an advantage to the consultant in that once the person with power is influenced, change can happen. Conservatism can also be an advantage in that it makes some avenues for change readily available. For example, if a consultant helps a business retain its name, identity, product line, and course, that may motivate a chief officer to make the changes that will allow those conservative goals to be met.

Consultation Processes

The demands of consultation situations are too variable and complex to allow for blanket generalizations, but ideally an important goal of any consultation should be enabling clients to deal with problems that will emerge in the future (Steele, 1975, pp. 3–4). A consultation should give an organization ways of solving problems and doing work that will help in dealing not only with immediate problems but also with future ones. In family businesses a successful consultation may, however, focus on a problem or issue that may never be faced again (for example, helping the founder organize a plan for succession to ownership), in which case problem-solving skills for the future may not be of much concern.

The first tool in a consultant's arsenal is a conceptual structure. A consultant needs a theory, a framework, a set of assumptions (Steele, 1975, p. 16). That does not mean that the consultant should be closed to what emerges or that the consultant should have a short list of diagnoses and cures to apply to all cases. But it does mean that the consultant needs to have some sense of what to look for in order to be able to see any-thing (Rosenblatt, 1981). This book provides a valuable set of ideas for approaching consultation with a family business, al-though people certainly are doing consultation with somewhat different perspectives (for example, Alcorn, 1982; Becker and Tillman, 1978; Danco, 1982a, 1982b; Danco and Jonovic, 1982; Jonovic, 1982; Kets de Vries and Miller, 1984; Levinson, 1983).

In approaching clients, a consultant needs to define a relationship with clients and to interpret the tasks to be accom-plished in terms that fit what the consultant can do. The goals of consultation are not to identify who is guilty and who is innocent, not to make others feel good, and perhaps not even to bring peace to organizations with inherent sources of conflict or to organizations that change and grow as a result of conflict. The goals of consultations are often multiple and subject to negotiation. For family businesses with problems, typically the primary goal of consultation is to help the client organization to change in some way in which the organization has been unable to change by itself. Perhaps most commonly, a consultant is called in when there is confusion over who does what, when a family member in a central role in the business seems to be doing poorly, when there are power battles between family members, when trouble occurs in the succession process, or when the business is doing badly although people do not con-ceptualize the issue as a family one.

Part of a consultant's definition of his or her relationship with a business should be to take the stance that different per-sons have different viewpoints and that the consultant needs to know them. From the beginning, the consultant should assert that each person's story is validly that person's story but that no person's story is "fact." Starting from that place, the con-sultant needs to elicit accounts of the business situation from more than one person. These accounts are important for sev-eral reasons. They are important because not everything to be known in order to consult effectively with a given business is on paper or otherwise obvious. They are important because good, interested listening can increase a consultant's rapport with the person speaking. And, of course, they are important because differing versions of reality will be present in different accounts and will need to be understood in order to provide effective consulting. Discrepancies between informants will point to lines of tension in interpersonal relationships and often to organizational problems such as overlap in jurisdiction or organizational goal conflicts. Discrepancies may represent miscommunication among persons involved in the business. In fact, to the extent that conflict produces misperception, it would be surprising if individuals in conflict had identical accounts.

The accounts people give will have a self-presentational aspect. Perceptions and understandings that people desire to communicate will be communicated; some things will be hidden. As various persons give their stories, the self-presentations will indicate to a consultant issues to be dealt with in order to facilitate change. One may not be able to see what is hidden, although it is certainly possible that some hidden things in one person's story will come out in another's. A consultant may not need to know what is unsaid in order to be useful, but a consultant may push family members either into dealing with what has been omitted from accounts or into seeing aspects of reality that they have been interpreting in ways that blocked apparently desirable change. Through the consultation process, for example, parental easing of an offspring's work load in a business may come to be seen by both parent and offspring as disenabling rather than helpful. Or a decline in the market share of a business may be seen not as a sign of massive advertising outlays by a nationally based competitor but as a sign of decision avoidance arising from difficult family relationships. Such "shadow realities" (Rosenblatt and Wright, 1984), when entered, may prove so threatening as to motivate family members to terminate the consultation, but helping people see things that they had been choosing not to see may also help family members recognize and talk about things that had been making serious trouble.

In promoting access to realities that family members had not been seeing, had been trying to keep others away from, had been ignoring, or had not been sharing, communication among family members may be very important. We certainly do not advocate rich, deep, and full communication as a cure-all or even as necessarily desirable. For people to come to terms with their problems and with each other, however, direct communication is a necessity. A consultant may facilitate communication by legitimating communication about troublesome areas (for example, concerns about the chief officer's health and plans for relinquishing control of the business, concerns about the equity of pay). Learning to speak about difficult issues may provide the means for much-needed change, but communication of that sort is not likely to happen without an outsider's help. People may even need help budgeting time for communication and finding a situation in which it can be carried out with sufficient privacy and sufficient freedom from interruption. People may also need help with basic communication skills —speaking for self, reflective listening, allowing the other to speak without interruption, and so on. Communication is important and is another of those areas in which a consultant either must be able to help or must be able to refer people to a competent specialist.

Another approach to promoting change is to get people thinking in terms of planning. Stuck in the here and now, making "that's the way I feel about it" decisions, people may be able to get unstuck if they can think, dream, and speak about where they would like to go. If a father/entrepreneur cannot talk about succession at the moment, he certainly can be helped to talk about his ideals for the future. Then the question becomes, how can you and the firm move toward those ideals? If your offspring does not seem ready to assume a major managerial role, how can she or he become ready, and how can that readiness be evaluated without attacking personalities or blaming?

When there are discrepancies among family members' hopes for the future, in dreams and ideals, the consultant may usefully mediate the differences. If Dad wants one future for the business and a daughter wants another but they both want the business eventually to be under the daughter's control, how can they work toward goals both can tolerate? Mediating conflicts may be an important element of consultation, one with important gains. Getting people committed to acting on plans to achieve distant goals may get them unstuck and may help them toward strategic planning in a broad array of areas (Peiser and Wooten, 1983).

Executive development may become more important as an entrepreneur ages. The issue may not only be one of eventual retirement of the chief officer or one of continued existence of the firm, it may also be one of retaining younger family members in the business. Training a younger family member to do high-level managerial work can be less threatening to a chief officer if it is clear that it is desirable to do such training while the current chief officer is still in a position to help, advise, evaluate, and head off major management errors (Cohn and Lindberg, 1974, pp. 207–208). Rather than waiting until the current chief officer is out of the picture, how much better it is to allow a younger family member to do substantial managerial tasks at a time when an experienced chief officer can still provide help! Furthermore, the stepping back from total control by the current chief officer can be understood to be a good thing if it is phrased in terms of freeing him or her to make key decisions or to do what she or he does best (Cohn and Lindberg, 1974, pp. 207–208). If, for example, the chief officer is best at product development, it seems reasonable to concentrate his or her efforts there and allow a younger family member who is learning about management more freedom in such areas as marketing or personnel management. Furthermore, a training period for a younger family member may give the chief officer freedom to develop new interests and ways of living that will allow a more comfortable and enriched retirement.

Planning becomes more obviously of value as a firm expands. For a family firm in which there is tension over how much authority the chief officer delegates or tension over decisions, managerial patterns that included very little rationalized, analysis-based planning may have sufficed when the business was smaller but may not work so well with the business expanding. In a sense, the business growth will have precipitated a family crisis that might have been forestalled, at least for a while, had the business remained small. In such a situation, the help of a consultant to get the family members who are in leadership roles in the business into a comfortable planning mode will help not only to deal with relationship issues but to be better able to cope with growth issues.

Perhaps the most common consultation process in a family business is organizational evaluation. Focusing on the functioning of the organization, one eventually can identify and analyze "family constraints" (Holland and Boulton, 1984) on organizational functioning. If there are, for example, problems in delegation of authority, tensions over who does what, or conflicts over the appointment of less competent family members to tasks that are beyond them, a consultant may sidestep the family issue by focussing on the organizational problem. It is not a question, for example, whether The Boss or The Kid is right about how to finance growth; the question is, given this type of business, of this size, in this market, in these times, are some approaches to financing more defensible than others? If family constraints have kept a business closed to a more defensible approach to financing, it seems wise to find ways to end the family constraints.

Organizational consultants who have worked with family businesses without having any particular sensitivity to the dynamics of families may have been helpful to the family as well as to the business. A push for an organizational change may have helped family members get past a relationship impasse. However, a consultant who is aware of relationship issues may be of even more help. Such a consultant may help family members to get perspective on their relationship problems, to reconceptualize things in a way that frees them up to deal better with their problems or to see how important it is to deal with family members not directly involved in the business but still important players in its tensions. Such a consultant may also be in a better position to refer family members to family counseling or to determine that what seems to be a family difficulty is likely to be resolved through organizational modifications. At another level, the question of consulting with sensitivity to family issues versus consulting without such sensitivity is a question of what is important in life. Is it important that the businesses do well, or is it important that people have good relationships with the persons who are important in their lives? Without in any way belittling the importance of business functioning, we take the position that family life is too important for serious dysfunction to be ignored and that success in one area does not have to be achieved at high cost to the other.

A final part of the consultation process to be mentioned here is the legitimation process. Consultants often choose to legitimate or are used to legitimate. What may be legitimated is a change or an evaluation already made in an organization—for example, that the chief officer will have to allow another family member more latitude in the organization or that a family member in the business is not up to doing the assigned job. What is legitimated may be a commitment to changes that the consultant has pointed to. The legitimation process may involve expert persuasion and authoritative endorsement, but it may also involve helping people feel better about what is inevitable. Among the more touching examples might be situations in which what is legitimated is a family member's leaving a business, the ending of a family's involvement in the business, the break-up of a business that cannot function without division, or a buyout in which a dream of shared ownership and/or control is ended. In such instances, one of the things that may be needed to legitimate the change is the engineering of some sort of grief ritual that acknowledges the difficulty of the changes, recognizes the value of what has been lost, and symbolizes the transition (see Albert, 1984; Rosenblatt, 1983; Rosenblatt, Walsh, and Jackson, 1976).

Consultants as Learners

An important element of consultation with family businesses, perhaps of any consultation, is the consultant's personal style. Some consultants choose to present themselves as decisive experts. However, from our perspective, each business and each family presents unique problems, and there is much yet to be known about families and family businesses. From that perspective, the preferred style for a consultant to a family business is that of learner, of somebody who may have substantial experience helping family businesses and who knows a great deal but who is open to the uniqueness of each case and to discovering new ways to facilitate problem solving. Such a stance may repel some clients, but a learner can be as helpful, tough, assertive, challenging, and strong as a consultant who comes across as a decisive expert. A consultant who is a learner will enter a new situation with considerable knowledge of other organizations and with conceptual frameworks for understanding organizations, but she or he will elicit client input and feedback and will use the actual situation of the business and the family as a guide to direction. Being a learner, one will be less likely to claim certainties that cannot legitimately be claimed in a field so young that is focused on entities so complex. A consultant who is a learner may enable clients to take more responsibility for the things they do that are consistent with consultant pushes for change. A consultant who is a learner makes clients partners in changes that may ensue from the consultation. If a recommended change is not backed by scientific certainty, clients will have to make their own choices and themselves be learners as they find ways to deal with their problems. A consultant can and often should provide strong leadership, but clients need to be committed to changes and to take responsibility for those changes (Beckhard and Dyer, 1983b). A consultant who is a learner models for clients a nondogmatic, open way of dealing with problems, which for many business families is an approach that might have prevented the problems that led to the need for a consultant.

Chapter Fifteen

Surviving While Working for a Relative

Perhaps a relative has hinted or said straightforwardly that some help is needed in the business the relative owns and manages. Perhaps the help is needed on a short-run basis, a few days, a few weeks, or a season; perhaps the help that is needed is only part-time. What should you do?

You need a job, want a higher income, want independence, or want to escape a job that is unchallenging, boring, or simply unpleasant. An opportunity seems to exist to enter a business run by a parent or other relative. You may already have worked in the business, and you may often have heard family members talk about it. The business sounds interesting, or perhaps it does not but you need an income. What should you do?

This chapter offers perspective on the decision to enter a family business. It offers suggestions for surviving in such a business and dealing with the family aspects of the situation. As the interviews we carried out made clear, there are opportunities when business system and family system are connected, and there are also potential problems. Whether people in the family call the business a family business or not, one cannot safely ignore the connection of business system and family system. The connection is there and must be dealt with.

Coping in Any Family Business

Although there is risk of family tension when family members are involved together in a family business, people are not without ways of dealing with tension. Perhaps the first thing to do with tension and with situations that could create tension is to put them into perspective. Seeing them as connected to being in the family business and seeing them as normal and understandable may make them less upsetting. For example, finding yourself in a situation that is tense because of role carryover or because of a power battle over relatives may be less upsetting if you can see what is occurring as common in businesses like the one you are in.

Putting things in perspective may head off or reduce some interpersonal conflicts. You may, for example, be less likely to blame somebody or to personalize a conflict if you can see that what is happening is a product of the situation everyone in the family/business system is in. If a relative/boss criticizes you in what seems a harsh manner for making an error, things may be more pleasant for you if you can take a mental step backward and say something like "This is his role" or "We are dealing with what just happened now, not with all of our relationship for all time." Similarly, if you are feeling irritated with what you are told to do or how you are told to do it, you may be able to handle things more comfortably if you can step back and recognize that your feelings arise in part from the fact that you are working for a relative or from your own distress at having a relative treat you that way. The additional perspective may lead you to decide that what happened was your relative's attempt to cope with the added difficulties and complexities of having you working in the business. You may decide, for example, that your relative may have been concerned about what nonrelated employees would think and so was more harsh with you. You may decide that your relative expected more from you than from a nonrelative and so was more upset with you when you did not understand something. When people have more perspective on things, they may be better able to cope with them. But that does not mean one should be passive in the face of difficulty.

Another important part of coping in a family business is speaking up about what bothers you. If, for example, you feel verbally abused or feel that you are expected to know more than you were taught, you may benefit from speaking up. Speaking up in any relationship is probably best done when the timing is appropriate, is best directed at the appropriate person (the person who seems to have made the trouble for you), and is best done tactfully. Although people cannot always do what is best, asking for what you want and speaking up when you feel things are wrong are generally good policies. Sometimes speaking up will improve how you are treated. You may learn, however, that you were living with wrong assumptions or that you missed something you probably should have learned. If having spoken up with good timing, with tact, and at the appropriate person does not seem to have worked for you, do not despair. Speaking up may have an impact later on, if not right away. It may enable you to feel some self-respect, even if it did not change things in a desirable way. It may enable you to learn, from the reaction you received, more about role boundaries as they are perceived by someone else and more about timing or tact. It may be a step toward eventual negotiation of something more desirable, a kind of initial bid or claim. If nothing else, speaking up may make it clearer to you where you stand and what you like or dislike, want or do not want.

Being together much of the time often means that people need distance the rest of the time. From a systems theory point of view, a system that is relatively closed and inward-looking becomes stagnant, instead of creative and adaptive. Closedness may force family members to an overdependence on one another that can be stifling. One may lose track of one's individuality, and the people one is with so much of the time may become satiating. With too much contact both at work and outside, many people develop tense or devitalized relationships. Hence, working together in the business often makes it important to arrange for some apartness, either at work or at other times. In order to have substantial contact outside the business, people often have to have considerable distance within the business, and in order to have substantial contact in the business, people often have to distance each other outside the business. Thus, a family business, for many people, is not a guarantee of a large amount of family togetherness. This is not to say that there are not relationship gains from working together. You may gain mutual respect, mutual knowledge, a broader base for interaction, and greater feelings of connectedness. But there also may be either substantial interpersonal distance or relationship problems.

Among the means of coping with a number of the potential problems of working in a family business is to move toward defining roles in the business. For example, defined roles will help to head off undesirable carryover of patterns of interacting from home to business or business to home. It is not a simple matter for a subordinate to define her or his role, but sometimes one can feel very strongly pressed to do so. For example, a man working in a family business said:

> "There have been situations where I felt what the other person was doing could extinguish my job, which causes a great deal of tension. My role in the business is never really clear; consequently clearing the air becomes sticky also" (048B).

Having a firm footing and clarity of role in the business would have helped him, his relationships with family members in the business, and perhaps the business itself. In a situation like that, perhaps the best approach to take at first is to press for role clarity, to try to elicit from supervisors clarification of what one is to do, and perhaps even to present a written description of what one thinks is one's position, as a first step toward negotiating a resolution of the difficulties. But one may, if one is going to stay in a business, have to learn to live with a more chaotic situation than one might hope for.

A general approach to living with and solving problems in a family business is to enter the situation with learning and flexibility as personal policies. Instead of feeling responsible for knowing it all or feeling down on oneself if one makes a mistake or is inept or ignorant, one can say, "I'll learn from my mistakes. I don't promise perfection." Instead of believing that there is a certain way things must be done and instead of having expectations that one is certain will be met, the business, one's family, one's coworkers, and oneself will benefit if one is able to accommodate to what is unpredictable, unexpected, or different from what one thought should be or would be. For example, a supervising relative may seem inept or may want to do things in ways that seem to you to be inappropriate. You may have to accept what is going on, learn how to accommodate to it, and be flexible in order to continue to function in the business. You need not agree and need not battle another in order to work with that person.

Given what has been said so far in this book, it certainly seems appropriate, if one is planning to work for a relative, to expect hard feelings at times. One should not be surprised to find oneself upset with oneself or upset with one's relatives. Expecting hard feelings may help cushion you from secondary effects of such feelings—for example, anger over anger or worry over worry. But there is another gain that can be had from expecting hard feelings: You may be able to get organized to deal with them through communication, through speaking and listening. Good communication may at times require you to hold off on dealing with some problems; at other times it may simply require you to acknowledge that you see things differently. But often it requires learning and flexibility, as you talk with others about feelings, differences, and how problems might be resolved.

A bottom line in working for relatives is to feel safe enough and free enough to leave the business. Although many work situations that at first seem hopeless turn out to be tolerable or even pleasant, occasionally the best way to maintain one's self-respect and morale and a congenial family relationship is to leave the business. It helps to have the confidence and self-awareness to do that if it seems necessary. Leaving is also easier on relationships if you enter the business with an understanding that for all parties involved it is a trying-out experience, that good people with the best of intentions sometimes find that they cannot work together in a family business.

Working for a Spouse

So far in this chapter, we have discussed matters that are applicable to anyone working for a relative. There are some special considerations when one works for a spouse. Since almost all the business families we studied in which a spouse worked for a spouse involved a wife working for a husband, that is a relationship we know much more about.

Whether you should come down to the store, factory, warehouse, or office to work for your spouse depends on how well both you and your spouse think you both can deal with the tension between equality and hierarchy. How well can your spouse handle differences of opinion? How well can you handle being told what to do by your spouse, being criticized by your spouse, being a learner with your spouse looking on, and perhaps even feeling exploited by your spouse?

The tension between equality and hierarchy can be dealt with in part by recognizing that the hierarchy is there but exploring how much you both can be comfortable with you talking about, commenting on, or raising questions about business issues. You may find that to work for your spouse, you will have to keep some opinions to yourself. Although the issue of what may be talked about and how it may be talked about may have to be worked out through experience, it may be useful to discuss the issue before working together. Legitimating discussion of the topic is a route to dealing more constructively with tension that may emerge over any topic.

We think it important that both partners enter the situation with the idea that it is an exploration, rather than a firm commitment, and that at any point either party has the legitimate right to end the working relationship. In the process of working for a spouse, you may minimize the irritation you or your spouse feels from too much time together by getting physical distance and role clarity. Role clarity also reduces the friction that comes from recurrent supervision. Roles may not be easy to work out in advance, but if you start by saying that you will want and need role clarity and if, as you work, you make efforts to come to a clear, mutually acceptable view of your intentions, your relationship with your spouse may be much more comfortable.

Working for a Parent

We found a number of parent/offspring relationships in which there seemed to be currently little or no tension. Working for a parent, you may make obvious gains in terms of income, having a place to work where you feel you belong, and learning. One big risk, however, is dependency. In a society that values moderate amounts of independence and autonomy, being involved in a parent's business may seem to you or to others to be too much like being taken care of. It may mean that you will need to put up with being ordered around, being treated like a child, and feeling powerless. A problem arising from such apparent dependency may be that you will resent and fight it, but the problem may be instead that you will like it and fail to do the growing-up things that most people do. You can be autonomous and still work for a parent; it involves having areas of life that you can govern by yourself and feeling free to take risks, even the risk of leaving the business. Although your parents cannot, in some ultimate sense, make you grow up (people cannot become autonomous solely by being nurtured and guided into it), your parents can help indirectly by giving you room to function and to try and perhaps even fail. The offspring differentiation process also requires that at times some business and home-life areas be out of bounds for offspring/parent interaction or at least for parent intrusion.

Unhappiness in parent/offspring business relationships is not solely the province of offspring. Parent issues have been discussed at various places in this book. One of the important issues is that parents may feel put down and unappreciated. It would probably be a good thing, if you work for a parent, not to take the parent for granted and not to express only the negatives. We are not advocating insincerity, but genuine praise and appreciation is valued by many people, even parent/employers.

Working for a parent seems to create the potential for nonrelated employees to resent one. They may feel that you are overpaid, are coddled, have an inside track to a top position, or are otherwise overbenefited. You may find yourself working much harder in a family business than you would somewhere else, partly as a way of showing to others (and maybe to yourself) that you deserve what you are getting. But that may not end the nonrelated employees' resentment. However, as you will know if you have worked outside the family business, in any work situation some people may have negative opinions and resentments about others. More generally, you may achieve some useful perspective on your family's business and on yourself if you have work experience elsewhere.

It might be better to be supervised by nonrelatives, but what if you are supervised by a relative? One approach toward doing that is to have had experience elsewhere being supervised. There are some things one has to learn in a supervision situation —for example, how to take criticism, how to seek more training if you find yourself doing something you don't feel competent to do, or how to correct a misunderstanding with a supervisor. Even a summer of part-time work in a fast foods restaurant may teach you how to be supervised and save you from inappropriately clashing with a supervisor/parent. Having learned how to be supervised will make life simpler when you work for a parent. Being supervised by a parent will also be simpler if you can keep in mind how things would be if you were not related. It will help you to recognize when either you or your parent oversteps a line. You may, for example, be asking your parent for too much indulgence, or your parent may, as a supervisor, be intruding into your private life. Clarifying those boundaries will make things easier for you and for your parent. Although you may, as an employee of a parent, feel powerless, you certainly have power. Parents have all sorts of incentives for paying attention to their offspring. Your parent may be angry with you, may not want to hear your opinions, and may disagree with you, but your parent is unlikely to send you to Siberia if you say that you are feeling too indulged or that business is not the place to discuss how you are spending your earnings or with whom you are spending leisure time.

If your work for your parent is leading or eventually will

lead to a role as a possible successor, you may find yourself in an especially demanding situation. As the discussions of succession in this book indicate, the succession process in a family business may have as many hazards as an eighteenth-century exploration of the Amazon jungle. Although succession situations are complex, there are some considerations that apply to most of them. One is that you would be well advised to learn what you will have to know to do the job you plan to succeed to, even if that means you will have to go away from the business for a while. It also pays to recognize that a parent whom you might succeed is human and has needs. We are not saying that you must protect your parent, but it may help you to be more patient if you understand that a parent may need to hang onto roles that were important, may need to have expertise and wisdom acknowledged, and certainly needs to have financial security.

Conclusion

Being willing and able to leave a difficult work situation is one's ultimate protection against misery. Short of quitting, keys to getting along well while working for relatives are tactful and timely communication, an openness to learning, tolerance of the foibles and frailties of others, flexibility about what one does and how one does it, and perhaps above all a willingness to work hard and to do one's best.

Chapter Sixteen

Conclusion: Putting Family and Business in Context

Family System and Business System

The theory on which this book rests is a very basic systems view. The key idea is that the family and the family business are separate but connected systems. There are two systems in that the goals, needs, tasks, and typically the personnel of the family and the business are not identical. That means that what is good for one system is not necessarily good for the other, and the two systems must inevitably compete some of the time for resources, including money and the time and energy of individuals in both systems.

One of the less obvious attributes of the interconnected systems is that it is not always clear who is in what system. In particular, a family member who never participates directly in the business may still be working hard to support the business— for example, by doing work at home that would otherwise have to be done by somebody in the business, who would then have less time and energy to devote to the business.

Because the systems interconnect, there are sometimes problems. One of the most frequent sources of problems in family businesses is that patterns of roles, rules, and so on that are the product of one of the two systems are carried over to the other system, where they are inappropriate. Although the carry-over of patterns may be no problem and may even be a benefit, with inappropriate carryover a pattern that may work well in one system makes trouble in the other. For example, a person who is appropriately the chief executive at work may not be appropriately the chief executive at home, or offspring dependence that is appropriate at home may be a source of problems at work. Sometimes the carryover is of patterns that are problems at both home and work—for example, consistently undermining the work or self-esteem of other family members.

Frequently what is needed when family system and business system seem in trouble because of patterns that are inappropriate in at least one of the two systems is greater separation of persons, roles, rules, and so on between the two systems. Consider some examples discussed in this book. Problems arise if the goals of one system are mistakenly seen as the only goals. Problems arise if a person is overidentified with the business, so that other family members are shortchanged or are even expected to work toward and serve only the business goals. Problems arise if it is not recognized that people may legitimately differ in how they feel about the business. Problems arise if offspring who work in the business are babied. Problems of many sorts may arise from inadequate separation of the two systems.

The ways of separating the two systems are many. One approach to the separation is at the conceptual level of individual family members. It is important that people see that the two systems are different. In that regard, the separateness of the two systems is clearer when it is acceptable to everyone in the family that family members differ in their commitment to work in the business. In some cases it helps to define roles in one place or both places, partly because that emphasizes that the systems are different and clarifies what is role-appropriate. In some businesses that operate in the home, it eventually is seen as desirable that the business be physically separated from the home. Still another approach to separating the two systems is for family members who work together to separate from one another in the workplace, both in business function and in physical distance. That reduces the chances for inappropriate carryover from one system to another.

Many business families get along very well. There is no absolute necessity for very sharp separation of family system and business system. Yet the overlap of the two systems means that each system is vulnerable to events (conflicts, griefs, disruptive changes) in the other, the more so the more closely the systems are connected. The connection between the two systems also means that change in one system is resisted in part because of the impact it may have on the other. For example, it may be difficult to move a son who is working in the family business to a position of less responsibility if family members not directly involved in the business will be upset by that. Again, with greater separation of business and family, a change in either will be easier to accomplish.

There is much more to this book than a simple statement of why systems should be separated or how they can be, but the key concept in the book is that family businesses and business families are special because of the connection of the two systems.

Developmental Cycles of Family Businesses

Family businesses have, to some extent, a kind of life course. We have, throughout this book, touched on issues of developmental cycles in businesses, and it is useful to emphasize some of those issues here. New businesses are more likely to be marginal and to require more time and commitment of the persons involved. Hence, there often is little contact between family members who are in the business and those who are not, and the latter often suffer a work overload at home. New businesses, to the extent that they are economically marginal, also require family members to live frugally and to take economic risks. When the business is new, there may also be pressure on family members who are not centrally involved in the business to come to work and help out.

Because new businesses tend to have few employees, whoever works there may have to do a greater variety of things, and the help of even one family member makes a bigger difference. At the same time, the newness of a business often means that work roles are poorly defined. It is not so clear what has to be done, what the best ways are to do things, who is best at doing what, and so on. That guarantees greater tension over work roles.

In new businesses, people are often learners. A boss may be learning how to boss. A spouse doing bookkeeping may be learning that for the first time. People working together may, for the first time, be facing what it means for two persons who have a relationship at home to have to deal with each other differently in the business. The newness guarantees the exhilaration and pain of learning.

In order to save money and because an away-from-home office or shop may not seem necessary, a new business may be run in the home. That may add to the tensions of family relationships, making it harder for the entrepreneur ever to get away from work, creating tensions over the use and appearance of places in the home, and putting other family members in a position to monitor the entrepreneur's activities and to be pressured to help, at least in small ways, with things like answering the phone and greeting customers. However, even when the business is run in the home, the entrepreneur may be very much out of contact with other family members. When businesses are new, children and spouses typically do not see an entrepreneurial parent/spouse very much.

In well-established businesses there may be some tension over whether to think of the business as a family one. Often the business was started as the entrepreneur's own business. Even if other family members have been directly involved, the business may not have been thought of as one that would involve other family members in important positions and be passed on to them. There may be a transition period, as a business moves toward being a family business, during which the entrepreneur wants family involvement but resists some aspects of it (for example, in decision making) and during which family members who are becoming more involved feel that they are invading the entrepreneur's territory. The transition of a business from the entrepreneur's own to the family's may take a substantial period of time, during which a number of emotional and relationship bumps and abrasions may occur.

The transition of a business from an individual's to a family's may be a result of a son's or daughter's involvement in the business. For people who want a business to stay in the family but who have no offspring or have none willing and able to do the job, the transition may hinge on a successful search for other kin who might fit in.

In a business that has become a family business, unrelated employees have to come to terms with the special relationship, special status, and place on the ladder of promotion of family members in the business. Managing nonrelated employees in such a situation is not simple. One may risk losing valuable people.

When offspring or other relatives work in the business, supervising them may be challenging. We have found, as have many others who have looked at family businesses in the United States, that supervision problems are often minimized when offspring in the business are physically and functionally separated from parents in the business and when offspring are supervised by nonkin.

As the business matures and as the chief officer matures, succession and estate planning become important. It is desirable that planning be done early, partly because nobody is guaranteed a full life span. But in practice, many entrepreneurs put off such planning. Even without planning, if there is an apparent successor in the business, as time goes by there will be some kind of beginning of a succession process. At the very least, tensions over how and when succession will occur may define some of the key issues. Even with a well-laid-out plan, there may still be stresses and strains as succession proceeds.

Paralleling the family transitions of a maturing business, there are often business transitions. Management may become dispersed as the size and scope of operations require more layers of supervision and decision making and more specialization. Credit may become more available and more of a necessity. Legal issues may become more salient. Whatever the entrepreneur was good at becomes, at some point, less obviously all that is necessary to be good at. For example, a great developer of products may turn out to be weak at financing or at recognizing when the balance sheet calls for product innovations. In this sense, a business is not a simple monolithic thing. To say, "I have had this business for thirty years," is not to say, "I have been doing the same things at the same place." Typically, those thirty years required many changes and much new learning.

In a business run by a second-, third-, or later-generation chief officer, the developmental cycle of the business does not usually go through the "new business" phase, but it does repeat to the extent that a new successor must be found and the succession process carried out. In a business that has gone through one succession, precedents for succession exist that may help or hamper business functioning and family relationships during the next succession process. A successor who has had to weather a succession process from the junior family member's side of things either will be locked into the precedents that have been set or will be intentionally different from the previous chief officer (for example, more sensitive or more planful).

Each generation of chief officer in a family business works in the shadow of the previous chief officer. The previous chief officer may actually be present and influential—for example, as a board chair or principal shareholder. In some businesses the transitions from one generation to another are longer than the periods when a single generation rules alone. Even if the previous chief is not actually present, the influence is there in how things have been organized, what employees have learned, what the new chief officer has learned to value, relations with creditors and customers, and a million other ways.

The new chief officer may have worked since childhood in the business and may have grown up in daily contact with the business, aware since childhood of the importance of the business in the family and perhaps even of a future as a chief officer. This socialization and the precedents of the business may be sustaining or stultifying for a new chief officer. However, the real issue in maintaining a family business across the generations is often one of finding successors. It is very difficult for a business to stay in the control of a family through generation after generation. It is difficult to find willing and able successors, although a family's connection may continue, for example, with the family's name remaining the business name or with family members retaining shares in the business.

Business Size

This book has touched, at many places, on matters of business size. Smaller businesses tend to be newer, so some of what is said in the previous section of this chapter about the business developmental cycle can be reread to illuminate issues of size.

People in smaller businesses may tend to have more trouble defining and sticking to roles. There is too much to do with the personnel available, and many tasks need to be done only occasionally. Smaller businesses may also have a different appeal, or draw, for family members than bigger businesses. A smaller business may have more need of family members to help out temporarily, to fill in, to serve as back-up help. But smaller businesses are not such a good draw to potential successors. It is partly a matter of whether one can earn a good living with a small business one has taken over, but it is also a matter of whether a business is big enough to support two boss-level nuclear families during the succession process and support the retirement of one executive and the continuing involvement of another.

Smaller businesses also provide the stage for more complexities in the education and development of executive autonomy of a potential successor. They are less likely to be divisible, so that an offspring can take over a piece in order to have more freedom to learn to manage. They are less likely to have a professional manager who is not a relative who can supervise a potential successor, freeing the family from the tension of supervision of close relative by close relative. One might further speculate that in many smaller businesses an entrepreneur will have had less contact with the culture of family businesses and may have had fewer educational interactions with accountants, attorneys, management consultants, tax experts, marketing firms, operations consultants, and an expert board of directors. As a consequence, there may be more rough edges and more rule-of-thumb management in smaller businesses. This roughness may lead to more difficult supervision of relatives and a more difficult succession process.

Larger businesses have some advantages for family involvement, but they also have some disadvantages. Many more relatives may want a piece of the profit, so there may be more jockeying for influence, roles, position, and control. There may be more family politics to deal with. A larger business may have more need for professional management, and certainly it will have more professional managers who will be in a position to step up the ladder to the top. That may put more stress on possible offspring successors; they will have to do well in comparison with professionals, or they will look like indulged mediocrities.

In a larger business that has grown from a small one, there may be tensions resulting from the changes in management needs. An entrepreneur may not have grown in knowledge and skills with the business. However, deficiencies may be remedied by professional managers.

Larger businesses may be more in contact with attorneys, CPAs, and tax experts who will push for the development of estate plans, succession plans, key-person insurance, and the like. Whereas in a smaller business these issues may have to come out of an intergenerational struggle, in a larger business the issues may have been resolved long ago as a result of recommendations from professionals. A small business may not even be able to afford expert advice when it is obvious to the business decision makers that the advice would be of value.

Although the preceding is merely a sketch of ways in which smaller and larger businesses may differ, it serves to illustrate a point made throughout this book—the considerable diversity found among business families and family businesses despite the issues and problems common to them. Business size is among many factors that are important in influencing the interaction of business system and family system, the problems that arise as a result of interaction of the two systems, and the ways that problems are resolved.

Realizing the Potential of Family and Business

It should be clear from what has been written in this book that it may not be possible to realize both the full potential of a business and the full potential of family life. Family and business compete for resources and are directed toward different goals. People who "want it all" are unlikely to succeed. Even within a family, what one person considers the realization of full potential for the family or the family business may be much less than that for another. People must, therefore, make choices among desirable ends, aware that something less than realization of full potential is likely in at least some area.

Many people in the business families we studied seemed to have felt generally satisfied with family life and business life. As Chapter Eleven points out, a number of respondents felt that the family business provided them with freedom, income, capital, a chance to be creative, connections with other family members, and much else. It also seemed clear, even from people in the families where relationships were in some ways difficult, that many respondents felt substantial satisfaction with relationships in the family.

There is no simple formula for success or happiness in family life or business life. There may be 10,000 separate skills, decisions, habits, and so on that must be optimal in order for a family or a business to do well. Moreover, the skills, decisions, habits, and so on that are appropriate are different in different families and businesses and different at different times within the same family or business. In this book, we do not address many of the issues that must be taken into account for a highly satisfying and fulfilling life, and in concluding this book we do not intend to summarize the dozens of suggestions concerning listening, talking, helpseeking, organizing the business, touching base with others, and so on that contribute to a better life in a business family. However, one general recommendation that appears repeatedly in this book deserves emphasis.

In one form or another, this book says that in order to move closer to realizing the full potential of family and business, it is important to cultivate difference, separation, and distinction. We speak, in this book, of the value of division of labor and position descriptions, the importance of allowing individuation to occur and of one's individuating from others. We speak of the value of separating kin from kin in situations where one relative might supervise the other or where there are inherent sources of relationship tension. We speak about making boundaries between entrepreneur and business, between home life and business life, between person and person. In each case we are saying that difference, separation, and distinction promote a better life.

The point can be understood in several ways. First of all, context affects relationship. Thus, not taking the context into account means that a relationship will be in trouble in some contexts. Division of labor, position descriptions, separation of kin in the business, and boundary building help people to adapt to context differences. Second, people differ, and not recognizing those differences creates problems. Individuation, boundaries, and separation can help to acknowledge, validate, and make the best use of those differences in promoting family life and the business. Difference, separation, and distinction need to be balanced by connection, but connection of family member with family member is much harder to achieve if there is insufficient attention to difference, separation, and distinction.

Appendix:
Studying Families in Business

Sampling

We began with the Yellow Pages telephone directories for Minneapolis and St. Paul and their suburbs. The phone book does not allow for perfectly random sampling. Some businesses are listed at several places, and in the Twin Cities some businesses are listed in both the Minneapolis and St. Paul directories. But the phone book still seemed a relatively unbiased place to begin.

Not surprisingly, given that such a large proportion of businesses in America are family ones, the majority of businesses we contacted were family businesses. Using the phone book means, of course, that we lost the newest businesses. But those businesses might not have operated long enough for family dynamics to have emerged clearly, and we might have found little in those businesses in the area of solutions to problems, which was a focus of our work.

The exact procedure for sampling from the phone books was as follows. For each case, a Yellow Pages phone book was chosen randomly (by means of single digits in a random number table), with the random numbers weighted in proportion to the number of pages in the Yellow Pages phone books for the two cities (1,372 pages in the Minneapolis directory, which was represented by the numbers 5 to 9 and 0 in the random number table, 897 pages in the St. Paul directory, represented by the numbers 1 to 4). Then a page was chosen randomly, then a column, and then an entry within a column, all by means of a random number table. Display advertisements were ignored, so that a company that had a regular listing and also a display advertisement could be sampled only if the regular listing was hit. This procedure weighs heavily those businesses that are listed in columns with relatively few listings.

Excluded from the sample were professionals (accountants, physicians, lawyers, social workers, counselors, chiropractors, psychologists, and so on), public agencies, associations and clubs, local outlets and subsidiaries of national companies unless the local operation seemed at all likely to be a franchise operation, and businesses not in Minneapolis, not in St. Paul, and not in a suburb immediately adjacent to one of the two cities. The first-tier suburbs included in the sample frame were Brooklyn Center, Columbia Heights, Edina, Falcon Heights, Fridley, Golden Valley, Lauderdale, Lilydale, Maplewood, Mendota, Mendota Heights, Newport, Richfield, Robbinsdale, Roseville, St. Anthony, St. Louis Park, South St. Paul, and West St. Paul. If a firm was listed on more than one line in a Yellow Pages column, only the first listing in the column was counted in drawing the sample. If a firm's subsidiary or outlet was picked and the subsidiary or outlet seemed entirely controlled by a local parent firm (for example, the plastics plant of a Twin Cities chemical firm), the decision was to go to the parent firm for an interview.

After a firm was picked, community directories were consulted to determine the name of the firm's president, head, owner, manager, or senior officer. The intent was to contact a particular person. If a senior person could not be identified by this procedure, the firm was dropped from the sample. Failure to identify a particular person seemed to occur most often because the firm was too new to be listed in the community directory.

Our Yellow Pages sampling procedure seemed to us to weigh established and larger firms more heavily, because firms that appeared in the Yellow Pages and those with multiple listings would be more likely to be chosen. This bias is not undesirable, since established and larger firms are relatively rare, and it seemed important to include in the sample enough established and larger businesses so that we could compare family dynamics in those businesses with family dynamics in smaller and younger businesses, so that we could be assured of looking at businesses with two or more adult generations with long-term involvement, so that we could be in a position to distinguish family relationship dynamics that prevent intergenerational transfer of the family businesses from those that do not, and for other reasons. Nonetheless, it became clear a short way into the interviewing that we were not drawing many businesses with annual gross sales in excess of $1,000,000 or with more than 100 employees, although we knew we needed a range of business sizes.

We therefore augmented our sample as follows. There is an annual directory of larger businesses in the Twin Cities called the *Corporate Report Fact Book,* published by *Corporate Reports* magazine. We sampled from the 1980 edition of this directory. From the list of privately held firms, we chose pages randomly and firms within pages, producing a sample of twenty-two larger privately held firms. From the descriptions of publicly owned local firms, we established a list of thirteen that, though publicly owned, seemed to be substantially owned, directed, or operated by people with a single surname. From this list, we randomly chose five firms. Thus, we had a list of twenty-seven firms that seemed to be large. Our goal was to interview people from at least ten large firms from the *Corporate Report* list.

We eventually interviewed at least one person from fifty-nine business-operating families; thirty-three cases involved an interview of a second family member. Fifty-nine cases is a very small number if one wants to study unusual or infrequently occurring things or to track down statistical complexities. But that

number seemed sufficient to define and explore the major problems in family relationships. We knew fifty-nine would be
enough to identify and document those problems and the most
common approaches people have taken to dealing with them.

A sign of the times and of the risk involved in any business venture was that even though we chose our sample by a
procedure that ought to minimize the number of businesses that
would have gone under, 6 of the 114 businesses we tried to contact were no longer in operation. Of the 108 businesses we contacted that were still in operation, one was not a local family
business; at 22 of them we were told the business was not a
family business, that it was not owned or operated within a single family. We think that in some of those 22 cases the business
was a family one by our definition but the person we contacted
found a denial of the family connection to be the easiest way to
turn us down. Among the 85 local businesses we contacted that
were avowedly family businesses, we were refused interviews at
26. The reasons given for refusal included that the person contacted was too busy (and judging by the activity of people we
did interview, people in family businesses are ordinarily very
busy), that there was no profit in being interviewed, that the
key family member was ill, that family matters were none of
our business, that the recent death of a family member made
participation in the study too burdensome, and that the issues
that would be discussed were too touchy. In several cases, we
never reached the person we wanted to interview but were
blocked by a secretary or other employee. Our interviewed
sample was thus 69 percent of the 85 local businesses we contacted that apparently were family businesses.

We are fully aware that the sample is a limited one. The
Twin Cities in the 1980s may provide a sample that is unusual in
economic situation, ethnic group distribution, the influence of
long winters, and many other ways. That the sample in the present study is not totally unrepresentative of families in business
is indicated by the many points at which the findings of the
study meshed with the findings of previous studies carried out
in the United States, in Britain, in France, and elsewhere. The
ultimate test of the adequacy of the sample is whether the find-

ings fit past studies, whether the findings are replicable, and whether the findings and the theory associated with them make sense to people in business families or people who work with such families.

The Businesses and the People Interviewed

We will not identify the nature of individual businesses that are unique in the Twin Cities or are among a small number in the Twin Cities. To do so might disclose the identity of the people interviewed, and we promised all respondents that we would guard their privacy. The other businesses in our sample included manufacturing firms, restaurants, retail stores, automobile service stations, insurance agencies, local franchise dealerships for national manufacturers, building contractors, and an impressive array of firms with unusual specialties. Table 1 summarizes the general characteristics of the businesses.

Table 1. Characteristics of the Businesses.

	Annual Gross Income	Number of Employees Who Were Not Relatives	Number of Relatives Currently in the Business (Including Respondent)	Years of Family Involvement in the Business
Mean	$ 4,778,000	67	3.6	25.6
Range	30,000–46,000,000	0–562	1–12	1–72
Median	1,200,000	11	3	26

Note: When family members disagreed about some figure, their separate reports were averaged in making calculations for this table. There were figures for 57 businesses on annual gross income and for 59 businesses on the three other variables.

We had hoped to obtain a range of size among our businesses, and as Table 1 shows, we succeeded. The first column gives figures on size as measured by money turnover; the second and third columns, figures on number of employees. Several businesses reported no part-time or full-time employees, although at least one of those used volunteer help from friends or relatives on occasion. Comparing the means and medians for annual gross sales and number of employees who were not relatives indicates that our sample included a small number of very large businesses but that businesses of more modest size were more typical.

In 57 of the 59 business families we studied, we were able to interview someone in the firm who was senior in the sense of power to make decisions and to hire and fire. In ten of the fifty-nine businesses, the senior person we interviewed was the founder of the firm. Table 2 summarizes the characteristics of the senior persons interviewed. It can be seen in Table 2 that

Table 2. Characteristics of Senior Persons in the Businesses.

Average age	51.5
Gender	54 men, 3 women
Average number of years in role of chief officer	11
Average education	2 years of college
Had nonmanagerial official role in the business	22 of the 41 who could be evaluated on this dimension

the senior person was generally male, although it seemed to us that in one firm a senior male was actually quite a bit under the influence of his mother, who was subordinate to him in the organizational chart. She had, for example, reorganized the business and changed the product line while he was on a vacation.

For thirty-five of the fifty-nine businesses in the sample, we also interviewed a family member who was not a senior person in the firm. Twenty-nine of those thirty-five persons currently or previously had an involvement in the family business. Table 3 provides information about the thirty-five respondents who were not senior persons in the family firm. They included mothers, fathers, husbands, wives, sons, daughters, grandchildren, and brothers of the senior person interviewed.

Table 3. Characteristics of Family Members Interviewed
Who Were Not Senior Persons.

Average age	38.3
Gender	19 men, 16 women
Average education	3 years of college
Had nonmanagerial official role in the business	24 of 27 who could be evaluated on this dimension

Contacting People

Our initial contact with a business was by letter. We wanted to contact businesses by letter in order to give people a chance to think over whether they might want to be involved in the study, which was described in a minimal way in the letter, and so that if they were going to have questions about the study, they might think about them in advance. A letter on a University of Minnesota letterhead helped to legitimate the telephone request for an interview, making it easier for an interviewer to deal with the person contacted. A letter also helped us to get past protective secretaries and junior executives, although we did not succeed in two cases. A week or two after our letter was sent out, one of us would call the recipient and ask for an appointment. Of the ninety-two interviews in the study, twenty-nine were done by Anderson, forty-two by de Mik, twelve by Johnson, and nine by Rosenblatt.

In trying to interview some family member in addition to our primary respondent from a business, we started the study with a quota system. Each of us would try to get a secondary respondent in some business in a particular kin category before trying to find, in another business, a relative in the next kin category on our list. That proved unworkable; we were missing lots of interesting people while waiting for a case with involvement by a relative in the right kin category. So we went to a system of trying to find another relative to interview. That other relative was always somebody who lived in the metropolitan area. The other relative chosen was chosen because of involvement in the business, because of a central role in the business, and because of availability. We asked the primary respondent for permission to contact the person we wanted to use as a secondary respondent. All but one granted permission; that one asked us to contact a different relative. It seemed appropriately respectful to grant primary respondents the right to prevent us from creating trouble or embarrassment for them. We had some concern that the secondary respondents might be a biased sample in that the primary respondents would somehow steer us away from people who would report unpleasantness and toward people who were the primary respondents' allies and supporters. That may be so, but as the text of this book indicates, we found plenty of reports of disharmony when we interviewed our secondary respondents.

When we contacted the secondary respondents, some knew about our study and some did not; a few had seen the letter we sent initially, and many had talked with the primary respondent. No prospective secondary respondents declined to be interviewed.

The Interview Schedule

Our interview schedule asked for background information about the respondent and the business and then went through a list of possible problem areas, asking whether there had been any tension or stress in each area. For any area in which there had been tension or stress, we obtained the respondent's narrative. In some cases a narrative elicited later in an interview illuminated matters discussed earlier. For each problem area we wanted a description of the problem, a statement of how it had been dealt with, and ideas about how it might have been headed off. The list of tensions and stresses was derived from our own familiarity with family businesses, from our understandings of tensions and stresses in enterprise-operating families (Rosenblatt and Anderson, 1981), from pilot work, and from the available scholarly and popular literature on family businesses. The interview concluded with questions about the advantages of having a family business.

Did Members of a Family Tell Things
in the Same Way?

One reason for using two respondents was to assess bias in perspectives and in reports of problems, problem solutions, and facts about the business. On more objective matters—duration of family involvement in the business, business gross sales, number of employees, and number of employees who were relatives—agreement was imperfect but very high.

Table 4 summarizes agreement between paired respondents on the more objective matters. For some issues the cor-

**Table 4. Agreement Between Respondents Connected
to the Same Business.**

Question	Correlation (r)	N
Number of persons involved in the business	.81	26
Number of employees who are not relatives	.97	24
Annual gross sales	.99	16
Number of years the family has been in business	.96	23

	Percentage Agreement	N
Other family members are involved in the business	97	29
Other family members not in the business now were there in the past	83	21
There has been a shift in ownership or control from parent to offspring	68	19
Who owns the business	72	29
Who manages the business	69	26

Note: N = number of cases on which the correlation coefficient or the percentage is based.

relation coefficient (r) is the appropriate indicator of agreement; for others the appropriate indicator is the percentage of agreement between respondents from the same family.

Although some respondents could not answer or declined to answer questions in each area, agreement was high on number of employees who were relatives, number of employees who were not relatives, annual gross sales, number of years the family had been in the business, and whether other family members were currently involved in the business or had been involved in the past. Agreement was somewhat weaker but still substantial on whether there had been a shift in ownership or control from parent to offspring, on who owned the business, and on who was managing the business.

Agreement was probably imperfect on involvement of relatives in the business because people may interpret differently the unpaid help that some spouses and offspring occasionally give and the meaning of being a corporate officer on paper without having any work involvement in the business. For example, a brother who was on paper a member of the board of directors but who never worked in the firm and who was never paid or a wife who helped without pay in emergencies may have been counted as in the business by some people and not by others.

Agreement was lower on past involvement of relatives in the business because some younger family members did not know of past business involvement of a mother, a grandparent, an uncle, aunt, or cousin. Imperfect agreement between family members on whether there had been a shift in ownership or control from parent to offspring stems in part from younger family members' sometimes not having a clear idea about what had happened in the relationship of parental and grandparental generations. But there was also some disagreement about whether ownership or control had shifted recently. For example, an offspring may have been the nominal manager of the business but still have been dominated by a parent. On paper or in an estate plan there may have been an actual or prospective shift in ownership, but nothing may actually have changed. Father, for example, may still have been making all significant decisions.

Agreement on ownership was imperfect in part because some family members failed to mention and perhaps did not even know of minority shareholders. There was also some discrepancy between family members over whether a wife who on paper was a separate shareholder for a firm that was in fact entirely in her husband's control should be counted as a separate owner. In another instance of ownership unclarity, a mother reported herself to be 42 percent owner of a business, a son who had founded the business to be a 42 percent owner, and each of two other sons to be an 8 percent owner. The son who had a larger share of the business than his brothers reported that only he and his mother were owners. Our inclination is to interpret the discrepancy to mean either that the son did not get into details with us (that is, he did not mention the 8 percent owners) or that he had little use for his brothers. In fact, his interview seemed to support the latter viewpoint. From his perspective, a major problem in the family business was that subordinates (his brothers) did not accept subordinate status.

Discrepancies in reports of who was managing a business can be attributed partly to ambiguities in the level of management our question called for. Some people apparently reported only a senior manager, whereas others reported on the whole array of people who could, in some sense, be called managers. Some disagreement on management arose, however, from problems in some of the businesses we studied. For example, a father might report that his son was the general manager of the family firm, whereas the son said that his father managed because his father still "pulls all the strings." In one case a son reported that he was the manager, but the father considered himself to be the manager. In several cases one family member considered a professional manager, a nonrelative, to be the manager of the business, whereas some other family member reported that a family member was manager. These discrepancies are an indicator that objective facts are not easily established in a study like this one, and the discrepancies are also potential symptoms of business and family tensions. For example, the businesses with disagreement between family members about who managed tended to be the businesses in which tensions were reported over decision making.

In considering agreement between family members over presence or absence of stress, we often heard a person say self-contradictory things. In some cases a person said there was no problem and then went on to talk about the area in a way that made clear that, by our standard, there was a problem. By our standards, people had tension or stress in an area, even when they said at some point in the interview that they had none, if—

1. They talked about the area in a way that seemed to show upset feelings (anger, sadness, agitation, and so forth).
2. They reported unresolved differences of opinion on major issues.
3. They reported behavior, such as theft, that outsiders would consider a tension-creating way of solving a disagreement.
4. They said someone in the family had experienced tension or stress in an area.
5. They said that they had had tension or stress in the area in the past but had none anymore.

Agreement between family members about tensions and stresses was adequate but not great. Table 5 reports agreement between family members for the areas of tension and stress that were the focus of this study. To evaluate agreement between family members, two of us independently judged the audiotape of each interview. The number of businesses for which paired respondents gave us material we could judge is comparatively small in the area of tensions and stresses. The interviews were relatively unstructured and sometimes did not get to focal issues. If the two coders disagreed on whether tensions and stresses over a particular issue were expressed in an interview, we dropped that interview from our tabulations on that issue.

In processing the taped interviews and the interviewer notes, two persons made independent judgments on the attributes of interest to us. Rosenblatt and Anderson coded thirty-seven cases; de Mik and Rosenblatt coded fifty-five. The major risks in having persons central to a research project do coding are that they may be influenced by the study hypotheses and that they may have developed understandings of descriptive terms that are different from what those terms would mean to most people. However, there are advantages of using coders who are central to a project. They are less likely to have idiosyncratic understandings of terms, they are better motivated to

Table 5. Agreement Between Relatives on Presence or Absence
of Tension and Stress.

Issue	Percentage Agreement	N
Who does what	63	22
Fairness of compensation or work load	67	18
Whether some family member should be in the business	78	14
Who should inherit or fairness of inheritance	80	15
Who should be a partner or fairness of someone's being a partner	90	10
How or when control of the business passes from one person to another	69	13
Too much time together or apart because of the business	65	17
Carryover of roles from home to business or business to home	69	16
Conflict between loyalty to the business and loyalty to family members not in the business	64	14
Conflict between what's good for the business and what's good for the family	56	18
Firing or refusing to promote someone	83	11
Fairness of a promotion or nonpromotion	80	15
Offspring in the business being pushed too hard or not hard enough	62	13
Problems resulting from one relative's supervising another	86	14
An important business decision or decision making in general	61	18
Whether someone should be in the business	55	11
Whether the family should continue to operate the business	71	14
Money	81	16

code carefully, and biases and errors would be a greater embarrassment to them than to anyone else who might code.

Table 6 presents interrater agreement on all variables except the tension and stress measures. Table 7 provides reliability data on those tension and stress measures. The number of cases for which reliability figures are reported is, for many variables, less than the number of individuals interviewed because one or both coders thought the information was insufficient in one or more interviews. Information was insufficient because interviews

Table 6. Interrater Agreement on All Variables
Except Measures of Tension and Stress.

	Correlation or Numbers of Cases on Which Coders Agreed	
Variable	Interviews Coded by Anderson and Rosenblatt	Interviews Coded by de Mik and Rosenblatt
Respondent age	$r = 1.00, N = 37$	$r = 1.00, N = 55$
Respondent gender	37/37	55/55
Years of education[b]	$r = .97, N = 35$	$r = .98, N = 54$
Respondent official title in business[e]	36/37	49/55
Years in current role[c]	$r = .95, N = 34$	$r = .86, N = 48$
Age when began working in business[c]	$r = .93, N = 37$	$r = .96, N = 51$
Had other formal roles in business[e]	28/35	43/50
Had full-time posteducation job outside this business[e]	16/17	26/27
Starting role in this business[e]	24/33	37/53
Had nonmanagerial official role in this business[e]	30/34	38/47
Current marital status[e]	35/36	50/50
Number of living sons[e]	$r = .94, N = 17$	$r = .84, N = 33$
Number of living daughters[e]	$r = 1.00, N = 18$	$r = .74, N = 33$
Number of living sons aged 18 or older[c]	$r = .95, N = 14$	$r = .88, N = 35$
Number of living daughters aged 18 or older[e]	$r = 1.00, N = 17$	$r = .86, N = 35$
Age of eldest offspring[a]	$r = 1.00, N = 7$	$r = 1.00, N = 21$
Age of youngest offspring[a]	$r = .87, N = 9$	$r = 1.00, N = 21$
Number of brothers living[c]	$r = .96, N = 11$	$r = .98, N = 25$
Number of sisters living[e]	$r = 1.00, N = 10$	$r = .97, N = 22$
How respondents entered this business[e]	20/27	39/45
Duration of interview tape[d]	$r = .96, N = 34$	$r = .97, N = 52$
Relationship around which the most tension is reported[e]	19/35	28/53
Respondent currently in business full-time[e]	34/36	48/48
Respondent considers it a family business[e]	35/37	41/42
Who owns the business[e]	24/37	35/51
Who manages the business[e]	33/37	43/50
Number of relatives involved in the business[c]	$r = .81, N = 36$	$r = .75, N = 51$

Table 6. Interrater Agreement on All Variables
Except Measures of Tension and Stress, Cont'd.

| | Correlation or Numbers of Cases on Which Coders Agreed | |
Variable	Interviews Coded by Anderson and Rosenblatt	Interviews Coded by de Mik and Rosenblatt
Number of nonrelated employees[a]	$r = 1.00, N = 35$	$r = .96, N = 47$
Annual gross sales[a]	$r = 1.00, N = 33$	$r = .99, N = 39$
How long ago did family get involved in the business[e]	$r = .81, N = 36$	$r = .94, N = 48$
Other family members currently in business[e]	33/36	51/52
Other family members in business in past[e]	34/35	42/44
Current spouse is or was in business[e]	26/29	36/38
Spouse role if now in business[e]	13/14	18/21
Spouse role when in business in past[f]	1/1	3/4
A previous spouse ever in the business[f]	1/1	1/1
Respondent divorced since business begun[e]	11/11	7/8
Number of sons ever in business[e]	$r = .82, N = 24$	$r = .95, N = 22$
Number of sons now in business[e]	$r = .90, N = 24$	$r = .96, N = 21$
If son in business now, role of highest-ranking one[e]	6/11	10/12
If any sons in business now, at least one lives with respondent[e]	12/12	8/8
If any son not in business, respondent desires a son to be in business or regrets his leaving[e]	8/9	8/10
Number of daughters ever in business[e]	$r = .96, N = 24$	$r = .92, N = 21$
Number of daughters now in business[e]	$r = .65, N = 23$	$r = .89, N = 16$
If any daughter in business now, role of highest-ranking one[e]	2/5	6/6
If any daughters in business now, at least one lives with respondent[e]	5/5	2/2

(continued on next page)

Table 6. Interrater Agreement on All Variables
Except Measures of Tension and Stress, Cont'd.

	Correlation or Numbers of Cases on Which Coders Agreed	
Variable	Interviews Coded by Anderson and Rosenblatt	Interviews Coded by de Mik and Rosenblatt
If any daughter not in business, respondent desires a daughter to be in business or regrets her leaving[e]	1/1	2/3
Respondent's father ever in business[e]	35/36	39/40
If respondent's father now in business, respondent and father coresident[e]	7/7	11/12
Father's role if now in business[e]	6/7	14/15
If father in business in past, most long-term role[e]	3/4	13/13
There hás been a shift in ownership or control from a father to an offspring[e]	30/34	38/43
Respondent's mother ever in business[e]	30/33	22/24
If respondent's mother now in business, respondent and mother coresident[e]	3/3	4/4
Mother's role if now in business[f]	0/0	0/0
Number of siblings ever in business[e]	$r = .98, N = 30$	$r = .79, N = 38$
Number of siblings now in business[e]	$r = .93, N = 31$	$r = .91, N = 43$
If any siblings now in business, current role of highest-ranking[e]	6/11	9/11
Any grandparent ever in business[e]	31/31	13/14
If any grandparent in business, role of top-ranking one at height of power[e]	1/1	4/4
Any grandchildren ever in business[e]	31/31	11/11
Number of nephews, nieces, aunts, uncles, cousins, and in-laws ever in business[c]	$r = .68, N = 31$	$r = .53, N = 28$

Table 6. Interrater Agreement on All Variables
Except Measures of Tension and Stress, Cont'd.

	Correlation or Numbers of Cases on Which Coders Agreed	
Variable	Interviews Coded by Anderson and Rosenblatt	Interviews Coded by de Mik and Rosenblatt
There has been a shift of owner-ship or control to a son-in-law[e]	9/9	49/53

Notes: Correlations are given for variables for which there is a continuum, such as age. Numbers of cases of agreement are given for variables for which there is no continuum, such as gender.

The letters *a* through *f* after names of variables indicate how cases of coder disagreement were resolved in combining coder judgments: a, coder judgments averaged; b, coder judgments averaged, cases with discrepancies greater than 2 were dropped; c, coder judgments averaged, cases with discrepancies greater than 5 dropped; d, coder judgments averaged, cases with discrepancies greater than 20 dropped; e, cases with disagreement between coders dropped; f, this variable dropped from the study, as there were too few cases.

Table 7. Interrater Agreement on Measures of Tension and Stress.

	Proportion of Cases on Which Coders Agreed	
	Interviews Coded by Anderson and Rosenblatt	Interviews Coded by de Mik and Rosenblatt
Who does what	30/33	42/44
Fairness of compensation or work load	28/30	39/46
Whether or not a particular relative should be in the business	24/31	34/41
Inheritance	24/31	39/42
Partnership	27/31	31/36
How or when control of the firm passes from one person to another	27/29	30/33
Togetherness and apartness	30/34	37/43
Carryover of roles from home to business or business to home	28/31	31/36

(continued on next page)

Table 7. Interrater Agreement on Measures of Tension and Stress, Cont'd.

	Proportion of Cases on Which Coders Agreed	
	Interviews Coded by Anderson and Rosenblatt	Interviews Coded by de Mik and Rosenblatt
Conflict between loyalty to the firm and loyalty to someone not in the firm	32/33	29/31
Conflict between what's good for the firm and what's good for the family	26/32	39/45
Firing or refusing to promote	26/28	26/26
Fairness of promotion or non-promotion	30/32	24/29
Offspring in firm pushed too hard or not hard enough	25/30	27/30
Supervision of relative by relative	29/33	28/38
Decisions	30/35	38/43
Whether someone should be in the firm	23/30	29/36
Whether the family should continue in the business	28/32	28/36
Money	26/32	35/40

Note: In combining coder judgments, all cases with disagreement between coders were dropped.

were only semistructured, because people did not want to answer particular questions or could not, because interviews were cut short as people interviewed had to tend to business matters, and in several cases because of tape recorder failure.

In generating the "data" for use in analyses, the judgments of the two coders for a given attribute of a given case were combined. However, when coders disagreed, it was not always possible or safe to combine the coders' judgments. When coders made judgments that could not be averaged, the decision was to omit that variable for that particular case. If averaging was possible, it was done, unless the coders seemed too discrepant. The letters *a* through *f* following the names of variables in Table 6 indicate how cases of coder disagreement were resolved in the combining of coder judgments.

Imperfect agreement is plausible because on many issues of tension and stress, people's differences in perspective are connected to the tensions and stresses. An offspring, for example, might have felt tension over supervision, whereas a supervising parent might have been unaware of tension or did not want to admit to self or to another that it was there. Imperfect agreement about tensions and stresses also arose because some problems had existed in the past and were known only to a family member long in the business. Some problems were not known to family members who had been little involved in the business or who had not been present during crucial interactions. Some tensions were private ones in that what could have been an interpersonal tension went on mostly in one person's mind—for example, a man who knew his wife and children would feel upset if he went on a long business trip but for whom most of the tension was a matter of private wrestling with what to do.

The overwhelming impression we get from the data on agreement between family members over presence or absence of tensions and stresses is that one person may have had difficulty with something that was not reported as a tension or stress by the other, made no great impression on the other, or was not even perceived as a tension or stress by the other. The issues we studied are family issues, but the tension or stress seemed often to operate mainly in one family member. However, as the discussions in the text indicate, in all areas of tension and stress there was substantial interpersonal entanglement and strife.

References

Albert, S. "A Delete Design Model for Successful Transitions." In J. R. Kimberly and R. E. Quinn (Eds.), *Managing Organizational Transitions*. Homewood, Ill.: Irwin, 1984.

Alcorn, P. B. *Success and Survival in the Family-Owned Business.* New York: McGraw-Hill, 1982.

Ambrose, D. "Transfer of the Family-Owned Business." *Journal of Small Business Management,* 1983, *21,* 49–56.

Anderson, R. M., and Rosenblatt, P. C. "Intergenerational Transfer of Farm Land." Unpublished manuscript, University of Minnesota, 1984.

Baizerman, M., and Hall, W. T. "Consultation as a Political Process." *Community Mental Health Journal,* 1977, *13,* 142–149.

Barnes, L. B., and Hershon, S. A. "Transferring Power in the Family Business." *Harvard Business Review,* 1976, *54,* 105–114.

Barry, B. "The Development of Organization Structure in the Family Firm." *Journal of General Management,* 1975, *3,* 42–60.

Becker, B. M., and Tillman, F. *Management Checklist for a Family Business.* Fort Worth: United States Small Business Administration, 1976.

Becker, B. M., and Tillman, F. A. *The Family Owned Business.* Chicago: Commerce Clearing House, 1978.

Beckhard, R., and Dyer, W. G., Jr. "Challenges and Issues in Managing Family Firms." Working paper, Alfred P. Sloan School of Management, Massachusetts Institute of Technology, 1981.

Beckhard, R., and Dyer, W. G., Jr. "Managing Continuity in the Family-Owned Business." *Organizational Dynamics,* Summer 1983a, pp. 5–12.

Beckhard, R., and Dyer, W. G., Jr. "SMR Forum: Managing Change in the Family Firm—Issues and Strategies." *Sloan Management Review,* 1983b, *24*(3), 59–65.

Benedict, B. "Capital, Saving and Credit Among Mauritian Indians." In R. Firth and B. S. Yamey (Eds.), *Capital, Saving and Credit in Peasant Societies.* Chicago: Aldine, 1963.

Benedict, B. "Family Firms and Firm Families: A Comparison of Indian, Chinese, and Creole Firms in Seychelles." In S. M. Greenfield, A. Strickon, and R. T. Aubey (Eds.), *Entrepreneurs in Cultural Context.* Albuquerque: School of American Research/University of New Mexico Press, 1979.

Benedict, M., and Benedict, B. *Men, Women, and Money in Seychelles.* Berkeley: University of California Press, 1982.

Bennett, J. W. *Northern Plainsmen.* Arlington Heights, Ill.: AHM, 1976.

Bennett, J. W. *Of Time and the Enterprise.* Minneapolis: University of Minnesota Press, 1982.

Berger, P., and Kellner, H. "Marriage and the Construction of Reality." *Diogenes,* 1964, No. 46, 1–24.

Bertaux, D., and Bertaux-Wiame, I. "Life Stories in the Bakers' Trade." In D. Bertaux (Ed.), *Biography and Society.* Beverly Hills, Calif.: Sage, 1981.

Boss, P. G. "Normative Family Stress: Family Boundary Changes Across the Life-Span." *Family Relations,* 1980, *29*, 445–450.

Boss, P. G., McCubbin, H. I., and Lester, G. "The Corporate Executive Wife's Coping Patterns in Response to Routine

Husband-Father Absence." *Family Process,* 1979, *18,* 79-86.

Boswell, J. *The Rise and Decline of Small Firms.* London: Allen and Unwin, 1973.

Bowen, M. "Family Therapy and Family Group Therapy." In H. Kaplan and B. Sadock (Eds.), *Comprehensive Group Psychotherapy.* Baltimore: Williams & Wilkins, 1971.

Broderick, C., and Smith, J. "The General Systems Approach to the Family." In W. R. Burr, R. Hill, F. I. Nye, and I. Reiss (Eds.), *Contemporary Theories About the Family.* Vol. 2. New York: Free Press, 1979.

Campbell, D. T. "Common Fate, Similarity, and Other Indices of the Status of Aggregates of Persons as Social Entities." *Behavioral Science,* 1958, *3,* 14-25.

Cates, J. N., and Sussman, M. B. "Family Systems and Inheritance." *Marriage and Family Review,* 1982, *5,* 1-24.

Christensen, C. R. *Management Succession in Small and Growing Enterprises.* Boston: Graduate School of Business Administration, Harvard University, 1953.

Cohler, B. J., and Grunebaum, H. U. *Mothers, Grandmothers, and Daughters.* New York: Wiley, 1981.

Cohn, T., and Lindberg, R. A. *Survival and Growth: Management Strategies for the Small Firm.* New York: American Management Association, 1974.

Dailey, R. C., Reuschling, T. E., and DeMong, R. F. "The Family Owned Business: Capital Funding." *American Journal of Small Business,* 1977, *2*(2), 30-39.

Danco, L. A. *Beyond Survival: A Business Owner's Guide for Success.* Cleveland, Ohio: University Press, 1982a.

Danco, L. A. *Inside the Family Business.* Englewood Cliffs, N.J.: Prentice-Hall, 1982b.

Danco, L. A., and Jonovic, D. J. *Outside Directors in the Family Owned Business.* Englewood Cliffs, N.J.: Prentice-Hall, 1982.

Davis, P., and Stern, D. "Adaptation, Survival, and Growth of the Family Business: An Integrated Systems Perspective." *Human Relations,* 1980, *34,* 207-224.

Deeks, J. *The Small Firm Owner-Manager.* New York: Praeger, 1976.

Donnelley, R. G. "The Family Business." *Harvard Business Review*, 1964, *42*(4), 93–105.

Edison, B. "As the Family Business Grows, or Why Didn't Grandfather Tell Us?" In J. D. Glover and G. A. Simon (Eds.), *Chief Executive's Handbook*. Homewood, Ill.: Dow Jones-Irwin, 1976.

Feldman, L. B. "Dysfunctional Marital Conflict: An Integrative Interpersonal-Intrapsychic Model." *Journal of Marital and Family Therapy*, 1982, *8*, 417–428.

Greenberg, G. S. "The Family Interactional Perspective: A Study and Examination of the Work of Don D. Jackson." *Family Process*, 1977, *16*, 385–412.

Greiner, L. E., and Metzger, R. O. *Consulting to Management*. Englewood Cliffs, N.J.: Prentice-Hall, 1983.

Gullotta, T. P., and Donohue, K. C. "The Corporate Family: Theory and Treatment." *Journal of Marital and Family Therapy*, 1981, *7*, 151–158.

Hedley, M. J. "Rural Social Structure and the Ideology of the 'Family Farm.'" *Canadian Journal of Anthropology/Revue Canadienne d'Anthropologie*, 1981, *2*, 85–89.

Henry, J. *Culture Against Man*. New York: Vintage, 1965.

Hirschhorn, L., and Gilmore, T. "The Application of Family Therapy Concepts to Influencing Organizational Behavior." *Administrative Science Quarterly*, 1980, *25*, 18–37.

Holland, P. G., and Boulton, W. R. "Balancing the 'Family' and the 'Business' in Family Business." *Business Horizons*, 1984, *27*(2), 16–21.

Jonovic, D. J. *The Second-Generation Boss: A Successor's Guide To Becoming the Next Owner-Manager of a Successful Family Business*. Cleveland, Ohio: University Press, 1982.

Kantor, D., and Lehr, W. *Inside the Family: Toward a Theory of Family Process*. San Francisco: Jossey-Bass, 1975.

Karpel, M. A. "Family Secrets." *Family Process*, 1980, *19*, 295–306.

Kepner, E. "The Family and the Firm: A Coevolutionary Perspective." *Organizational Dynamics*, Summer 1983, pp. 57–70.

Kets de Vries, M. F. R. "The Entrepreneurial Personality: A

Person at the Crossroads." *Journal of Management Studies,* 1977, *14,* 34-57.

Kets de Vries, M. F. R., and Miller, D. *The Neurotic Organization: Diagnosing and Changing Counterproductive Styles of Management.* San Francisco: Jossey-Bass, 1984.

Kohl, S. B. *Working Together: Women and Family in Southwestern Saskatchewan.* Toronto: Holt, Rinehart and Winston of Canada, 1976.

L'Abate, L., and L'Abate, B. L. "Marriage: The Dream and the Reality." *Family Relations,* 1981, *30,* 131-136.

Lansberg S., I. "Managing Human Resources in Family Firms: The Problem of Institutional Overlap." *Organizational Dynamics,* Summer 1983, pp. 39-46.

Levinson, H. "Consulting with Family Businesses: What to Look For, What to Look Out For." *Organizational Dynamics,* Summer 1983, pp. 71-80.

McGivern, C. "The Dynamics of Management Succession." *Management Decision,* 1978, *16,* 32-42.

Marcus, G. E. "Law in the Development of Dynastic Families Among American Business Elites: The Domestication of Capital and the Capitalization of Family." *Law and Society Review,* 1980, *14,* 859-903.

Marcus, G. E. "The Fiduciary Role in American Family Dynasties and Their Institutional Legacy: From the Law of Trusts to Trust in the Establishment." In G. E. Marcus (Ed.), *Elites: Ethnographic Issues.* Albuquerque: University of New Mexico Press, 1983.

Menchik, P. L. "Primogeniture, Equal Sharing, and the U.S. Distribution of Wealth." *Quarterly Journal of Economics,* 1980, *94,* 299-316.

Miller, E. J., and Rice, A. K. *Systems of Organizations.* London: Tavistock, 1967.

Peiser, R. B., and Wooten, L. M. "Life-Cycle Changes in Small Family Businesses." *Business Horizons,* 1983, *26*(3), 58-65.

Pine, C., and Mundale, S. " 'Til Death Do Us Part." *Corporate Reports,* 1983, *14*(9), 77-83.

Pitts, J. R. "The Structural-Functional Approach." In H. T.

Christensen (Ed.), *Handbook of Marriage and the Family.* Chicago: Rand McNally, 1964.

Renshaw, J. R. "An Exploration of the Dynamics of the Overlapping Worlds of Work and Family." *Family Process,* 1976, *15,* 143–165.

Rosenblatt, P. C. "Needed Research on Commitment in Marriage." In G. Levinger and H. Raush (Eds.), *Close Relationships: Perspectives on the Meaning of Intimacy.* Amherst: University of Massachusetts Press, 1977.

Rosenblatt, P. C. "Ethnographic Case Studies." In M. B. Brewer and B. E. Collins (Eds.), *Scientific Inquiry and the Social Sciences: A Volume in Honor of Donald T. Campbell.* San Francisco: Jossey-Bass, 1981.

Rosenblatt, P. C. *Bitter, Bitter Tears: Nineteenth Century Diarists and Twentieth Century Grief Theories.* Minneapolis: University of Minnesota Press, 1983.

Rosenblatt, P. C., and Anderson, R. M. "Interaction in Farm Families: Tension and Stress." In R. T. Coward and M. W. Smith (Eds.), *The Family in Rural Society.* Boulder, Colo.: Westview, 1981.

Rosenblatt, P. C., and Keller, L. O. "Economic Vulnerability and Economic Stress in Farm Couples." *Family Relations,* 1983, *32,* 567–573.

Rosenblatt, P. C., Nevaldine, A., and Titus, S. L. "Farm Families: Relation of Significant Aspects of Farming to Family Interaction." *International Journal of Sociology of the Family,* 1978, *8,* 89–99.

Rosenblatt, P. C., and Titus, S. L. "Together and Apart in the Family." *Humanitas,* 1976, *12,* 367–379.

Rosenblatt, P. C., Titus, S. L., and Cunningham, M. R. "Disrespect, Tension, and Togetherness-Apartness in Marriage." *Journal of Marriage and Family Therapy,* 1979, *5,* 47–54.

Rosenblatt, P. C., Titus, S. L., Nevaldine, A., and Cunningham, M. R. "Marital System Differences and Summer-Long Vacations: Togetherness-Apartness and Tension." *American Journal of Family Therapy,* 1979, *7,* 77–84.

Rosenblatt, P. C., Walsh, R. P., and Jackson, D. A. *Grief and Mourning in Cross-Cultural Perspective.* New Haven, Conn.: Human Relations Area Files Press, 1976.

Rosenblatt, P. C., and Wright, S. E. "Shadow Realities in Close Relationships." *American Journal of Family Therapy*, 1984, *12*, 45-54.

Savage, D. *Founders, Heirs, and Managers: French Industrial Leadership in Transition.* Beverly Hills, Calif.: Sage, 1979.

Schneider, D. M. *American Kinship: A Cultural Account.* (2nd ed.) Chicago: University of Chicago Press, 1980.

Simmel, G. "Conflict." (K. H. Wolff, Trans.) In G. Simmel, *Conflict and the Web of Group Affiliations.* New York: Free Press, 1955. (Originally published 1908.)

Steele, F. *Consulting for Organizational Change.* Amherst: University of Massachusetts Press, 1975.

Titus, S. L., Rosenblatt, P. C., and Anderson, R. M. "Family Conflict over Inheritance of Property." *Family Coordinator*, 1979, *28*, 337-346.

Trow, D. B. "Executive Succession in Small Companies." *Administrative Science Quarterly*, 1961, *6*, 228-239.

Wertheim, E. S. "The Science and Typology of Family Systems II. Further Theoretical and Practical Considerations." *Family Process*, 1973, *14*, 285-309.

Woodburn, L. T., and Barnhill, L. N. "Applying Family Systems Therapy Principles to Couples Counseling." *Personnel and Guidance Journal*, 1977, *55*, 510-514.

Index

311

Informant Index

005:
41-42, 43-44, 48, 60, 65, 95, 103, 113-114, 132, 150, 155, 178, 180, 185, 190-191

006:
25-26, 45, 46, 51, 55, 62, 90, 102, 126, 151, 169-170, 171, 186, 207, 224

011:
1, 106, 119, 128, 130

014A:
129

015:
4, 61, 71, 74-75, 102, 153, 154, 165

018:
30, 52-53, 79, 104, 114, 115, 141

025A:
32, 41, 52

025B:
37, 43, 45, 81, 130, 134, 158, 160, 191, 202

027:
41, 84, 111, 166

031A:
25, 35, 48, 86, 103, 111, 163, 203

031B:
37, 58, 158

032A:
28, 73, 93, 182

032B:
170

033A:
23-24, 83, 158-159, 170

033B:
50, 109, 120, 156, 164, 191

036A:
35, 36, 45, 99, 128, 159, 175, 179, 227, 251